Advances in Visual Methodology

Advances in Visual Methodology

Edited by
Sarah Pink

Los Angeles | London | New Delhi
Singapore | Washington DC

First published 2012

SAGE Publications Ltd
1 Oliver's Yard
55 City Road
London EC1Y 1SP

SAGE Publications Inc.
2455 Teller Road
Thousand Oaks, California 91320

SAGE Publications India Pvt Ltd
B 1/I 1 Mohan Cooperative Industrial Area
Mathura Road
New Delhi 110 044

SAGE Publications Asia-Pacific Pte Ltd
3 Church Street
#10-04 Samsung Hub
Singapore 049483

Library of Congress Control Number available

British Library Cataloguing in Publication data

A catalogue record for this book is available from the British Library

ISBN 978-0-85702-848-8
ISBN 978-0-85702-849-5 (pbk)

Typeset by C&M Digitals (P) Ltd, Chennai, India
Printed in India at Replika Press Pvt Ltd
Printed on paper from sustainable resources

CONTENTS

LIST OF FIGURES

ABOUT THE EDITOR AND CONTRIBUTORS

Sarah Pink is professor of social sciences at Loughborough University. She is known internationally for her work relating to visual and sensory methodology and her publications in this area include the books: *Doing Visual Ethnography* (2001, 2007, also published in Polish by Jagiellonian University Press in 2009), *Doing Sensory Ethnography* (2009), *Working Images* (co-ed., 2004), *Visual Interventions* (ed. 2007) and *The Future of Visual Anthropology* (2006). Her methodological work is often developed in the context of research projects that seek to connect theoretical scholarship with applied research, currently with a focus that includes questions concerning digital media and sustainability.

Elisenda Ardévol is professor at the department of arts and humanities of the Open University of Catalonia (UOC), and resident researcher at the Internet Interdisciplinary Institute (IN3) of the same University in Barcelona (Spain) where she coordinates the research group in digital culture *mediaccions*. As social and cultural anthropologist, she has published *La busqueda de una mirada* (2006) on visual anthropology and ethnographic film, analysing the theoretical and methodological perspectives of doing research with visual data, as well as other academic papers related to new media practices and online research methods. She has taught courses at different Spanish and Latin-American universities, having been lecturer and visiting scholar at the Centre for Visual Anthropology, at the University of Southern California, Los Angeles. Currently, her main line of research is media anthropology and cultural production in Internet and related digital technologies.

Marcus Banks is professor of visual anthropology at the University of Oxford. After his doctorate at the University of Cambridge he trained in documentary film production at the National Film and Television School. He has published widely on ethnographic film and visual research methodology. His books include *Rethinking Visual Anthropology* (co-edited with Howard Morphy, 1997), *Using Visual Data in Qualitative Research* (2007), and *Made to be Seen: Perspectives on the History of Visual Anthropology* (co-edited with Jay Ruby, 2011). His previous research includes a study of film in colonial India and a short study of image use on the social networking site Facebook. He is currently in the early stages of research on image use in forensic science.

Andrew Clark is a lecturer in sociology at the University of Salford. His research focuses on the interaction between space and society. Past research projects have explored representations of deprived neighbourhoods and social inter-actions in public places. He recently completed a three-year research project funded by the ESRC on the interaction between social networks, neighbour-hoods and community that developed visual methods as part of a qualitatively driven multi-method approach. His recent articles have been published in *Art and Health: An International Journal for Research, Policy and Practice*, *The International Journal of Research Methodology*, and *Journal of Youth Studies*.

Roderick Coover is an associate professor at Temple University, Philadelphia, USA. Several of his works, including the CD-ROM, *Cultures in Webs: Working in Hypermedia with the Documentary Image* (Eastgate), the DVD, *From Verite to Virtual: Conversations on the Frontier of Film and Anthropology* (Documentary Educational Resources) and the co-edited book, *Switching Codes: Thinking Through Technology In The Humanities And Arts* (Chicago), examine relation-ships between visual practices and scholarly research practices. His interactive and video works include: *Unknown Territories* series (Unknownterritories.org), *Inside/Outside*, and *The Theory of Time Here* (Video Data Bank), which explores questions in the representation of place and visual technologies. He has also made ethnographic films such as *The Language of Wine: An Ethnography of Work, Wine and the Senses* (languageofwine.com), which looks at how the words of an occupation – winemaking in Burgundy – shape the metaphors lives are lived by. Coover exhibits his work internationally and is a recipient of Mellon, Fulbright and Whiting awards. His essays and artist papers can be found in journals such as: *Ethnographiques*, *Visual Studies*, *Visual Anthropology*, *Film International* and *Film Quarterly*, among others (www. roderickcoover.com).

Cristina Grasseni, MPhil, PhD, Radcliffe Institute and Film Study Center fellow at Harvard University (2011/12) lectures anthropology at Bergamo University (Italy). Amongst her research interests are visual knowledge, sense of place and local development in the Italian Alps. Amongst her recent pub-lications are: *Skilled Visions: Between Apprenticeship and Standards* (ed. 2007), *Developing Skill, Developing Vision: Practices of Locality at the Foot of the Alps* (2009) and *Luoghi Comuni. Antropologia dei luoghi e pratiche della visione* (*Common Places. Anthropology of Place and Practices of Vision*, 2009 – in Italian).

Jon Hindmarsh is professor of work and interaction in the department of management at King's College London. His research involves studies of social interaction and communication in a variety of organisational settings and has focused on issues of 'embodiment', 'materiality', 'teamwork' and 'training'. He also engages in interdisciplinary research to explore the potential for these kinds of studies to inform the design of new technologies. His recent books include *Video in Qualitative Research* (2010, co-authored with Christian Heath and Paul Luff); *Organisation, Interaction and Practice: Studies in Ethnomethodology and Conversation Analysis* (2010, co-edited with Nick Llewellyn); and *Communication in Healthcare Settings* (2010, co-edited with Alison Pilnick and Virginia Teas Gill).

Susan Hogan is professor of cultural studies at the University of Derby. Professor Hogan has research interests in the history of medicine. She has written extensively on the relationship between the arts and insanity, and the role of the arts in rehabilitation. She is also very interested in the treatment of women within psychiatry and in antenatal care. Her books include *Healing Arts: The History of Art Therapy*. Susan Hogan has also undertaken training in social science research methods in sociology and social policy, and has become very interested in visual methodologies. Her most recent research with the University of Sheffield has been on women's perceptions of ageing, using a range of visual methods.

Christina Lammer has a PhD from the University of Vienna, department of sociology. She lives and works as a sociologist, lecturer and artist in Vienna. She recently finished her collaborative research activities, *CORPOrealities* (2004–2009) on empathy and somatic perception at Medical University Vienna (MUV). In 2009 she started the art(s) and science project *Surgical Wrappings* (2009–2014) and explores the material culture of surgery. In a further study, *FEATURES – Vienna Face Project* (2010–2014), Christina Lammer investigates portraiture in plastic and reconstructive surgery and in the visual and performative arts. For this she is affiliated with the University of Applied Arts in Vienna. She is the author of *Die Puppe: Eine Anatomie des Blicks* (1999), *doKU: Kunst und Wirklichkeit inszenieren im Dokumentarfilm* (2002) and *Günter Brus: Kleine Narbenlehre* (2007). Christina Lammer is editor of *Schneewittchen: Ein Eiskristallbuch* (1999) and *CORPOrealities* (2010). She is co-editor of *Puppe.Monster.Tod.* (1999) and *Verkörperungen/ Embodiment* (2007). She is currently writing a book *Empathographie* (2013) about breast cancer and the reconstruction of body image in patients of plastic surgery.

Francesco Lapenta is associate professor in visual culture and new media at the department of communication, business and information technologies, at the University of Roskilde. He is a member of the editorial board of the journal *Visual Studies*, Taylor and Francis, Cambridge, and a member of the executive board of the International Visual Sociology Association. He is currently a visiting professor at the sociology department of New York University. Lapenta's most recent work includes the special issue 'Autonomy and Creative Labour' of the *Journal for Cultural Research* (2010), and the article 'Geomedia: on location-based media, the changing status of collective image production and the emergence of social navigation systems' (2011). He recently edited the special issue of *Visual Studies*, 'Locative media and the digital visualisation of space, place and information' (2011).

Lydia Martens is senior lecturer in sociology at Keele University. The ESRC-funded Domestic Kitchen Practices project, which provides the inspiration for her chapter, piloted various video recording techniques in kitchens as a means for examining routines, temporalities and materialities in mundane domestic life. Her publications include: *Eating Out: Social Differentiation, Consumption and Pleasure* (2000, with Alan Warde) and *Gender and Consumption: Domestic Cultures and the Commercialisation of Everyday Life* (2007, with Emma Casey). Publications on this specific project have appeared in the journals *Home Cultures* and *Consumption, Markets and Culture*.

Maggie O'Neill is professor in criminology in the school of applied social sciences at Durham University. Maggie has a long history of collaborating with artists to conduct what she calls ethno-mimetic research – a combination of ethnographic and arts-based practice. Her interdisciplinary research career has developed at the intersections of cultural, critical and feminist theory; renewed methodologies for socio-cultural research – including arts based methodologies; and praxis through participatory action research (PAR). The outcomes of recent AHRC-funded research with four community arts organisations can be accessed online (www.guardian.co.uk/society/gallery/2009/jan/13/sense-of-belonging-exhibition).

Luc Pauwels is a professor of visual culture at the University of Antwerp (department of communication studies), Belgium. He is the director of the Visual Studies and Media Culture Research Group and Vice-President of the International Visual Sociology Association (IVSA). As a visual sociologist and communication scientist, he has written extensively on visual research methodologies, visual ethics, family photography, website analysis, anthropological filmmaking, visual corporate culture and scientific visualization in various international journals. Books include: *Visual Cultures of Science* (UPNE, 2006), *The Sage Handbook of Visual Research Methods* (2011, together with Eric Margolis), and a forthcoming monograph with Cambridge University Press: *Reframing Visual Sociology*.

Dylan Tutt is a senior research fellow at the Innovative Construction Research Centre at the University of Reading. His qualitative research focuses on social interaction, communication and technology, although he maintains a wider interest in quite diverse areas of cultural sociology, stemming from his background in sociology and visual culture. He specializes in visual ethnography and video-based studies of communication and (work) practice in diverse settings, including construction sites, research labs, GP clinics, and the home. Dylan has also explored ways to apply these ethnographic studies to the development and design of new systems and technologies. His publications reflect a strong interest in the social shaping of technology, workplace studies, ethnographic interventions, construction sociology and the sociology of the family. Dylan is currently co-editing a book with Sarah Pink and Andy Dainty for Routledge: *Ethnographic Research in the Construction Industry.*

ACKNOWLEDGEMENTS

An edited book is always a collaborative work, created from the work of its contributors, and my first thanks must go to the scholars and authors who have written the chapters from which its *Advances in Visual Methodology* are made. I have enjoyed every moment of reading and discussing their chapters during the months of the book's development – it has been an inspiring experience to work with a group of scholars who are really pushing forward the boundaries in visual methodology. The majority of the work on this volume was developed during my sabbatical leave from the Department of Social Sciences at Loughborough University during the academic year 2010–11, which I spent as a visiting scholar at the Internet Interdisciplinary Institute of the Universitiat Oberta de Catalunya in Barcelona. I am very grateful to both universities for their support during this year.

As ever, I would like to thank Patrick Brindle and the Sage editorial team for all of their support and work with me in the production of this volume.

PART 1
KEY DEVELOPMENTS AND ISSUES

Advances in visual methodology are always accompanied by (and indeed in some ways participate in the constitution of) their history, wider intellectual and technological contexts and ethical and practical questions. This book starts with an exploration of some of the key developments and issues that form the context that the advances discussed in this book bring to the fore, and with which they are simultaneously framed.

Chapter 1, by Sarah Pink, introduces a series of key theoretical, technological and practical issues that shape both the context in which visual methodologies are practised, and the form of this volume. This chapter is a guide to the reasons why this book is needed, and what it stands for in a contemporary ecology of theoretical waves, digital media technologies, drives towards public engagement, and interdisciplinary collaborations. It describes this context, assesses how it has become interwoven with and participates in producing advances in visual methodology, and maps out how these intersections are represented in the different chapters of this book.

Chapter 1 does not discuss visual ethics. Not because this topic is unimportant. But rather because in recent years, along with the increasing interest in both visual methods and more generally in ethical regulation, there has been a surge in academic interest in questions around the ethical practices of visual researchers. Because the field of visual methodologies is itself a diverse and interdisciplinary arena of scholarship, the combining of this with the question of visual research ethics has created a complex area for discussion. It has indeed become something of a research sub-field in its own right, the topic of conference panels, articles and book chapters. It might therefore in itself be considered an advance in visual methodology.

Following these developments, Chapter 2, by Andrew Clark, is dedicated to the question of advances in visual methodology through the discussion of visual ethics, thus seeing the evolution of the field of visual ethics as a topic of study as an advance in its own right. Indeed the growing interest in visual methods across a range of academic disciplines and the increase in formal mechanisms for institutional regulation of research ethics converge to produce a new context. This new context situates the question of visual ethics in new ways. Yet, as Clark argues, visual ethics are also and inevitably situated within particular projects and relationships with participants, and are part of an epistemological debate, rather than simply standing for institutional, practical and/or moral hurdles that researchers navigate in the course of their projects.

1

ADVANCES IN VISUAL METHODOLOGY
An Introduction

Sarah Pink

It was surely no coincidence that just at the turn of the 21st century four books about visual methodology were published: Marcus Banks' *Visual Methods in Social Research* (2001), my own *Doing Visual Ethnography* (2007a [2001]), Gillian Rose's text book *Visual Methodologies* (2010 [2000]) and Theo van Leeuwen and Carey Jewitt's edited volume *The Handbook of Visual Analysis* (2001). This marked a moment in the social sciences and humanities where for a number of reasons the visual was becoming more acceptable, more viable and more central to qualitative research practice. As the century moved on these works were accompanied by an increasing number of further publications, conferences, seminars and training events focused on visual methodologies. The field has since developed in exciting and divergent ways. It is losing none of its momentum and indeed continues to inspire innovative and important studies across a range of disciplines as well as further theoretical and methodological reflection. It is, moreover, an area of academic and applied research that demonstrates particularly powerfully that the relationship between theory, technology and method should not be separated. Understanding methodology is concerned with comprehending how we know as well as the environments in which this knowing is produced; as such, it involves engaging with a philosophy of knowledge, of practice and of place and space. Research methods and the practical engagements they entail are inextricable from this process. It is therefore important to engage with both simultaneously and in doing so to depart from the theory/methods divide. In the case of visual methodology this means understanding and engaging not only with the newest and latest theoretical developments in our fields, but also with the ways that these are co-implicated with technological developments and media practices. *Advances in Visual Methodology* contributes to this task. It draws together in a single volume a set of key advances and explorations that sit at the innovative edge of theory and practice in contemporary visual methodologies. It presents a critical and reflexive engagement with interdisciplinary practice in the field of visual research and representation as it is currently developing and emerging, and casts of a series of inspirations and challenges for its future.

We now find ourselves at a new stage in the development of visual methodology as a field of interdisciplinary and post-disciplinary practice that spans scholarly and applied concerns. This era in visual methodological work is of course characterised by both continuities and departures from the past trajectories of visual and media theory and practice as they have been developed in, across and between various different academic and applied disciplines. To understand this emergent context, as well as to project it as a continuing endeavour as the 21st century unfolds, here I take visual methodology to be a field of practice. It is not my aim in this introduction to review the vast and ever increasing literature that has gone before. Rather, first I map out some of the key themes and strands in this field in order to suggest how and why they are becoming interwoven in contexts that are increasingly post-disciplinary and multi-method.

This volume considers visual methodologies as a set of approaches to working with the visual in research and representation that are constantly in progress and development. Every piece of research has the potential to be used to respond to the methodological frame through which it was originally conceived. For some scholars the methodology is a tool through which to achieve research findings, and for them it is the latter that are most important as a contribution to knowledge. Yet for others, including those who contribute to this volume, methodology is something that should be critically reflected on as a crucial component in the processes through which we produce knowledge. From this latter perspective the research process and the methodology that informs it cannot be separated from the findings of the research, right through from research design to its representation. This problematises practices such as data sharing, complicates team working, and requires thorough interrogations of perspective, epistemology and the philosophical and moral commitments of researchers in collaborative and interdisciplinary work endeavours.

In part, such rethinkings of methodological principles are provoked because the very tools of visual research have undergone radical transformations. Some would argue that these technological developments produce shifts that change the very way that we are able to conceptualise and experience the social and electronic realities in which so many of us live. Others would stress the continuities that are apparent in how researchers engage with technological innovations, echoing the uses they had for earlier designs. Indeed ethnographers, who more typically focus on the ways in which technologies, software and images become part of social relations, tend to stress how technologies are appropriated rather than how they change the basis of the world we live in (e.g. Coleman, 2010; Miller, 2011). Whichever is the case (and I would suggest that this in fact varies for different methods, media and researchers), something is definitely happening that requires us to engage with the advancement of visual methodologies in a new technological context. This book inevitably confronts this question and below I scrutinize this new digital media context in more detail. Some of the chapters of this book also deal with the question of web-based technologies directly, yet in the context of other theoretical and epistemological shifts with which they are implicated. In fact most of the contributors to this book engage with the digital context of visual research, even if not directly, since practitioners and scholars of visual methodologies are for the most part essentially engaged with working in a digital environment. This does not however mean that 'old' media are not advancing in visual research; as we see in other chapters, the manual drawing, crafting and making of images is also moving forward in new ways.

An equally important feature of the contemporary advances in visual methodology is the series of theoretical shifts that in particular characterized the first decade of the 21st century. Theories and philosophies of phenomenology, space and place, practice, the senses and movement have come to the fore across the 'visual' academic disciplines, sub-disciplines and interdisciplines. These approaches, which are often used in ways that are interconnected, are advancing the field of visual methodology by offering theoretical paradigms through which the visual, vision, images and media practices can be reworked. This book is in part structured in response to these moves, with sections that respectively engage with the issues they raise and highlight examples of advances in these areas.

Another increasingly important element of contemporary research is represented in the ways that a growing number of visual researchers are seeking to develop engaged, applied or public research agendas and collaborations. This has always been a feature of my own work, in that I have sought to maintain a balance and importantly a bridge between 'visual' research projects that are theoretical, scholarly and applied. There has been a strand of applied and intervention-based visual research ever since the field developed (see Pink, 2007b) although this might be regarded as a 'hidden' part of its history (Pink, 2006, 2007b), which has only recently been more explicitly recovered. Yet this area is now thriving with a continuous series of new developments (see Pink, 2011c) along with an inspiring enthusiasm for collaborative and participatory filmmaking amongst graduate students.

Visual methodology as a field of scholarship

One of the key developments that proved an inspiration for this book is reflected in what I propose is the emergence of visual methods and visual methodology as a field of interdisciplinary scholarship and practice. Along with the increasing number of conferences and seminars dedicated to visual methods, and the vast number of other 'visual' conferences, workshops, master-classes, seminars and courses that are ongoing around the globe, *Advances in Visual Methodology* stands as a marker of the momentum with which visual methodology as a field in its own right is moving on. Its contributors examine how new practice-based, theoretical and methodological engagements are developing and emerging; the impact they are having on the types of knowledge visual research produces and critiques; the ways these intersect with new media; and the implications of this for social and cultural research, scholarship and intervention. As the different chapters of this book demonstrate, there are different approaches and practices within the field, and in some cases these are also being openly debated (see Pink, 2011a) as visual researchers from one field start to ask why and how it could be that those from another who, on the surface of it, use the same technologies and ask similar questions, could actually be doing something so different.

As an edited volume, *Advances in Visual Methodology* connects with existing and established methods discussions (by covering areas including ethics, visual ethnography, social interaction analysis and virtual ethnography) as well as with newer issues (visual digital and locative media, arts practice and social intervention and possibilities for public scholarship). Yet it also extends the discussion in critical ways that link to theoretical debates (e.g. relating to practice theory, spatial theory and the senses). In doing so it sits alongside and in a constructive relationship to contemporary visual methods texts, such as Luc Pauwels and Eric Margolis's recent edited volume, *The Sage Handbook of Visual Methods* (2011). However, rather than taking a conventional textbook angle on presenting each approach and its rationale for re-use, *Advances in Visual Methodology* is concerned with critically advancing the debates in the disciplinary and interdisciplinary areas with which its authors engage. Around a decade earlier, Theo van Leeuwen and Carey Jewitt edited *The Handbook of Visual Analysis* (2001), which represented the work of a set of visual scholars from across different disciplines. In common with that volume, *Advances in Visual Methodology* is concerned with developments across disciplines. Yet, as part of its agenda, it also accounts for how the field of visual methodology scholarship is moving on.

Given the increasing focus amongst scholars and students on research methodology as a field of interest and research in itself, this book seeks to extend the debates in visual ethics and in visual methods and practices, and expand the field. In developing it, the idea of visual methodologies as routes to knowledge becomes a fundamental way of thinking about what it is we are seeking to do as we use visual methods and media in research. Following on from this, the question becomes one that considers the different routes through which visual methodologies might take us to new types of knowledge, the ways of knowing that these imply, and the ways in which they are engaged by different groups of people. In doing so I am not seeking to argue for hierarchies of knowledge or to pitch one discipline against another (although I admit I might have done this in other publications). Rather, I see each section of this book as focusing on how the visual becomes a way of arriving at particular types and layers of knowledge or ways of knowing.

This perspective is not about a refusal to take a theoretical stand and argue for it. Instead, it is my concern to permit the question of how visual methodology has by now emerged as a field of academic scholarship to be demonstrated through the chapters written by the contributors. In recent years much has been written about visual methods and methodologies, which crosses disciplines and media practices. It is a field of scholarship that I believe we should see as open and constantly shifting. Scholars who participate in it are united both in their concern for investigating how the visual might enable routes to knowledge and their commitment to innovating through the practical use of constantly changing (audio)visual media in research. In this context their work is influenced not only by theoretical developments but also by the relationship between theoretical and technological fields of study and practice. Therefore this book does not define or crystallise visual methodology at a specific moment in its development. But rather through a focus on *advances* it examines the multiple routes that are developing and the way that they constitute visual methodology as a field of scholarship. I argue that when thinking about visual methodologies we need to be aware of the emergences, intertwinings and points of contact between different approaches, and the implications of these. *Advances in Visual Methodology* invites readers to reflect not just on the past and on present developments, but to think in a more processual way. This is intended moreover to lead us to consider how the methodologies discussed here might take us into the future of our disciplinary and interdisciplinary work through new combinations and the imaginings for future work that it seeks to inspire. Therefore, *Advances in Visual Methodology* is not directly designed to replace or to contest any existing text or paradigm. Rather it seeks to contribute to scholarship in this field by engaging and *advancing with* the existing visual methodology and methods texts that form part of the field of scholarship it participates in. These interlinkages are all the more clear when we consider how the authors or editors of some of the leading edited volumes and single-author books in this field are participating as contributors to this volume, signifying its relevance to existing debates and their advancement. Indeed, in Chapter 14, the final chapter of this book, Luc Pauwels critically reviews the state of visual research, in a call for a continuing series of developments in the future.

Elsewhere I have outlined the (sometimes intersecting) histories of visual anthropology, visual sociology and visual culture studies to trace their significance for a visual ethnography (Pink, 2007a [2001]). I have likewise approached the work of applied visual ethnography and anthropology by arguing that it has a history (Pink, 2006, 2007b). Other authors have equally discussed the historical contexts and debates that frame visual methods in their own fields. I will not repeat the detail of these historical summaries here. It is sufficient to say that disciplinary and cross-disciplinary histories of visual methodology can be seen as providing a trajectory through which contemporary uses of visual methods are informed and also from which they depart. When one begins to trace the use of visual methods over time it also becomes clear that, as theoretical and disciplinary contexts shift, other 'advances' in visual methodology have occurred. Historically it might be argued that there were two key shifts during the 20th century. The first involved the push for visual methods and visual representation during the 1970s and 1980s when these were still highly contested and often marginalised ways of working, accused of being overly subjective. By the late 1980s and into the 1990s, along with the reflexive and postmodern turns in theory and methodology, visual methods had begun to become more accepted and there was an increasing interest in their practice, even though they could not be in any way described as mainstream. Yet by the turn of the century, further changes were underway, along with digital technologies and further theoretical shifts towards a focus on mobility, flows, the senses, spatial theory and practice. These ideas have been pivotal in shaping the advances that are represented in the current visual methodologies represented by the contributors to this book.

The question of defining visual methodology as a field of practice is further complicated by the fact that within it discipline and also task-specific uses and understandings of the visual exist alongside and in relation to visual work that is self-consciously interdisciplinary. By interdisciplinary I mean research that combines the practices, theories and ideas of different disciplines to produce novel outcomes and contributions to knowledge, theory and applied interventions. Yet interdisciplinary practice is not always simple: because visual methods have developed across disciplines it would be impossible to say they have one single common heritage, or aim. Indeed it is often their shared focus on the visual that can be seen as a common factor with their variable assessments of the status of visual images, such as, for example, documentary film, art, research footage, data, or materials for content analysis. A review of some of the (increasingly vast) existing literature gives a sense of the patterns of discipline-specific and interdisciplinary works that have emerged.

For example, some existing volumes have tended to be identified according to discipline – focusing on a visual sociology (Knowles and Sweetman, 2004) or visual anthropology (Banks and Morphy, 1997; Banks and Ruby, 2011; Pink,

2006; Pink et al., 2004). Others have brought together different disciplines and practices to represent a range of visual methods in edited volumes (e.g. Prosser 1998, van Leeuwen and Jewitt, 2001). Some authored books have proposed visual methodologies in ways that need not be discipline specific (e.g. Banks, 2001; Heath et al., 2010; Mitchell, 2011; Pink, 2007a [2001]; Rose, 2010 [2000]) but nevertheless advance different theoretical and epistemological standpoints. Other moves have brought together disciplines or practices in specific ways. For example, Arnd Schneider and Chris Wright's two groundbreaking books bring together anthropology and arts practice (2006, 2010) and other work specifically attends to the relationship between visual methods, social intervention and/or participatory research (Mitchell, 2011; Pink, 2007b). These developments in the relationship between social-science research practice and visual media have also been accompanied by a stream of literature that focuses on the theory and practice of ethnographic film (including, for example, the work of Crawford and Turton, 1991; El Guindi, 2004; MacDougall, 1998, 2005; Ruby, 2000). The ethical, practical and epistemological foundations of ethnographic filmmaking have historically been (and often still are) quite different from those of other uses of visual methods in the social sciences. Yet as a field of practice and theory, ethnographic filmmaking has had an undeniably important influence on the development of visual methodology as a field of scholarship.

Therefore, as a field of scholarship, visual methodology is complex and diverse. Its uniting themes tend to be the focus on the (audio)visual; the media and technologies engaged; and attention to a specific range of ethical issues. There are sometimes vast differences in terms of the ways that the status of the image is understood, and the theoretical and discipline-specific foundations that distinguish some approaches to the visual in research methodology. Part 5 of this book focuses specifically on interdisciplinarity. The first two chapters in this part show that there is no single rule for working with the visual across disciplines. As Marcus Banks demonstrates in Chapter 12, in some cases it is not appropriate to borrow methods from other disciplines. Instead, sometimes one needs to dig deeper into the resources of one's own disciplinary practices and perspectives to find a methodological solution. In contrast, in Chapter 13, Susan Hogan and I discuss a productive relationship between feminist art therapy and visual ethnography methods by identifying theoretical and practical coherences between these two disciplines which are not often mutually engaged. Yet, as I outline in the next section, recently a series of theoretical themes and practical issues that have swept across the social sciences and humanities have also been highly influential in ways that imply their common impact across the 'visual' disciplines. This offers ways both of theming the visual methodologies discussed in this book and of potentially creating stronger connections between disciplines.

Changing thought: theoretical turns and visual methodologies

Theoretical developments, debates, 'turns' and critiques form part of the ongoing flow of academic practice. Their developments frame the routes that scholarship and analysis take, and they also have important implications for methodological developments. In my own view it is crucial that theoretical coherence should be achieved throughout a project. By this I mean that the methodological approach should be informed by the same theoretical commitments that underpin any analysis of culture, society, persons or materialities produced through qualitative research. For example, in my book *Situating Everyday Life: Practices and Places* (Pink, 2012), I seek to achieve this continuity. Here, in the present volume, we also see that theoretical shifts in recent years have been implicated in the production of new types of analysis and subjects for research but also of 'innovative' research methods, and openness to 'new' ways of doing visual research of which digital and visual media are a part. Indeed, as I argue below, it has often recently been the case that digital media can inspire us to rethink theoretical paradigms in ways that have implications for the way we also understand 'old' media (Pink, 2011b). Yet there are also a series of broader theoretical shifts that are having a noticeable impact on not only visual methodologies, but more widely on both the research questions that are being asked and the way researchers go about trying to answer them. Interestingly, because more generally visual and digital media are tending to be increasingly integrated into a number of research methods and approaches, it would be easy to see visual methods as specifically implicated in these changes. While this might or might not be the case, we can be certain that they are having an impact on the way visual methods are engaged.

In *Advances in Visual Methodology* these theoretical shifts are treated in two different ways. First, in the following two parts of the book, contributors focus on what might be seen as two of the central theoretical strands of our time: practice and spatial theory. While neither of these paradigms are by any means new, they have recently come to occupy a level of importance in the social sciences and humanities that goes beyond disciplinary boundaries to inform the way scholars have formulated their research questions, understood their research practices and analysed their findings. There by no means exist standard and commonly agreed-on theories of practice, place or space – and indeed the terms have tended to be used in ways that are even sometimes contradictory, ranging between the descriptive and the abstract and so forth (see Pink, 2012, for a discussion of this). However, in recent scholarship they have been employed in an increasingly coherent way to offer understandings of both research practices and findings. In Parts 2 and 3 of this book respectively, contributors consider on the one hand, practice, and on the other, place and space. Collectively the authors of these chapters invite novel perspectives in both systematically addressing these theoretical strands through their visual research, and conceptualising their visual research methods through these theoretical paradigms.

While what have been called the 'practice turn' (Schatzki et al., 2001) and the 'spatial turn' (Hubbard et al., 2004) are addressed through groupings of chapters, the questions they raise endure throughout the book. For example, the idea of visual research itself as practice is developed particularly by Lydia Martens (Chapter 3), Jon Hindmarsh and Dylan Tutt (Chapter 4) and Elisenda Ardévol (Chapter 5). These contributors were invited to discuss the implications of the 'practice turn' for visual methodologies, in part due to their expertise in the study of practices themselves. Yet it is perhaps not surprising that they have turned their analytical gaze not only to the question of how visual researchers are analysing other people's practices in novel ways, but also to the very practice of visual research methods. This interest in research itself as practice is reflected across the volume, and clearly with a greater or lesser degree of emphasis it is often precisely practices that visual researchers study. The focus on practices and spatial theory is moreover inextricable from two other theoretical 'turns' or themes that are fundamental to contemporary thought about the visual and the way we do research – the senses and the focus on mobilities and movement.

What is often now referred to as a 'sensory turn' has had a profound impact on the way visual research is currently conceptualised. This has brought about a rethinking of visual culture studies with an acknowledgement of the relationship between the visual and the other senses. While developed explicitly in Elizabeth Edwards and Kaushik Bhaumik's (2009) *The Visual Sense*, this shift was already being acknowledged in earlier writings in the 21st century. A multi-sensory approach (Pink, 2009) has also played a key role in our understandings of anthropological film, rooted in the work of David MacDougall (1998, 2005), and is becoming a strand in the teaching and practice of visual anthropology. The re-situating of the visual in relation to the other senses has a series of implications for visual researchers. But, as I have pointed out elsewhere (Pink, 2009), it does not imply that a focus on the visual is no longer relevant. Rather it demonstrates that we need to rethink how the visual and its relationality to other sensory categories come into play in the ways that we create routes to knowledge in our research processes. As some of the contributors to this volume show, an appreciation of the senses has become increasingly integrated into the methodological frameworks that inform visual research. Therefore Cristina Grasseni (Chapter 6) writes of 'sensescapes' when discussing community mapping; Elisenda Ardévol's (Chapter 5) and my own

(Chapter 7) chapters remind us of the sensory dimensions of visual Internet research; and Christina Lammer (Chapter 10) discusses the use of her own body as 'a sensory research instrument'.

Movement and mobility are likewise increasingly popular questions for social research and in the practice of research. This has been no less so in the development of visual research methods. These themes become particularly pertinent in the chapters of the book that focus on digital technologies in visual research. For example, in Chapters 5 and 8 respectively, Elisenda Ardévol and Francesco Lapenta bring our attention to the potential of mobile and locative media and in Chapter 7 I suggest that movement is a useful metaphor through which to understand our experiences of digital ethnographic places.

Changing media: digital technologies and methodological reflection

Developments in digital, mobile and locative media inspire both new theoretical and practical engagements in the methodological process. Collectively, the contributors to this volume reinforce this point, and some chapters specifically address this issue. Digital media have inspired advances in research, media and arts practices, which create new routes to knowledge and its representation, and new ways for audiences to engage with visual research. Simultaneously, however, it becomes clear that existing theoretical frameworks that have been used to understand media practices and processes do not always accommodate the new types of digital, social, spatial and mobile encounters in which contemporary visual researchers become implicated. This demands that we develop advances in the ways we understand both the phenomena that we are researching *and* our positioning as researchers within these complex social-technological-environmental contexts. Significantly, these advances in practice and theory are not only relevant to understanding new ways of doing visual research in a digital era. They also enable us to rethink the ways in which media(ted) research and the ethnographic encounter is understood more widely. Thus they constitute part of wider theoretical advances with the arts and social sciences. In this sense, the work of these contributors shows that scholarship around visual/ digital methodology is not simply an isolated field that is aimed at the development of new research methods, but that it is just as likely to produce theoretical insights that are relevant to mainstream academic scholarship. Such works indeed suggest that the importance of achieving theoretical and methodological coherence is not only a one-way process of ensuring that we understand the methods we use with the same theories with which we understand our findings. Rather, it means that we might understand our research findings through theoretical frameworks developed in relation to the knowledge processes that are part of our methodological advances. Examples of such revisions in relation to technological changes are evident across this volume even when the chapters concerned are not directly 'about' the Internet. For instance, in Chapter 6, while her main focus is on community mapping, Cristina Grasseni shows how choosing a specific means of multimedia representation is a key step in the research process. With a more specific focus on visual Internet research Elisenda Ardévol points out in Chapter 5 how a visual/virtual ethnography creates new challenges for the researcher. In Chapter 7, I discuss how new visual ethnography environments that span Internet and face-to-face relations demand alternative non-locality-based theoretical framings, as does Francesco Lapenta in Chapter 8, through his discussion of the implications of the development of what he calls 'geomedia'. Similarly, in Chapter 11, Rod Coover argues that 'digital technologies have altered fundamental theories about how documentary images work and how to work with them'. Our experiences of new technologies are therefore encouraging us to think in new ways theoretically which in turn reflect back on how we theorise old media and on how we engage with media as researchers.

Changing the world: public and applied visual methodologies

Visual methodologies are used across a wide range of research contexts. I have stressed the interdisciplinarity of this field of scholarship and this is explored more fully in the final section of this book. Yet its boundary crossing does not stop in the way it fluidly associates itself with a range of different disciplines, albeit in different ways. Visual methodologies also create important bridges between what were in the past the rather separate worlds of academic social-science scholarship on the one hand, and on the other, the domains of applied and public research and of arts practice. These contexts, all of which engage the (audio)visual for research and communication about the works that are produced in them, are becoming increasingly interwoven in a contemporary context. Part 3 of this book looks at how research that engages with both the social sciences and the arts, and is intended to take on a public or applied profile, is pushing forward new advances in visual methodology. This raises a number of significant questions, including the issue of how such methodological advances made in the contexts of digital arts, documentary or participatory arts programmes might be seen as impacting on visual methodology as a field of scholarship. As recent works show, such as my own edited volume focusing on applied visual anthropology (Pink, 2007b) and Schneider and Wright's two edited texts exploring the connections between anthropology and art (2005, 2010), these are not entirely new combinations. Yet brought together we can see how social science, art and intervention invite new ways of thinking about how we might do visual research; how we might engage participants and publics in the processes of research and in the dissemination of such work; how in a digital context this invites new ideas and new practices; and thus what advances in visual methodology this brings.

The chapters in Part 4 directly approach this question. Maggie O'Neill (Chapter 9) and Christina Lammer (Chapter 10) both bring social science and visual and arts practice together to create works that are applied, public and scholarly, and Rod Coover (Chapter 11) brings us the collaborative methodology of writing in conversation to discuss new practices in non-fiction image-making with digital tools. Yet the themes of this part are not bounded, and both the application of visual methods outside academia and questions of their politicisation resurface across the volume. Lydia Martens (Chapter 3) discusses the politics of looking and policy debates about hygiene and nutrition; Cristina Grasseni's (Chapter 6) work with community mapping was an applied anthropology project developed with an ecomuseum; Jon Hindmarsh and Dylan Tutt (Chapter 4) discuss video analysis methods that are used in academic and applied work; and Susan Hogan and I (Chapter 13) discuss art therapy practice. Thus demonstrating a range of contexts where applied and scholarly research fields are bridged in contexts of interdisciplinarity.

Futures

This volume sets out a carefully selected set of critical and contemporary advances in visual methodology that are not only pushing forward the field of visual and generally qualitative research practice, but also offering new routes to knowledge that also have wider implications for scholarly and applied practice. I urge readers to engage with them as sources for thinking with and through the social, and as ways of participating in understanding the world and also as a set of practices that could lead to a range of new and equally innovative future scholarly, applied and public interventions. The future is not in this book, but in what we do with the ideas that its contributors propose.

References

Banks, M. (2001) *Visual Methods in Social Research*. London: Sage.
Banks, M. and Morphy, H. (eds) (1997) *Rethinking Visual Anthropology*. London: Routledge.

Banks, M. and Ruby, J. (eds) (2011) *Made to be Seen: Perspectives on the History of Visual Anthropology*. Chicago, IL: University of Chicago Press

Coleman, B. (2010) 'Ethnographic approaches to digital media', *Annual Review of Anthropology*, 39: 487–505.

Crawford, P.I. and Turton, D. (eds) (1991) *Film as Ethnography*. Manchester: Manchester University Press.

Edwards, E. and Bhaumik, K. (eds) (2009) *Visual Sense: A Cultural Reader*. Oxford: Berg.

El Guindi, F. (2004) *Visual Anthropology: Essential Theory and Method*. Walnut Creek, CA: Altamira Press.

Heath, C., Hindmarsh, J. and Luff, P. (2010) *Video in Qualitative Research: Analyzing Social Interaction in Everyday Life*. London: Sage.

Hubbard, P., Kitchin, R. and Valentine, G. (2004) *Key Thinkers on Space and Place*. London: Sage.

Knowles, C. and Sweetman, P. (eds) (2004) *Picturing the Social Landscape: Visual Methods and the Sociological Imagination*. London: Routledge.

MacDougall, D. (1998) *Transcultural Cinema*. Princeton, NJ: Princeton University Press.

MacDougall, D. (2005) *The Corporeal Image: Film, Ethnography, and the Senses*. Princeton, NJ: Princeton University Press.

Miller, D. (2011) *Tales from Facebook*. Cambridge: Polity Press.

Mitchell, C. (2011) *Doing Visual Research*. London: Sage.

Pauwels, L. and Margolis, E. (2011) *The Sage Handbook of Visual Methods*. London: Sage.

Pink, S. (2006) *The Future of Visual Anthropology: Engaging the Senses*. Oxford: Routledge.

Pink, S. (2007a [2001]) *Doing Visual Ethnography*. London: Sage.

Pink, S. (ed.) (2007b) *Visual Interventions: Applied Visual Anthropology*. Oxford: Berghahn.

Pink, S. (2009) *Doing Sensory Ethnography*. London: Sage.

Pink, S. (2011a) 'Multimodality, multisensoriality and ethnographic knowing: social semiotics and the phenomenology of perception', *Qualitative Research*, 11 (3): 261–76.

Pink, S. (2011b) 'Sensory digital photography: re-thinking "moving" and the image', *Visual Studies*, 26 (1): 4–13.

Pink, S. (2011c) 'Images, senses and applications: engaging visual anthropology', *Visual Anthropology*, 24 (5): 437–54.

Pink, S. (2012) *Situating Everyday Life: Practice and Places*. London: Sage.

Pink, S., Kurti, L. and Afonso, A.I. (eds) (2004) *Working Images*. London: Routledge.

Prosser, J. (ed.) (1998) *Image-Based Research: A Sourcebook for Qualitative Researchers*. London: Falmer Press.

Rose, G. (2010 [2000]) *Visual Methodologies* London: Sage.

Ruby, J. (2000) *Picturing Culture: Explorations of Film and Anthropology.* Chicago, IL: University of Chicago Press.

Schatzki, T., Knorr-Cetina, K. and von Savigny, E. (2001) *The Practice Turn in Contemporary Theory.* London: Routledge.

Schneider, A. and Wright, C. (2006) *Contemporary Art and Anthropology.* Oxford: Berg.

Schneider, A. and Wright, C. (2010) *Between Art and Anthropology: Contemporary Ethnographic Practice.* Oxford: Berg.

van Leeuwen, T. and Jewitt, C. (eds) (2001) *The Handbook of Visual Analysis.* London: Sage.

2

VISUAL ETHICS IN A CONTEMPORARY LANDSCAPE

Andrew Clark

Introduction

Recent years have witnessed a burgeoning debate about how researchers working with visual materials and methods can act in ethically appropriate ways (Allen, 2009a; Papademas, 2004; Perry and Marion, 2010; Prosser, 2000; Wiles et al., 2011) that has coincided with critique of the increasing bureaucratisation and regulation of social research by institutional review boards (Dingwall, 2008; Hammersley, 2009; Martin, 2007). The ethical concerns of researchers working with visual methodologies in respect to these debates can be summarised as follows: first, that visual research methods and the data they produce raise particular ethical issues because the visual is somehow different in form or method to word- and number-based data (Prosser, 2000; Prosser and Loxley, 2008); second, that existing institutional ethical review procedures, ethical frameworks and codes of practice are unsatisfactory for visual material (Papademas, 2004; Perry and Marion, 2010; Wiles et al., 2010b); and third, that there is some uncertainty about how to proceed when ethical conventions applied to other methods and data seem inappropriate for visual material (Riley and Manias, 2004; Wiles et al., 2008; Wiles et al., 2010a). Although wide-ranging in scope, much discussion about visual ethics frequently focuses, on the one hand, on the practicalities of doing such research ethically, addressing concerns about how to gain informed consent, and dealing with confidentiality and anonymity; and on the other, about the role of review boards and ethical frameworks in visual research practice. However, while certainly important, concern about the practicalities of doing visual research or how to meet the regulatory requirements of institutional ethics review boards should not be the sole drivers of ethical practice. In this chapter I argue that ethical decision-making in visual research should be considered with regard to epistemological approaches, specific research contexts, and in relation to researchers' and participants' own moral frameworks.

This chapter provides an overview of current ethical debates in image-based research including the influence of institutional structures and ethical issues surrounding data collection and dissemination, as well as issues of informed consent, anonymity and confidentiality, and ownership. I then reflect on these in the context of a recent qualitatively driven multi-method research project to illustrate the ways in which they are negotiated in situated visual research practices. This is not because I think this research offers exemplary practice in ethical visual research, but rather to show how situating ethical issues in particular contexts offers ways of thinking about what constitutes 'visual ethics'. I argue that a situated approach to image-based ethics may more appropriately take account of the concrete, everyday situations within which ethics are negotiated between researchers and research participants. The intention is not just to provide an overview of the ethical dilemmas visual researchers face, but also to outline ways in which research ethics intersect practicalities of method and technique with questions about the ontological status of visual data, and broader debate about how we might recognise and practise ethically appropriate research. In doing so, I suggest that alongside important developments in the production, analysis, and (re)presentation of data, advances in visual methodologies are placing ethics at the forefront of knowledge production.

The turn to the visual and ethical anxieties

It is widespread practice for social researchers to draw upon ethical frameworks and codes of practice when planning and conducting research. Common principles underpinning these ethical codes of practice include mutual respect, non-coercion and non-manipulation, and support for democratic values and institutions (Israel and Hay, 2006), outlined by Papademas as:

> Respect for person and the moral requirement to respect autonomy and the requirement to protect those with diminished autonomy; Beneficence and complementary requirement to do no harm and to maximise possible benefits and minimise possible harms; Justice and the fair distribution of the benefits and burdens of research. (Papademas, 2004: 122)

Put simply, ethical practice is about researchers 'figuring out what is the "right" research approach for a given project' (Martin, 2007: 321) with regard to data collection and analysis, treatment of participants, and responsibilities to society (Singleton and Straits, 2005). In research practice, this tends to be addressed through attention to informed consent, anonymity, confidentiality, dissemination, secondary usage, copyright and legalities. Of course, these issues are not unique to visual research, and it is important not to declare visual material a 'special case' that is somehow ethically different to other methodologies or types of data. However, while institutional inspection and regulation impacts on all social researchers, those working with visual material have expressed concern that they may be disadvantaged because of a lack of familiarity among ethical review panels with regards to their methods and methodologies, the nature of the data they collect and analyse, and the inappropriateness of existing, normative ethical frameworks. This has prompted the development of codes of ethical conduct tailored to visual methods and material such as that produced by the International Visual Sociology Association (Papademas and IVSA, 2009) and the British Sociological Association (VSG/BSA, 2006). Implicit in the development of these visually tailored codes is a spirit of 'aspirational' (Papademas and IVSA, 2009: 250) rather than prescriptive or exhaustive instruction that infer that the ethical conundrums facing visual researchers are not straightforward to resolve in the abstract (Clark et al., 2010; Gross et al., 2003; Papademas, 2004; Perry and Marion, 2010; Wiles et al., 2011). Perhaps because of this abstract uncertainty, concerns have been raised that visual methods afford particular scrutiny by institutional review boards, or may discourage neophyte researchers to work visually (Prosser and Loxley, 2008). Although there is some evidence to indicate regulatory uneasiness towards visual methods (e.g. Allen, 2009a, 2009b; Bradley, 2007), there are also accounts of visual researchers receiving less ethical interrogation at the hands of review boards than they might have been led to expect (Wiles et al., 2010b).

This is not to deny that the production, analysis and display of visual material raise specific ethical dilemmas (Pauwels, 2008; Perry and Marion, 2010; Wiles et al., 2010b). Indeed, as recent initiatives funded by the UK-based Economic and Social Research Council indicate, there remains demand among visual researchers themselves about how best to tackle issues such as anonymity, informed consent, protecting participants from harm, complexities about the ownership of visual data, and the ethics of dissemination and display (e.g. Prosser and Loxley, 2008; Wiles et al., 2008, 2010b). How some of these issues impact on visual research is outlined below.

Key issues impacting on visual researchers

Informed consent

Obtaining informed consent involves not only gaining agreement or permission to produce visual material but also to reproduce or display it among different audiences and in different contexts. In providing informed consent participants are expected to not be deceived or coerced into taking part in research, are informed of the purpose of the research and the research process, and understand the uses the research will be put to (Sin, 2005). Gaining informed consent for visual material could be particularly important since visual data alone may provide limited understandings of the meanings and experiences recorded in that data but requires further exploration through elicitation and discussion with others (Banks, 2007; Harper, 1998). The public display, publishing, or wider dissemination of visual data without the consent of individuals pictured has also been described as ethically questionable (Pink, 2007).

However, obtaining informed consent is not always straightforward, or possible, in visual research (Clark et al., 2010). It is not always clear that participants fully understand what it is they are consenting to, especially given that the meaning of consent, and cultural understandings and significance of visual materials more broadly, vary across societal, cultural and relational contexts (Becker, 1988; Pink, 2007; Ruby, 2000). Indeed, even if research participants collaborate fully in the production of visual data it is unlikely they will be fully aware of the intentions driving its production (Gross et al., 1988; Prosser, 2000), particularly if these change following reflection, further data collection, or deeper analytical understanding (Emmel and Clark, 2011). A further issue concerns who might be in a position to provide consent, such as when filming or photographing in public spaces or at public events, where it may be impractical to gain informed consent from all those present (Schwartz, 2002). Harper (2005) reports on how some point to precedents in photojournalism and photo-documentary, arguing that harm to subjects is unlikely to occur from 'showing normal people doing normal things' (2005: 759). While it may be impossible to gain consent from everyone in a crowded public arena, some may query the recording of visual images of unknowing individuals in public, or their subsequent display of such material. Finally, questions over consent arise when research participants produce visual data themselves, for example, through video diaries or photo-elicitation (e.g. Allen, 2009b; Holliday, 2007; Marquez-Zenkov, 2007; Mizen, 2005), especially if images include other people. Here, researchers are reliant on consent being obtained by participants acting as ethical mediators as well as data producers, and while those photographed are able to consent to being photographed by the participant, it is less certain that they will know all the purposes to which those images could be put. Of course, it may be possible to subsequently request permission through whomever took the image, but this is a complex issue to manage.

Anonymity and confidentiality

Rose (2007: 251) has critically pointed out that previous versions of the UK-based Economic and Social Research Council's (ESRC, 2006: 1) ethics framework recommended that 'all information supplied by informants should be confidential, and all informants guaranteed anonymity (in the case of photographs, this would entail ensuring no individuals were identifiable, by blurring faces digitally, for example)'. While the current, revised Framework does not explicitly make such prescriptive instruction (ESRC, 2010), such statements have contributed to the unease with which visual methodologists have to approach existing ethical frameworks. They also indicate how anonymity and confidentiality, while perhaps considered central to good ethical practice for text-based data, present particular challenges to visual researchers (Wiles et al., 2010a, 2010b). To put it bluntly, it is often impossible, impractical, or even illogical to maintain the anonymity and confidentiality of individuals in artwork, photographs and film. Visual methods are often justified on the grounds that they can reveal information that text-based methods cannot, enable participants to present particular aspects of their identities, and have a broad appeal as aesthetic cultural artefacts (Chaplin, 2004; Harper, 2005; Holliday, 2007). Consequently, altering visual material by 'disguising' participants in order to preserve their anonymity and maintain confidentiality may destroy the very purpose of producing data visually. In this regard, visual material presents a significant challenge to conventional ethical practices surrounding the anonymity of participants.

That said, if participants are to be made anonymous, researchers have adopted a range of strategies and techniques including computer software packages that offer pixelation techniques or that can blur faces (see, for example, Hindmarsh and Tutt, Chapter 4, this volume). While the effects may be variable and not always appreciated by those who are being 'protected' (Wiles et al., 2008), technological advances are making such initiatives more effective and sensitive to those they strive to protect. Other researchers have adopted more creative approaches to displaying visual data such as not publishing images containing recognisable individuals in them (e.g. Barrett, 2004; Schwartz, 2002), or making individuals harder to recognise by using pseudonyms alongside the seemingly unaltered images of those same individuals in order to unhitch participant names from their visual identifiers (Marquez-Zenkov, 2007; Mizen, 2005). However, while issues of anonymity have been a particular concern of those working with still images, there is a successful tradition in ethnographic filmmaking of explicitly not anonymising visual material, in part because (historically at least) of a lack of technological capability but also, and more significantly, because anonymising such material is contrary to the purpose of producing such films (Pink, 2007).

While technological developments have facilitated more creative, and satisfactory, ways of anonymising moving and still images, the assumption that preserving anonymity and confidentiality is the only ethical position to adopt is being questioned with researchers obtaining explicit consent from participants to display images unchanged (Sweetman, 2008; Wiles et al., 2010a). This partly stems from concern about the difficulties of achieving full anonymity given the ease with which 'internal confidentiality' (Tolich, 2004) – whereby individuals within a studied community can recognise themselves and others despite attempts at anonymity – can be broken in the display of visual material. However, additional concerns have also been raised about how some techniques to anonymise visual material draw connotations with criminality and victimhood in its parallels with techniques used in media representations (Wiles et al., 2010b). While deciding not to anonymise visual material clearly circumvents the issue of how to anonymise it, this is about more than the need to overcome practical and technical concerns (Sweetman, 2008). Presenting identifiable visual data enables it to be considered in ways that may be closer to how producers intended, and heralds a more participatory approach to ethical decision-making. Moreover, the questioning of often taken-for-granted practices such as anonymisation and confidentiality also echoes reports of participants' demands that their experiences and narratives are explicitly attributed to them and, potentially, offer some (albeit tentative) resistance to top-down institutionally imposed codes of ethical practice.

Purposefully rejecting ethical conventions such as anonymising all data is more than an appeal as a pragmatic solution to what at times can be rather unsatisfactory attempts at partial anonymity. For it parallels wider debates about how social research can better empower participants through the research process, engaging with them as individuals able to enter into ethical dialogue with researchers rather than being represented merely as research subjects in need of protection. Clearly, the decision to not anonymise images needs to be justified and discussed with participants, and, of course, while participants may have consented to the display of images this does not necessarily mean researchers have carte blanche to display those images as they choose. Indeed, there are occasions when researchers may be required to go against participants' wishes if they have consented to having their identities revealed in the dissemination of visual images (Barrett, 2004). Consequently, rather than seeing the rejection of anonymisation of participants as an 'easy' way of circumventing the challenges of anonymising visual material for display or dissemination, it needs to be considered in relation to questions of paternalism, empowerment and respect for participant voice.

Ownership and the display and dissemination of images

Although important in their own right, the complexities surrounding consent and anonymity are heightened in the context of debate about the ownership and public display of visual materials. Specifically, there are questions around who owns visual data and who has the 'right' to use, display and reuse it. Usually, the person who creates an image retains copyright ownership unless sold or explicitly retained by the producer's employer, and can subsequently use the images for a range of purposes including archiving (Clark et al., 2010). However, what may be considered legal in copyright terms is not necessarily ethical in terms of ownership and usage. Given visual data is frequently the product of a researcher-participant collaboration, the 'ownership' of images is not straightforward, with the researcher, the photographer, and the individuals depicted in images all potentially having a claim in how those images are used. While some of these issues may be resolved if the researcher also produced the image, there are further questions to address if researchers are using archived or existing data and when the keeper of the images did not produce, or is not featured in, the image (Wiles et al., 2008). Questions of ownership of images then, are not simply about determining who has legal ownership, but also about who can consent to the inclusion of images in research, and about who has a say in how images are used.

An advantage of working with visual materials is the ways in which they can be used in research outputs that focus on public engagement. It is increasingly common for findings of research to be presented not just in published outputs but also in the form of exhibitions, displays and online galleries where the visual becomes far more than neutral representations of everyday life. For example, the 'Look at me! Images of women and ageing project' (www.representing-ageing.com) is explicitly challenging stereotypical images of older women by enabling 'ordinary' older women to comment on, or create, their own images of ageing. Here, the visual becomes both practice and outcome of attempts to destabilise stigmatising, gendered discourses of ageing. Far from a neutral tool through which to view society, the visual offers an explicitly political act of looking at and displaying inequality (see www.representing-ageing.com and Chapter 13, this volume). Approaching the visual as a political practice and 'product' of research requires ethical consideration of questions about the display of images and their release into the public realm where it is interpreted in different ways and becomes liable to re-use. Researchers have to consider how to negotiate consent between producers of the image and those featured in it, as well as explain the possible implications of the display. No matter how ethically appropriate researchers act when displaying such material, it is important to recognise that the public display of visual material means they relinquish control of how those images are read and interpreted, and especially in the case of online display, potentially re-used by unknown viewers. Once in the public realm, participants and researchers have no control over how images are read, and will struggle to prevent them being used for different purposes by others (Pauwels, 2006; van Dijck, 2008).

Consequently, there are differences between consenting to take part in research and consenting for an image to go in a book, on display, or on the Internet. Consent may be required not only to produce a photograph or film footage, but also for the specific formats and contexts in which the image is displayed, such as books, conference papers, exhibitions, or for general illustrative purposes (Pink, 2007). While participants might consent to having their photograph taken, they may not be consenting to the subsequent display of those images. Researchers need to be aware that consent to the display of images at one point in time does not necessarily mean a participant is happy to consent to the use of the image in the longer term. To put it bluntly, if a participant changes their mind about the use of an image of themselves in the future there may be little a researcher can do about this. Thus dissemination is far from a fixed, one-off activity for visual material, and much like all data, lingers to be reworked, reinterpreted, and perhaps re-presented, in different contexts.

From ethical debate to ethical practice

As outlined then, researchers working with visual methods and data clearly face a significant number of ethical dilemmas. While it is easy to raise such dilemmas, ways of addressing them are less forthcoming. Faced with the challenges of inappropriate institutional regulations, some have inferred that visual researchers attempt to circumvent review boards by presenting their work as journalism or documentary filmmaking rather than research, pointing to ethical practices in journalism that tend to offer seemingly less restrictive assumptions on how visual material is collected and reproduced. Bradley (2007), for example, comments on how members of his institutional ethical review board queried whether his proposed video-documentary method was better addressed as journalism rather than social science: 'because a journalist does not interpret data . . . only collects and presents it' (2007: 342). While Bradley submitted his research proposal for ethical approval 'just to be safe' (2007: 342), it is important that visual researchers do not simply comply with ethical regulations simply for their own security. If visual methodologies are to be presented as rigorous and credible practices to other researchers, ethical review boards, and research funders, it is important that it is afforded the same ethical consideration and respect as other, perhaps more 'conventional', methodologies. This is not to suggest that journalism does not have its own code of ethical conduct, but rather to recognise that journalism and social science research are not the same. It is important to question whether attempts to pass visual research as some kind of (imitation) journalism may cause others to question its social science credentials.

Alternatively then, and as already discussed, advances in visual ethics have encouraged the questioning of some normative assumptions behind ethical decision-making. There are also reflective accounts of how visual-orientated researchers have worked with institutional review boards in order to better negotiate the ethical terms of their research (Wiles et al., 2010a). Other responses have included calls to share best practice (Riley and Manias, 2004; Wiles et al., 2008, 2010b); provide more explicit training (Wiles et al., 2011); and for visual methodologists to join research ethics boards themselves or engage in broader debate about ethical practices in research (Clark et al., 2010). For instance, relating to the later, the concerns of participatory researchers about the lack of understanding of the ethical challenges presented by their own approach amongst members of review boards resulted in calls for new ways of thinking about not only disciplinary codes of practice but also the nature of what constitutes ethical research (Askins, 2007; Khanlou and Peter, 2005; Perry and Marion, 2010).

These responses clearly move beyond calls for 'how to do' ethical visual research to address wider methodological and epistemic debate about the nature of knowledge, power, and critical research practice. This includes re-situating ethics-related debate beyond the requirements of regulatory frameworks and codes of practice (important though these are) in an emergent landscape of alternative ethical practices. Some, though certainly not all, of the ethical dilemmas visual researchers face arise from a legacy of biomedical, or at least positivist-orientated, ethical principles that fail to fit with their predominantly post-positivist methodological frameworks (Clark et al., 2010). This is not to suggest that visual researchers are engaging in naïve ethical practices, but rather hints at how ethical practice is as much about questions of epistemology as it is about research method and technique. Viewed from this perspective, it may be more appropriate to consider ethical issues part of an ongoing process of negotiation and reflection. Such situated ethics recognise that it is unlikely that a 'one-size-fits all' ethical framework will be appropriate for all visual research and demonstrate how ethical decisions can be made (and appraised) in the context of particular cases rather than according to a set of prescriptive regulations that are rigidly adhered to or adopted whole (Simons and Usher, 2000a). In the final section then, I outline how some of the ethical issues discussed above were negotiated in one particular research context.

Situating and negotiating ethics in practice

The Connected Lives[1] research project investigated how social networks, neighbourhoods, and communities are perceived and represented in a heterogeneous inner city neighbourhood. It sought to understand how social networks are built, maintained, and break down within particular geographical and temporal contexts. In doing so, we were interested not just in what networks are for, but also in the ways in which social relations are situated within, and reproduced through, localised spaces that constitute neighbourhood life and broader associations under the banner of community (Clark and Emmel, 2009; Emmel and Clark, 2011). A range of qualitatively driven methods were developed to investigate the multi-dimensionality of the real-life experience of networks, neighbourhoods, and communities including walking interviews, participatory mapping, and day-diaries of communication practices with 24 participants along with our own (researcher) participant observation. These methods made prominent use of the visual, including diagrammatic representation of social networks, researcher-produced photography, and participant-produced photograph and elicitation interviews. Towards the end of the research we held workshops for stakeholders and policy makers to discuss findings, and a Community Exhibition, attended by a number of participants and other local residents, where substantive findings were represented through specifically produced images, images produced during the research, and submissions to a 'community photography' competition (Emmel and Clark, 2009).

Over the course of the research we were faced with a number of the ethical issues discussed above. Would a review board have ethical concerns about our methods? Would it be necessary, or even possible, to anonymise the visual data? How could we display the data in ways that protected our participants from harm or revealing that they had participated? How would we gain informed consent from participants to produce, analyse and display images of them? How would we manage the informed-consent process for images showing other people that participants produced? Would we be able to use the images in publications or at conferences given this would clearly break anonymity and confidentiality?

These questions are more than 'problems' to be overcome, but are also indicative of a wider set of issues about the position of visual methodologies relative to knowledge production. As a research team we accepted that we did not have all the 'right answers' upfront, but rather recognised, to use Usher's (2000) phrase, our 'ethical anxieties' as fruitful ways of facilitating dialogue drawing upon recognised ethical conventions for guidance. Rather than adopting universalist principles, we pursued a more iterative and flexible ethical approach that was adaptive to and situated within specific contexts. This included engaging in dialogue with participants about what would make our research ethically appropriate for them as well as us.

While we gained verbal informed consent at the onset of each interaction with a participant, we returned to the issue throughout an encounter (or method) and, when wanting to use data in particular outputs such as at conferences, we requested permission, and ensured that such permission, if possible, was granted for future display. Certainly, we were fortunate that the use of multiple methods enabled us to return to participants over a period of time and develop potentially stronger relationships with them. This may have afforded greater opportunities to share our ideas about how we wanted to use the data, and to negotiate further consent about the use of visual material. Central to our broader approach to research was our belief in engaging with participants as active agents in the research process, able to contribute to how we proceeded with the development and deployment of research methods, and wider methodological concerns. As participatory researchers have highlighted, institutional review boards construct participants as potentially vulnerable 'subjects' to be protected by a 'codified set of procedures that assumes a standardized, researcher-driven model of scholarship' (Martin, 2007: 322) rather than individuals capable of engaging in a collaborative and negotiated research process. By not assuming that, as researchers, we 'knew best', we could navigate a path through the ethical maze (Prosser, 2000) with the support of participants. Thus, when providing their consent, participants were able to consider some of the ethical issues outlined above, guided by our questioning and directed discussion about the potential implications of engaging with visual methods.

When producing visually orientated data, participants modified the methods in ways they considered ethically, as well as practically, appropriate. For instance, when producing photographs to accompany their day-diaries that included other individuals, participants reflected on how they had discussed the research before asking for permission to take their photographs, having been guided by their prior discussions with the research team about the nature and importance of gaining such consent. Others deliberately avoided taking photographs of people because they were not sure it was 'fair' that they could be included in the research without their explicit consent. Some took photographs of family and friends, but specified that they were not shown beyond the research team and requested that they were only used for analysis purposes. One participant took photographs of several individuals but decided not to hand the photographs over, preferring to maintain control (and outright ownership) of them by showing us the images but taking them away afterwards. Similar flexibility emerged during the walking interview method. For instance, participants declined to take photographs of people, or chose to conduct the 'walk' by car in order to avoid being seen, and potentially recognised, with a researcher. Frequently, we encountered other people known to them during the walks. In such cases, the participant would often 'take control' of the interaction, explaining what they were doing, providing an outline of the research, requesting permissions to take a photograph, and informing those we met that, in entering into discussion with us, they might become part of the research. In other cases, participants prompted discussion about their queries of the ethics of photographing others.

When discussing and collecting visual data we were careful to ensure participants' consent that the images form part of the dataset for analysis, and/ or could be used for dissemination purposes. This enabled participants to make distinctions between visual material they were happy to have included in the research but not shown or displayed beyond the research team. When selecting images to display in the exhibition we discussed the implications of recognition to those participants whose images we wanted to use. For the most part, because our reasons to display an image were in order to make a more abstract argument that drew upon a range of data and analysis rather than a particular story or issue unique to the individual in the image, we found that participants were prepared to provide consent. However, because it would prove too complicated to return to all the individuals featured in images taken by participants, we did not display images of individuals we could not obtain direct consent from. For while we were satisfied that we had consent from such individuals for their image to be part of the data-set, we did not know for certain that they had consented to the image being used for any other purpose, including display. We also arranged for photographs to be produced specifically for the exhibition that, we felt, represented important findings, including a theme around the rather generic title of 'people make places'. For these images, we were keen that a number of individuals were featured. In these cases, we obtained verbal consent for permission to produce and display the images un-anonymised. A number of the individuals included in this set of images came to the exhibition and expressed pleasure at seeing themselves on public display.

In this way, the visual became both a practice and a site where we could situate and reflect upon ethical concerns. Throughout the research we adopted 'layers' of ethical practice regarding the production, analysis, storing and display of images in different contexts. While this could potentially be an administratively onerous process, we relied on verbal consent and 'non-consent' for the use of images in particular ways. Thus we dealt with issues of production, ownership, and display throughout the research project in collaboration with participants. That said, we found that some images, much like other kinds of data, are more amenable to 'public disclosure'. In a small number of instances, while participants were keen that we show to others particular images of specific places, we did not follow this up. This was not because of what the images showed per se (in these cases, they included community centres, cafes and public houses), but because of the narratives associated with those images. Here, it was the significance of intentions behind the production of the image that made some less appropriate to display. A situated approach to ethics does not mean going with whatever participants request, but rather enables researchers to make informed decisions in collaboration with participants and in consideration of the contexts in which those images will subsequently be viewed and interpreted (Pink, 2007; Wiles et al., 2010b). Moreover, in negotiating the ethical terrain with participants as the research progressed, we were able to side-step prescriptive structures that could have been imposed at the outset of the research, reframing our visual ethics as a relational practice situated within the sites and scales of data production, analysis and presentation.

Visual researchers demonstrate how the process of doing visual research is just as important as the outcome. So too should ethical considerations be considered part of the process of knowledge production rather than a 'bolt on' to visual research design. Research ethics are not just about getting a proposal past an ethics panel, or ensuring that participants sign an informed consent form, but are intrinsic to the entire research process (Humphries and Martin, 2000). Situated visual ethics approach the issues discussed earlier as part of an ongoing negotiation between researchers and participants rather than part of a potentially paternalistic relationship between them. With some notably important exceptions (perhaps when working with some marginalised groups or among societies where visual media and technologies may be uncommon), visual cultures are a familiar part of the everyday lives we aim to understand, though this is not to state that such cultures are all the same. In our case, we found that many participants were accustomed to determining appropriate production and display of visual material, in part due to their increasing familiarity with visual technologies including digital cameras (both still and film), and the display of visual materials on public-access Internet sites such as Facebook, Flickr and YouTube. Many participants dealt with the ethical complexities around the production, collection and display of visual material in their everyday lives, albeit in rather messy, inconsistent, and potentially chaotic ways. In encouraging our participants to play a role in ethical decision-making about how we work with visual material in research, so they draw on their own ethical compasses that they use to navigate comparable issues in their everyday lives. This is not to suggest that participants have the solutions to these issues, or indeed can agree on them given time, but rather indicates that negotiation can achieve more appropriate ethical positions that are sensitive to the visual social and cultural milieu the research is conducted within. Moreover, in problematising objective and universalist principles, so we were able to better recognise, discuss, and accommodate ethical differences among participants while maintaining broader ethical principles of mutual respect, non-coercion and support for democratic values.

I am not claiming that a situated approach to visual ethics a panacea. It is not clear, for example, how ethics committees respond to situated and contextualised approaches to ethical visual research that reject universalist frameworks. As discussed above, researchers may also be required to have the final say about a particular ethical issue, possibly overriding the wishes of participants who, for example, may be keen that particular, un-anonymised images are displayed. Similarly, it is important not to reify participants' views as necessarily being any more ethically appropriate than others (including those of researchers). Questions of power and control in the research process remain unresolved, though the approach at least attempts to position participants as active agents, alongside institutional review board members and researchers, at the heart of debates about visual ethics. Moreover, shifting visual research practice out of what Bauman (1993: 34) might term 'the stiff armour of artificially constructed ethical codes' makes any decisions liable to temporality, inconclusiveness, and potentially short of universal acceptance among participants and researchers within research projects, let alone across different projects or socio-cultural environments.

In reflecting on this example then, I am not proposing that it offers a kind of 'best practice' or a utopian framework appropriate to other research contexts. It has never been my intention to outline or provide prescriptive guidance for every ethical dilemma visual methodologists may face. I am conscious, for example, that it has not addressed the re-use of visual material in data archives (Rolph et al., 2009), working with 'vulnerable groups' (Boxall and Rolph, 2009), or researching potentially 'risky' subjects (Allen, 2009a). Indeed, to attempt to do so would be to defeat the purpose of a call to appreciate the situatedness of ethical concerns. For as Simons and Usher note:

> the whole point about a situated ethics is . . . that it is situated, and this implies that it is immune to universalization. A situated ethics is local and specific to particular practices. It cannot be universalized and therefore any attempt to formulate a theory of situated ethics, given any theorization strives for universality, is doomed to failure. (Simons and Usher, 2000b: 2)

Rather, my aim has been to demonstrate the ways in which visual methodologists address ethical dilemmas in the contexts, relationships, and sites in which they arise. While this is open to critiques of relativism and an 'it all depends' or 'anything goes' attitude, this does not mean we are unable to agree on culturally situated 'good' and 'bad' ethical practices. How such practices are arrived at becomes central to ethical practice, and speaks to important debates about biomedical ethics or the ethics of care, researcher paternalism and participant agency (Blum, 1988; Gilligan, 1982; Singer, 1991), and the impact of ethical regulation. In this sense, the development of recent ethical frameworks that deal explicitly with visual methods and material (Papademas and the IVSA, 2009; VSG/BSA, 2006) may not only demonstrate the strength of demand for such guidance (paradoxically at a time when concern over ethical regulation appears to be growing), but may also be indicative of the dissatisfaction with predetermined codes and frameworks designed for other epistemological and methodological contexts, as well as ongoing concern among visual researchers that we conduct research that is ethically appropriate.

Conclusion: beyond fixing ethics

In reflecting on how a situated ethical approach framed my own work with visual data and methods, this chapter has suggested that ethical visual research is better practised in particular contexts. Situated visual ethics are not about 'fixing' ethics, but about recognising that ethical decisions and practices run throughout research practice, and cannot be resolved by adherence to pre-determined codes or universalist principles. This is not to suggest that visual researchers disregard existing guidelines, but rather consider them as guidance to draw upon when considering the social, political and cultural contexts that ethical issues arise within.

Those working with visual material are clearly advancing the frontiers of technical, empirical and methodological research. In doing so, they call into question some of the assumptions behind ethical codes of practice and the discourse of institutional review boards. Debates about visual research ethics do not just involve negotiating ethical regulation or attending to the somewhat practical matters of whether and how to anonymise material or gather informed consent, but also engage in critiques of what may have become 'taken-for-granted' ethical practices, and challenge positivist-inspired, universalist, protectionist and objectivist thinking about research ethics. Moreover, in pursuing agendas around the politics of participation, and recognising those who choose to participate in research as active individuals able to engage in ethical debate, whilst still adhering to core ethical foundations, so visual methodologists are demonstrating how their advances in ethical practices have the potential to reach far beyond their own visual landscapes.

Note

1 'Connected Lives' (Principal Investigator Nick Emmel) was part of the Manchester/Leeds Real Life Methods Node of the National Centre for Research Methods funded by the Economic and Social Research Council (ref 576255017).

References

Allen, L. (2009a) '"Caught in the act": ethics committee review and researching the sexual culture of schools', *Qualitative Research*, 9 (4): 395–410.

Allen, L. (2009b) 'Snapped: researching the sexual cultures of schools using visual methods', *International Journal of Qualitative Studies in Education*, 22 (5): 549–61.

Askins, K. (2007) 'Codes, committees and other such conundrums', *ACME: An International E-Journal for Critical Geographies*, 6 (3): 350–9.

Banks, M. (2007) *Using Visual Data in Qualitative Research*. London: Sage.

Barrett, D. (2004) 'Photo-documenting the needle exchange: methods and ethics', *Visual Studies*, 19: 145–9.

Bauman, Z. (1993) *Postmodern Ethics*. Oxford: Blackwell.

Becker, H. (1988) 'Forward: images, ethics and organisations', in L. Gross, J. Katz and J. Ruby (eds), *The Moral Rights of Subjects in Photographs, Films and Television*. New York: Oxford University Press. pp. xi–xvii.

Blum, L. (1988) 'Gilligan and Kohlberg: implications for moral theory', *Ethics*, 98 (3): 472–91.

Boxall, K. and Rolph, S. (2009) 'Research ethics and the use of visual images in research with people with intellectual disability', *Journal of Intellectual and Developmental Disability*, 34 (1): 45–54.

Bradley, M. (2007) 'Silenced by their own protection: how IRB marginalizes those it feigns to protect', *ACME: An International E-Journal for Critical Geographies*, 6 (3): 339–49.

Chaplin, E. (2004) 'My visual diary', in C. Knowles and P. Sweetman, P. (eds), *Picturing the Social Landscape: Visual Methods and the Sociological Imagination*. London: Routledge. pp. 35–48.

Clark, A. and Emmel, N. (2009) 'Connected lives: methodological challenges for researching networks, neighbourhoods and communities', *Qualitative Researcher*, 11: 9–11.

Clark, A., Prosser, J. and Wiles, R. (2010) 'Ethical issues in image-based research', *Arts and Health*, 2 (1): 81–93.

Dingwall, R. (2008) 'The ethical case against ethical regulation in humanities and social science research', *21st Century Society: Journal of the Academy of Social Sciences*, 3 (1): 1–12.

Economic and Social Research Council (2006) 'Research Ethics Framework' (previously available from: www.esrcsocietytoday.ac.uk/ESRCInfoCentre/Images/ESRC_RE_Ethics_Framework_tcm6-11291.pdf).

Economic and Social Research Council (2010) 'Framework for Research Ethics (FRE)' (retrieved 25 October 2011 from: www.esrc.ac.uk/_images/Framework_for_Research_Ethics_tcm8-4586.pdf).

Emmel, N. and Clark, A. (2009) 'The methods used in connected lives: investigating networks, neighbourhoods and communities', ESRC National Centre for Research Methods: Real Life Methods Node working paper no. 06/09 (retrieved 10 July 2011 from: http://eprints.ncrm.ac.uk/800).

Emmel, N. and Clark, A. (2011) 'Learning to use visual methodologies in our research: a dialogue between two researchers', *Forum Qualitative Sozialforschung / Forum: Qualitative Social Research*, 12 (1): Art. 36 (retrieved 10 July 2011 from: http://nbn-resolving.de/urn:nbn:de:0114-fqs1101360).

Gilligan, C. (1982) *In a Different Voice: Psychological Theory and Women's Development*. Cambridge, MA: Harvard University Press.

Gross, L., Katz, J. and Ruby, J. (1988) 'Introductions: a moral pause', in L. Gross, J. Katz and J. Ruby (eds), *Image Ethics: The Moral Rights of Subjects in Photographs, Films and Television*. New York: Oxford University Press. pp. 3–33.

Gross, L., Katz, J. and Ruby, J. (eds) (2003) *Image Ethics in the Digital Age*. Minneapolis, MN: University of Minnesota Press.

Hammersley, M. (2009) 'Against the ethicists: on the evils of ethical regulation', *International Journal of Social Research Methodology, Theory and Practice*, 12 (3): 211–26.

Harper, D. (1998) 'An argument for visual sociology', in J. Prosser (ed.), *Image-based Research: A Sourcebook for Qualitative Researchers*. London: Routledge Falmer. pp. 24–41.

Harper, D. (2005) 'What's new visually?', in N. Denzin and Y. Lincoln (eds), *Handbook of Qualitative Research* (3rd edn). Thousand Oaks, CA: Sage. pp. 747–62.

Holliday, R. (2007) 'Performances, confessions and identities: using video diaries to research sexualities', in Stanczak, G. (ed.), *Visual Research Methods: Image, Society and Representation*. Thousand Oaks, CA: Sage. pp. 255–79.

Humphries, B. and Martin, M. (2000) 'Disrupting ethics in social research', in B. Humphries (ed.), *Research in Social Care and Social Welfare: Issues and Debates for Practice*. London: Jessica Kingsley. pp. 69–85.

Israel, M. and Hay, D. (2006) *Research Ethics for Social Scientists: Between Ethical Conduct and Regulatory Compliance*. Thousand Oaks, CA: Sage.

Khanlou, N. and Peter, E. (2005) 'Participatory action research: considerations for ethical review', *Social Science and Medicine*, 60: 2333–40.

Marquez-Zenkov, K. (2007) '"Through city students' eyes": urban students' beliefs about school's purposes, supports and impediments', *Visual Studies*, 22 (2): 138–54.

Martin, D. (2007) 'Bureaucratizing ethics: institutional review boards and participatory research', *ACME: An International E-Journal for Critical Geographies*, 6 (3): 319–28.

Mizen, P. (2005) 'A little "light work"? Children's images of their labour', *Visual Studies*, 20 (2): 124–39.

Papademas, D. (2004) 'Editor's introduction: ethics in visual research', *Visual Studies*, 19 (2): 122–6.

Papadamas, D. and IVSA (International Visual Sociology Association) (2009) 'IVSA code of research ethics and guidelines', *Visual Studies*, 24 (3): 250–7.

Pauwels, L. (2006) 'Discussion: ethical issues in online (visual) research', *Visual Anthropology*, 19 (3/4): 365–9.

Pauwels, L. (2008) 'Taking and using: ethical issues of photographs for research purposes', *Visual Communication Quarterly*, 15 (4): 243–57.

Perry, S. and Marion, J. (2010) 'State of the ethics in visual anthropology', *Visual Anthropology Review*, 26 (2): 96–104.

Pink, S. (2007) *Doing Visual Ethnography* (2nd edn). London: Sage.

Prosser, J. (2000) 'The moral maze of image ethics', in H. Simons and R. Usher (eds), *Situated Ethics in Education Research*. London: Routledge. pp. 116–32.

Prosser, J. and Loxley, A. (2008) 'Introducing visual methods', National Centre for Research Methods Review Paper 010 (retrieved 10 July 2011 from: http://eprints.ncrm.ac.uk/420/).

Riley, R. and Manias, E. (2004) 'The uses of photography in clinical nursing practice and research: a literature review', *Journal of Advanced Nursing*, 48 (4): 397–405.

Rolph, S., Johnson, J. and Smith, R. (2009) 'Using photography to understand change and continuity in the history of residential care for older people', *International Journal of Social Research Methodology*, 12 (5): 421–39.

Rose, G. (2007) *Visual Methodologies: An Introduction to the Interpretation of Visual Materials* (2nd edn). London: Sage.

Ruby, J. (2000) *Picturing Culture: Explorations of Film and Anthropology*. Chicago, IL: University of Chicago Press.

Schwartz, D. (2002) 'Pictures at a demonstration', *Visual Studies*, 17 (1): 27–36.

Simons, H. and Usher, R. (eds) (2000a) *Situated Ethics in Educational Research*. London: Routledge Falmer.

Simons, H. and Usher, R. (2000b) 'Introduction: ethics in the practice of research', in H. Simons and R. Usher (eds), *Situated Ethics in Educational Research*. London: Routledge Falmer. pp. 1–11.

Sin, C.H. (2005) 'Seeking informed consent: reflections on research practice', *Sociology*, 39 (2): 277–94.

Singer, P. (1991) 'Afterward', in P. Singer (ed.), *A Companion to Ethics*. Blackwell: Oxford. pp. 543–5.

Singleton, R. and Straits, B. (2005) *Approaches to Social Research* (4th edn). New York: Oxford University Press.

Sweetman, P. (2008) 'An ethics of recognition? Questioning immediate assumptions about issues of ethics and anonymity in visual research', paper presented at the Visual Methods Symposium, 10 July (retrieved from: www.education.leeds.ac.uk/research/visual-methods/masterclass.php).

Tolich, M. (2004) 'Internal confidentiality: when confidentiality assurances fail relational informants', *Qualitative Sociology*, 27 (1): 101–6.

Usher, R. (2000) 'Deconstructive happening, ethical moment', in H. Simons and R. Usher (eds), *Situated Ethics in Educational Research*. London: Routledge Falmer. pp. 162–85.

van Dijck, J. (2008) 'Digital photography: communication, identity, memory', *Visual Communication*, 7 (1): 57–76.

VSG/BSA (Visual Study Group of the British Sociological Association) (2006) 'Statement of ethical practice for the British Sociological Association, Visual Sociology Group' (retrieved 15 February 2011 from: www.visualsociology.org.uk/about/ethical_statement.php).

Wiles, R., Prosser, J., Bagnoli, A., Clark, A., Davies, K., Holland, S. and Renold, E. (2008) 'Visual ethics: ethical issues in visual research', National Centre for Research Methods: Methods Review Paper 011 (retrieved 10 July 2011 from: http://eprints.ncrm.ac.uk/421/).

Wiles, R., Coffey, A., Robison, J. and Heath, S. (2010a) 'Anonymity and visual images: issues of respect, "voice" and protection', ESRC National Centre for Research Methods Working Paper series, 07/10 (retrieved 10 July from: http://eprints.ncrm.ac.uk/1804/).

Wiles, R., Coffey, A., Robison, J. and Prosser, J. (2010b) 'Ethical regulation and visual methods: making visual research impossible or developing good practice?', ESRC National Centre for Research Methods Working Paper series, 01/10 (retrieved 10 July 2011 from: http://eprints.ncrm.ac.uk/1802/).

Wiles, R., Clark, A. and Prosser, J. (2011) 'Visual ethics at the crossroads', in L. Pauwells and E. Margolis (eds), *The Sage Handbook of Visual Research Methods*. Thousand Oaks, CA: Sage. pp. 685–706.

PART 2
VISUAL PRACTICES AND VISUALISING PRACTICE

The recent interest in practice-focused approaches in the social sciences is generating an interest in not only the practices of research participants but also of researchers themselves. Visual research practices are not exempt from this enquiry and indeed they are implicated in several different ways when a practice approach is taken.

The first and most obvious question is that of how we might go about using visual methods to investigate and analyse the practices of research participants. The three chapters in this section show how practice theories are being engaged in a range of different visual methodologies. In Chapter 3, Lydia Martens draws on sociological uses of practice theory to explore the use of CCTV cameras in the intimate domain of the domestic kitchen, a way that visual researchers can record and analyse practices as they are performed in everyday life. Martens shows how such an approach not only advances visual methods but also the type of policy-relevant and academic knowledge that is available about kitchen practices through visual means. In Chapter 4, John Hindmarsh and Dylan Tutt discuss the use of video in ethnomethodological approaches to workplace practices. Their chapter focuses on the case study of the 'data session' – a work practice in the ethnomethodological analysis of video recordings. In Chapter 5, Elisenda Ardévol approaches the question of how we might research and analyse other people's visual practices through Internet research. As Ardévol's chapter demonstrates, the Internet offers a digital showcase of other people's visual cultures and practices, offering multiple opportunities for visual researchers to engage with many types of (audio)visual productions. While Ardévol's discussion creates connections specifically between visual and virtual ethnography, her chapter shows that a much wider range of visual research methods can be (and have been) applied to Internet content.

The second issue these chapters raise is the notion of visual research itself as practice. Indeed, if we follow the arguments of practice theorists who place practice at the centre of the analysis this would be the starting point or unit of analysis for understanding any social and practical activity. By seeing visual research itself as practice we can then begin to understand, as Martens points out in Chapter 3, that it generates sets of standards just as do the practices of the participants. This approach also allows us to see visual research practices as embodied and sensory – a point made by both Martens in Chapter 3 and Ardévol in Chapter 5. Like Martens, Ardévol both writes about other people's practices, and reflects on the development of visual-virtual research as a field of practice. In Chapter 4 Hindmarsh and Tutt directly engage with the question of visual research as a practice, this time through a focus on analytical practice. Their chapter develops an explicit form of layered reflexivity as they focus on the practice of video analysis as it is performed in their own discipline, in the form of an analysis of a video recording of analytical practice, in which one of the researchers is in fact analysing his own practices.

Finally, when doing visual research through a practice approach we are compelled to consider practices of looking. These might be questions about how research participants, other researchers or we ourselves look. Technologies are implicated in these practices, and changing technologies, especially in a digital Internet context as outlined by Ardévol, invite new mediated practices of looking. These open up new methodological and practical challenges and ideas, which Ardévol outlines in Chapter 5. We need to attend to the mediated nature of the practices of looking of the visual researcher, whatever technology she or he is using. Another important theme is the question of the politics of looking, emphasised by Martens in Chapter 3. Drawing on the example of the domestic context, Martens points out how practices of looking and video recording are politicised, and imbued with power relations. Hindmarsh and Tutt in Chapter 4 likewise show how forms of professional vision are engaged as part of a collaborative practice in data sessions.

The practice approach therefore brings to the field of visual research a series of insights, not only about participants' practice, but also about our own research practices and our practices of looking.

3

THE POLITICS AND PRACTICES OF LOOKING
CCTV Video and Domestic Kitchen Practices

Lydia Martens

Introduction

Impassioned debate about the 'politics of observation' has accompanied the rising prominence of video as a technology that facilitates the comprehension of social and cultural life. Critics rehearse the sanctity of privacy in intimate settings and in public space, which is perceived as challenged by observational practices envisaged as surveillance and voyeurism (Lyon, 2002; Schaeffer, 1975). This 'politics of observation' is closely connected with recording technologies, notably with the rising prevalence of CCTV, in general use and as a facet of such criticism (Norris and Armstrong, 1999). But the emerging picture is complex. On the one hand, there is a social urgency to hold onto privacy and intimacy. On the other hand, we are part of a society fascinated by the private lives and practices of others. This attraction is nurtured and facilitated by various mediated developments, exemplified for instance by Reality TV programming (Palmer, 2008), whilst the normalisation of image making and observation of private life goes in tandem with the growth in recording technologies like digital cameras, camcorders and mobile phones, invariably targeted at the domestic market (Pantzar, 1997; Pink, 2007). These trends in cultural life are mirrored in research practice. Cultural tolerance of what is acceptable in terms of bringing matters of private and domestic concern into public focus has shifted quite considerably since Schaeffer observed in 1975 that the use of video recording in domestic settings should be avoided in research practice unless 'no other tools permit the acquisition of necessary data' (1975: 257). Notwithstanding the criticisms levelled at the invidious qualities of observation, there has been a growing interest in the use of visual and video methodologies in social and cultural research, traceable in the increasingly varied disciplinary areas in which video practices are being adopted and evident in growing methodological debate (Heath et al., 2010; Knoblauch et al., 2008; Pink, 2007). Having said this, the ways in which this contradiction has been incorporated into researchers' working practices vary substantially.

This chapter is located at the cusp of this contradiction. I do not seek to resolve it here, as arguably, it serves a useful purpose by keeping in focus not only the fact that observation, or preferably, 'practices of looking'[1] are politically charged, but also that research and scholarly commentary are always political activities in their own right.[2] What this chapter does offer is an opening up of the politics of looking in an attempt to challenge some resilient and unhelpful assumptions about the relationship between visual recording technologies and the politics of looking, in which the interconnectedness between the politics, practices and purposes of looking is overlooked. I do so by adopting a praxeological attention to frame a reflection on our experiences of looking at CCTV recordings of everyday life and practices in domestic kitchens. I start by locating the adopted praxeological framework at the intersection of anthropological and philosophical/theoretical reflections on the social nature of practices, followed by a discussion of the video work that formed part of our research. Moving onto praxeological concerns, I first discuss the situated quality of our looking practices and then consider how the technological 'solutions' adopted to access the 24/7 reality of everyday kitchen life created a distinct embodied research experience. The argument is concluded by returning to the issue of standards and politics in visually mediated research practices.

The politics and practices of looking in social research

The generic critique of surveillance in everyday life involves a politics of 'the look' that seems largely disconnected from an interest in the practices and purposes of looking in practical research contexts. When we do consider such practical contexts, it is clear that there exists considerable disparity in the manner in which politics comes into the research process when video practices are adopted. In the field of research relevant to my focus here, that of practices in mundane domestic kitchens, there is a contingent of researchers who engage in observational research in private domestic settings, and who appear to be insensitive to the notion that their work contains a political dimension (Anderson et al., 2004; Arnout et al., 2007; Jay et al., 1999; Redmond et al., 2004). With an absence of any reflective interest in the politics and practices of looking, it could be argued that this mode of research lies at one end of the political spectrum. Recent debate on video practices in social research suggests that such insensitivity is not a rule of thumb, though differences in approach are evident. Much recent debate has, for instance, focused on the politics of looking 'through the lens' (Büscher, 2005; Schubert, 2006). Useful for emphasising the socially constructed nature of visual and video data, this debate does not help us move beyond a questioning of the production of data to consider practices of looking at the video *products* created in and through such production. An important articulation of the connections between the politics, practices and purposes of looking during the work of *interpretation* may be found in Kindon's (2003) account of a participatory research project in which video was used. Her argument that there can be a feminist 'practice of looking' positions politics and purposes right at the centre of research practice, and as such, it is one of the earliest statements to that effect. Kindon's work may therefore be seen as situated at the other end of the political spectrum from the science/policy contingent and may be regarded as an example of the drive towards participatory and action research methodologies, where political engagement focuses on the 'right' treatment of research participants and illustrates an explicit sensitivity towards the consequences of research reporting.

Recent contributions by Grasseni (2007a, 2007b, 2008) signal a final set of work in which the politics, practices and purposes of looking come together. It forms part of the return in anthropology to the question of how 'enterprises of learning and knowing' connect with the embodied and multi-sensory nature of experience (Harris, 2007; Pink, 2009). Different types of everyday and skilled practices have been the focus of their investigation, but in furthering their understanding, anthropologists have at the same time questioned their research practices in what may be described as a 'dual praxeological[3] attention' characterising an ethnographic approach commonly known as apprenticeship. Grasseni's location in this debate is of particular interest precisely because she questions the role and place of looking in research practice. For Grasseni, vision is always a 'flexible, situated and politically fraught' (2007b: 2) dimension of culture and embodied practice. In the introduction to *Skilled Visions*, she seeks to move beyond the ambiguities which exist around the politics of looking in research practice, especially in the way it has been embedded in anthropological discourse, by emphasising how vision is located as an inevitable sensory dimension of the full-embodied character of everyday and scholarly practice. Moreover, following Ingold (1993), she argues that it is not looking per se that is politically fraught, but the purposes which guide the ways we look which are. Thus, rather than remaining stuck in the debilitating state that denies the frequently prominent role of looking in research practice, here is an invitation to actively interrogate research practices in which looking plays a prominent role, whilst maintaining sensitivity to the political relevancies and urgencies of such practices.

This chapter brings these lessons from anthropology together with reflections on the practices and politics of looking at mundane performances in the
intimate setting of domestic kitchens. The approach I adopt here is to locate
practices of looking firmly within a conception of 'research as practice' in its
own right. Like the anthropological directions discussed above, our work thus
involved a dual praxeological concern in the sense that the primary research
objective was to develop insight into common kitchen practices, like cooking,
cleaning and ordering. I locate our practices of looking within a conception of
'research as practice' by drawing on Reckwitz's formulation of a practice analytical attention as directing the researcher to an 'analysis of the interconnectedness
of bodily routines of behaviour, mental routines of understanding and knowing
and the use of objects' (2002: 258).

Whilst Reckwitz emphasises the interconnectedness of these 'three'
dimensions of practice, it is useful to consider the kind of questions which
each generates. Firstly, this formulation encapsulates the idea of research
practice as an embodied and multi-sensory practice. We may thus ask how
embodied routines are manifested in observational work with CCTV footage. Given the fact that visual researchers have not often focused on practices of looking at video 'as data', it may not be superfluous to point to the
centrality of practices of looking in our work. Whilst this raises the question
of how we looked at this data, it also raises questions about the location of
looking within a multi-sensory embodied engagement. Linked to the third
facet is the question of whether and how the embodied manifestation of our
practices is mediated, informed and shaped by the concomitant and creative
embedding of objects, tools and technologies in the research process. I therefore question how, in the process of developing our analysis practices, the
researcher's body is utilised and in what respect their senses become skilled
and their bodies disciplined in and through the mediation and aid of the
technologies used during the process.

Finally, in considering the second dimension, we may ask how 'mental routines of understanding and knowing' come into our work. This question points
to the presence of two types of 'practice communities'. The researchers were
at the same time 'practice-carriers' (Røpke, 2009) of kitchen practices and
research practices. As researchers with a conceptual and practical understanding of kitchen practices, it is clear that the 'mental routines of understanding
and knowing' in kitchen life came into the research in specific ways. I am here,
however, also interested in the 'mental routines of understanding and knowing'
associated with research practice, because this usefully opens up the presence
and role of *standards* in a practice and the question in what respect research practice may be regarded as guided by a community of practice (Grasseni, 2007a;
Wenger, 1998). Methodological discussion and debate, which has become

increasingly vibrant in recent years, may be regarded as an ongoing struggle over standards and procedures in research practice, in a community which is both diverse and evolving over time, and where innovation and improvisation occur concomitantly with sedimentation in investigative practices. These processes signify how politics has an inherent presence in research practices and how resilient hegemonic tendencies are 'institutionalised' in such practices through routines of understanding and knowing (Martens, 2010). These ideas are further supported in the philosophical elaboration on practices by Schatzki, in which a practice is defined as 'a "bundle" of activities, that is to say, an organized nexus of actions'. Practice thus embraces 'two overall dimensions: activity and organization' (2002: 71), with organisation tapping into culturally located and defined rules, principles and instructions. All engender a politics of standards. Moving between these foci in this praxeological reflection should be productive for destabilising some unhelpful 'routines of understanding' in this field, and will in addition illustrate how assertions about *standards* in the two practice domains are interconnected.

The visual exploration of kitchen practices: using CCTV technology

In *Domestic Kitchen Practices: Routines, Risks and Reflexivity*,[4] we conducted ethnographic work with a small set of families on their kitchen lives and practices. We actively trialled video recording in this project, using different technologies and techniques of recording. This included the 24/7 recording of everyday life in the kitchens of some families, using a CCTV camera and assorted equipment. There were two main reasons for pursuing this mode of recording. One was our questioning of the kinds of insights gained of *mundane practices* from techniques of research which centred on 'reported behaviour' (and thus, the range of research approaches in which data is generated through some type of discursive interaction between researchers and researched). The other was that, in considering the different possibilities for generating visual records of everyday kitchen life, it seemed to us that CCTV technology was especially promising for the opportunities it created to 'dwell on' the practical organisation of life in kitchens. Our choice to work with CCTV was further stimulated by the very real problems caused by the physical presence of a researcher in domestic kitchens, especially in small kitchens, and at times when such presence is socially and physically impossible. By virtue of its technical qualities, CCTV will operate 24 hours a day, day and night, without the very real lapse in embodied sensory attention as time moves on and the body understandably gets tired. CCTV can with ease 'sit through the night' just in case respondents have nocturnal habits, capturing what goes on there in a 'naturalistic' manner, whilst at the same time capturing hours of non-activity without falling asleep.

The use of CCTV technology in the examination of the 'real-time production of social life' in the kitchen (Mondada, 2006: 51) opens up the question of whether we sufficiently thought through the politics of our actions. Given the association of CCTV technology with surveillance and unequal power-relations, can it be rescued from this association and opened up as offering a potentially acceptable mode of researching everyday life in an ethically sensitive manner? Pessimists would point to the fact that CCTV-recording technology has been studiously ignored by visual researchers and that they have done so for good reasons. In their critical comment on the rise of CCTV recording in public and private life, and consequently its potential as a source for scholarly investigation, Schnettler and Raab (2008: 14) cite only one source to serve as example of this type of 'material' and the problems it creates. If anything, the common trend in 'politically sensitive' video research practice is embodied by Kindon's (2003) participatory approach (see also Kindon et al., 2007). They may nevertheless be surprised to discover that, like Kindon, our research had a feminist outlook. One of the rationales of our project was to engage actively with discursive allegations over the lack of domestic kitchen skills, which took shape during the 1990s, in relation to bacteriological food scares in the United Kingdom. If anything, the creation of bacterial food poisoning as a social problematic is more pronounced now than it was when we started our research in 2002 (e.g. Shapiro et al., 2011). The rationale for funding our research, we argued, was that existing evidence did not warrant the allegations made about domestic incompetence, and we proposed to develop methodological tools for enhancing knowledge of what people do in their kitchens, focussing especially on such mundane practices as cleaning and ordering. Politically, therefore, the discursive struggle over standards in domestic practice lies at the very foundation of our own concerns and interests.

The way in which we proceeded with our research follows some of the principles outlined by Kindon (2003). We had careful and detailed discussions with those interested in participating in our research about the different ways in which they could get involved, and the diverse options for developing visual materials were discussed and participation fully negotiated. In the end, four of the 12 participating families agreed to work with the CCTV technology in the production of a temporal and visual record of their kitchen lives. Other families made video tours or diaries, whilst yet others agreed to have their kitchens photographed. The CCTV technology was set up in the kitchens of participants after negotiation about where might be the best place for it and the other equipment that came with it. In addition to a small, single and immobile black-and-white camera, there was a VHS recorder, a small black-and-white TV monitor, an infra-red sensor and a microphone, along with their cables. Noteworthy is that prior to starting this work with participants, the CCTV technology was trialled in the kitchens of the researchers, thus generating first-hand experience of what it was like to be observed in this way. Researchers and participants joined in setting the system up – a process of collaboration that resulted in some mirth. Once set up the researcher left the home and it became the responsibility of the research participants to place VHS tapes into the recorder and to renew these when they were full.[5] In this way, the participants were recruited as active agents in the creation of the footage, whilst the researcher was physically absent, though noteworthy is that both were 'dependent' on the technology in the sense that it embodied a specific mode of recording. I here include the fact that, unlike modes of recording in situ, there are few possibilities for interacting with the researcher as the footage is created. As such, the use of CCTV in social research generates its own unique questions, diverting from those which have been at the forefront in reflective questioning of video research (Büscher, 2005; Mondada, 2006).

Participants were invited to look at the footage created and to record over any instances where things happened they did not want to share. Of course, the number of hours of footage created made it impractical for participants to watch all of the footage. There were also some comments about the boring nature of what was on the footage, so much so that one participating family decided to treat the researchers to a musical duet, performed on a Saturday evening. Along with some other occurrences, these were examples of participants finding their own ways of communicating with the absent researcher and joking with the technology itself (see also Laurier and Philo, 2009). At the end of the recording period, the researcher collected the VHS tapes and the equipment and took these back to the office for analysis. The researcher then returned at a later date to discuss the experience of working with the recording equipment in the kitchen and to watch and talk about some selected footage. In her discussion of watching and talking about the videos created by her participants, Kindon develops interpretation as a practice where video operates as a visual medium to stimulate discursive interaction between researcher and participants, an interaction in which the voice of participants comes to the fore in a strong and assertive way. As such, participatory video research is appreciated especially for stimulating comprehension of the 'often-complex perceptions and discourses of local people' (Johansson et al., 1999: 36, also quoted in Kindon, 2003: 143). In our work, CCTV was useful exactly because it offered a means of moving away from dialogic engagement, and consequently, an opportunity to concentrate on the 'doing' of everyday life, using vision as the main interpretative medium.

Situating looking in the kitchen

The way in which we as researchers came to 'look' at practice performance in domestic kitchens is quite different from the way we or other practice carriers might utilise our/their eyes during practice performance, or to 'look on' whilst practices are performed by others in everyday contexts. This suggests different practices of looking, each following divergent contexts and purposes for looking. These include the 'relaxed observation' of a socially accepted bystander in the kitchen who is 'looking on' whilst someone is getting on with their work. It may be that the bystander's presence in the kitchen is of a solely social nature, and thus 'looks on' without much necessity for the need 'to see' much of what is going on. Contrast this with another instance of 'looking on', where the observation may be of a more pedagogic kind and thus more reflective and attentive. This may for instance happen during intergenerational interaction in the kitchen when children or other 'learners' are practising cooking. Here there is a clearer need to see what is going on and to respond to this through interaction. In their performance, however, the practitioner uses vision in combination with the other senses in order to practically perform the tasks identified in and through the objectives they are pursuing. This mode of looking is closely connected with that internal 'visualisation' that links our normative understanding and relevant teleoaffective pre-occupations (e.g. purposes, emotions) with the practical understanding of how to carry out practices (Schatzki, 2002). Visualisation is thus an expression of the ways in which expertise or skill (and imagination) is lodged into our memories, linking the practical and conceptual modes through which we understand a practice (Schatzki, 1996, 2002) and suggesting ways in which to proceed. Whilst the utilisation of our visual capabilities may well be very intense during practice performance (cooking practices could form an example here), arguably this is an attentive vision directed purely at the practical carrying out of the practice in question. Contrast this to the reflective purposes of looking that connect with the conceptual and contemplative requirements of scholarly understanding. One type of visual skill pertains to the practical purposes of performing practical kitchen tasks in time and space; the other to the questioning and intellectual purpose of scholarly observational practice. From the point of view of interpretation, it is important to note that the look of the kitchen 'practice carrier' and the look of the scholar 'practice carrier' came together in an important way in our efforts to understand mundane practices in domestic kitchens.

We have already offered an account of the diverse scholarly ways of looking which we explored, developed and employed, with varying degrees of perseverance, during our analysis (Martens and Scott, 2004). Each had different purposes, and thus arguably entailed different modes of looking and, in their developed form, skilled vision (Grasseni, 2008). First of all, we looked *at practices* to get an overview, trying not to stop the video player but simply to get a sense of the goings-on of life in the kitchen (and, of course, also the lengthy periods of inactivity there). This way of looking allowed us to develop insight into the cultural dynamics of life in domestic kitchens, and it answered typical sociological and ethnographic questions about family and domestic life (e.g. who did what in the kitchen; when and how the kitchen was used; what interpersonal activities occurred there, what we could tell about the family's interpersonal relations, and so on). Given we were kitchen 'practice carriers', this mode of looking and interpretation was less challenging than the modes discussed below, in part because there was a lot here that was 'familiar' (e.g. the spatial organisation of the kitchen and how it is used). In some respects, the purpose of looking *at* the kitchen practices of others was an invitation to be sensitive to variations between modes of performance, between family members, across participating families and between the researcher's own practices and those of the participants.

The second approach we developed for looking at the data was to focus in on the main kitchen practices (washing dishes, other types of cleaning and ordering in the kitchen, cooking and socialising) in order to develop understanding of how these were 'carried out'. We here looked *in practices* to see how these were organised. In accordance with the research objectives, we were interested in finding out more about how mundane practices were constituted as routines; what tasks were brought together in their performance; in what sequence doings and tasks were performed; and how objects and bodies were utilised in the process. Possibly the most exciting feature of video recordings – their quality as an archive to be accessed at a time and a place that is convenient and best suited to the researcher – came into its own here. As observed by others (e.g. Lomax and Casey, 1998), the technology offers viewing possibilities, such as fast-forwarding, slow motion and rewind/repeat viewing, that create flexibilities in modes of looking. In our work, the fast-forward function was useful for developing an overview of when pockets of activity occurred in the kitchen, and broadly speaking, what happened during that time. The rewind function was very useful, for instance, for returning to a small part of the footage just seen, sometimes more than once, in order to clarify what was happening in it. In view of the fact that the visual 'information' recorded in video contains a high level of complexity (Schnettler and Raab, 2008: 33), this points to one of the ways in which video-facilitated observation may be more powerful than direct eye observation. These tools thus open up opportunities for *dwelling* on the minute details of performance, and through which practices become realised – something which would be impossible to do during face-to-face interaction, when in addition to the limits of what is possible for the eye–brain to 'take in' during looking, the interpersonal dynamics of the situation might intervene with the researcher's desire to focus on the minute before one scene is replaced by another.

A third mode, which may be conceived as looking *for practices*, was preoccupied with identifying practices and quantifying specific features of them and the way they are performed. Drawing on our experiences of looking *in practices* we explored ways of looking at this data that allowed us to quantify kitchen practices in a temporal way, considering when, how long for, and by whom the 'common' practice categories (those listed above) were performed. The CCTV data stimulated and facilitated such temporal ways of looking at the data, because the footage included a date stamp, plus an ongoing time counter that included information on hours, minutes and seconds. In our report, we suggested other useful ways for looking at the data, for instance, by focussing on the kitchen's materiality, in movement and in immobility. Thus, the way in which bodies moved in the kitchen space and, for the purposes of exploring cleanliness, how common artefacts, like kitchen cleaning cloths, were used over time, seemed useful and relevant avenues to explore.

It is clear that these three modes of looking tap into different research purposes and they lead to different insights into kitchen life and mundane practices. By comparison, in the observational studies conducted by science/policy scholars, a focussed and partial gaze is adopted that looks out for specific types of hygiene practices to the exclusion of everything else. It intentionally excludes context from the adopted observational practices. That practices of looking are situated within specific communities of scientific practice and carry political baggage is therefore clear. In view of this, it is useful to reflect on the political subtext of our own modes of looking. I start with the observation that modes of looking *in* and *for* practices involve greater abstraction than is the case for looking *at practices*. In our first mode of looking: the practice of looking *at practices*, we were looking at people and their interactions in everyday kitchen life. In our second and third modes of looking, the practices of looking *in* and *for practices*, the focus shifted to practical organisation of performance and the enumeration of practices in performance. Abstraction is a common and unquestioned 'routine' and purpose in the mental practices of scholars, often leading to and informing theoretical conjecture. Arguably, the process of abstraction may be regarded as ethically questionable, certainly from the point of view of a participatory methodology, as it involves a distancing from the immediate concerns of research participants as the scholar's own creative interpretative work takes over. Thus, the closer we looked at practices, the less the looking was about 'knowing people', and the more it became about 'knowing practices'. As our focus became more abstract, there was a shift away from the politically significant issues of intimacy and privacy of domestic life, and from the interactional connotations of the voyeuristic gaze. In the literature on practice theory, this is conceived as a shift away from methodological individualism, and associated with the idea that a practice precedes performance, and thus the performer (Halkier and Iben, 2011). I will now elaborate this reflection by considering how the technological mediation of our observational practices shaped and facilitated our modes of looking.

Technology and embodiment in CCTV video analysis

The analysis process gained technological density as we moved through these modes of looking. Whilst looking *at practices*, most closely mirroring real-time and full embodied observation in ethnographic practice, our interpretation was rooted through the writing of field notes. Moving into modes of looking *in practices*, our note-taking became more 'technical' and detailed in an attempt to describe tasks and doings within a temporal frame that listed hours, minutes and seconds. In order to capture some of the considerable complexity in the data, we also used voice recorders in order to facilitate this detailed description of the action 'we saw evolving' on the video footage at a later date. As argued by one of the researchers, it usually took longer to write down what was seen than it took for participants to enact specific actions, making the need for replay or voice recording pertinent. Fine-tuning the focus was thus aided by different technological tools and we explored different tools to schematically represent the temporal unfolding of doings and tasks in performance. This included Coding Stripes in NVivo2 and Gantt Charts in Excel.

Work with CCTV video creates a research practice characterised by distinct embodied manifestations. One of the most striking features of this type of data is the distance it creates, temporally, spatially and interactionally, between the performance of practices and the observation of those performances, and thus, between the performers and the researchers. Whilst having benefits, there are also some clear disadvantages. Looking first at the interactional dimensions of this process and linking these to issues of interpretation, I finish by summing up the consequences of the primacy of looking for research as an embodied work practice.

In our work, the researchers did not need to engage in the no doubt very time-consuming work of becoming sufficiently close to the participants to be able to be present in their kitchens in the relaxed manner of a friendly observer. Whilst this allowed us to work with a broader range of families than would have been possible otherwise, it meant that the research process was simply less interactional (and possibly less satisfying) than might be the case in full embodied observational work. Because the research participants did not have the opportunity to get to know the researcher very well, whilst the researcher developed a detailed insight into the kitchen life of the participants, one of the consequences pointing to adverse ethics was that this created unevenness in mutual familiarity between the researcher and participants. This came out most clearly during visits following on from the CCTV video phase of the research, for instance, when participants engaged in video elicitation work with the researchers as part of a more general discussion about their experiences of working with the equipment in their kitchens.

The researcher's embodied absence during the performance of kitchen life clearly also makes discursive interaction in situ impossible, for both researcher and participant. Whilst this may make us dwell on the unsociable nature of this research, especially where we consider the ethnographic purpose of looking *at practices*, it also relates to some of the challenges encountered in analysing this data. In interpersonal contact in everyday life, people frequently make interpretive errors or encounter interpretive uncertainties. Language contains discursive conventions with which such uncertainties and errors may be rectified, for example, when we ask for clarification during a conversation. One reason why researcher comprehension may be a struggle in relation to CCTV video is because of ambiguities around the context of enactments, which cannot be verified through discursive interaction. In his elaborations on the constituent components of a practice, Schatzki (2002: 70) clarifies that the *doings*, which come to constitute a practice, may in fact constitute different *acts* because the context or intended meanings behind them may be varied. Drawing on his argument, different doings may represent the same action, or the same doing may represent different actions. This points to the ease with which the performance of a doing by one practitioner may be misread by an observing other, regardless of whether they are practice carriers, simply because the doing may carry different social meanings and it may not be immediately evident which meaning is harboured in the doing that is performed. Without the benefit of dialogic interaction, the researcher is left with the need to 'find' meaning using the only interpretative resource at their disposal: in other words, watching out for this meaning to become apparent in and through the ways in which doing and actions are organised in performance. There is a link here with the practice of reviewing sequences of actions in performance, for an interesting question is: what stimulates the researchers to go back and watch again? This may be a matter of there being too much going on at the same time and the inability of the researchers to see the multiplicity of doings that are unfolding before their eyes. It may also be a matter of uncertainty about the context in which specific actions are unfolding. In relation to this, it is important to recognise that it takes time to make sense of what is seen on video footage, time during which actions simply keep following one another.

Another way of thinking this through is to suggest that the technological quality of this type of video data *disables* the researcher. There is little doubt that kitchens are full of smell, touch, taste, sound and embodied knowledge, and that these are salient components in the multi-sensory comprehension of what goes on in them (see also Sutton, 2006). In our work, researchers did not have the benefit of this full embodied perception. Unique to our research was therefore the singling out of vision to the exclusion of the other senses in the interpretive process, with the exception that the researchers' practice-carrying presence could see the operationalisation of their multi-sensory memories (visualisation) of kitchen life and practices to 'fill in' some of the gaps in sense making. We must however concur that our looking was also in some respects disabled! Discussing the location of the camera in the operating theatre, Schubert (2006) touches on the possibility of moving the camera around the field, mimicking in some respects the movement of the human eye following goings-on that appear to be of interest, and as these evolve over time and space. In our project, we worked with a single black-and-white camera, fixed in one location, in the kitchen. The fixed frame footage which became the finished product was clearly deficient, hiding areas of the kitchen and of the domestic space beyond it. It was thus not possible to move with the practitioners as they themselves moved out of the frame. In addition, the fixed nature of the camera meant that it was not always possible to *see clearly* the performance of prac-tices as they unfolded, for instance, because the practitioners enacted certain practices with their backs towards the camera or because sun light through the kitchen window reduced the clarity of the footage. In these instances, too, the researchers were challenged to 'fill in the gaps' as best they could.

CCTV video recording compels the researcher to disconnect practices of looking from a fully embedded multi-sensory experience, and during the practice of looking the body is subjected to the priorities of watching and sense-making. This approach thus differs distinctly from the apprenticeship in ethnographic research. As such, vision is disabled, enskilled and disciplined, and this develops alongside the creation of a disciplined and docile researcher body. The four families who participated in the CCTV element of our research together produced in the region of 100 hours of footage. Behind the viewing of this material is a whole story of the time-consuming, creative, boring and frus-trating process of sitting, watching, sense-making and recording. I remember sitting 'like a couch potato', for hours on end, in an easy chair in front of the television, holding the remote control in one hand and the voice recorder in the other, in order to allow the eye to remain fixed on the footage as much as pos-sible. Analysis work like this needs strategies, for selecting footage (Schubert, 2006) and for coping; for our third mode of looking, for instance, it may be conducive to researcher sanity if the process is turned into a communal one, with plenty of beverage and breaks to share in between bouts of viewing. But there are also clear ways in which this type of material inspires the creative capacity of researchers, which was illustrated in thinking through our modes of looking and devising ways of representing our emerging understanding.

Conclusion

Acknowledging the fact that research is always located in particular politically charged domains of discursive engagement, in this chapter I have engaged with the question of how we can work with video in research practice in a politically engaged manner, when that video is created with the aid of CCTV technology. In doing so, I have not focussed solely on considerations of research participation and video production, but I have confronted the interrelationships between the *politics*, *purposes* and *practices* of looking in interpretive work, thus opening the politics of looking up to questions of its embeddedness in practical research contexts. In contrast to much debate in visual methodology, I have focused especially on the work of analysis, treating it as a practice (or set of practices) that throws up issues around the specific sensory and embodied manifestation of this work, located as it is in the heavily mediated character of CCTV technology and the specific foci of our research. Drawing on Reckwitz's (2002: 258) conceptualisation of practices as resident in the 'interconnectedness of bodily routines of behaviour, mental routines of understanding and knowing and the use of objects' was useful for homing in on these three dimensions in reflecting on our 'research practices', but also to acknowledge their inextricable interconnectedness. So even when we may think of our practices of looking as innovative and emerging from the specific concerns of our work, we might ask the question how looking *for practices* connects with principles and procedures of enumeration which are in essence already part of the 'mental routines of understanding and knowing' we find in the social science research 'toolkit'.

Thinking about 'research as practice' has also allowed *standards* to come to the fore. By thinking across widely varying working practices with video, from a science-policy directed approach in which practices of looking are very much taken for granted, to a participatory-action approach in which the relationship between politics and practices is scrutinised in considerable detail, it has been possible to locate our own work. It could be argued that these contrasting approaches to video research highlight different standards and politics in scholarly practice. Whilst methodological innovation is, perhaps unexpectedly, evident in both approaches, both also evidence sedimentation. On one side is a community of scholars who have grown into their community of practice by becoming routinised into standards of practice characteristic of scientific enquiry, but devoid of the kind of reflectivity we find elsewhere. This calls to mind 'the role of informal, mostly tacit knowledge in expert conduct' and 'the disciplined and disciplining aspects of memory and sensibility that are not spontaneous, personal and subjective but rather *embedded* in mediating devices, contexts and routines' (Grasseni, 2007b: 4). The argument developed by Grasseni (2007b, 2008) and Ingold (1993), that practices of looking relate to the purposes of looking, also connect with Harris's (2007: 3) argument on 'ways of knowing'. He argues: 'the general attraction of the phrase is its appeal to multiplicity and an inclusive sense of what is considered to be knowledge'. This opens up the idea that there is no such thing as one type of knowledge about, for example, kitchen practices, associated with one standard (rules about appropriate conduct) of practice. The emphasis on 'inclusivity' furthermore points to the politics behind knowing and knowledge, suggesting that knowledge may work in an exclusionary or even derogatory manner. Such allegations can certainly not be levelled at the participatory community of scholars, for whom reflectivity and an acknowledgement of the politics inherent in their research practices and the outcomes of research are crucial dimensions shaping those practices. Nevertheless, from my standpoint, it becomes possible to recognise in this 'trend' in visually mediated research a critique of looking that moves too far into the opposite direction, and which conflates 'reprehensible' technologies (i.e. CCTV) with 'reprehensible' research practices. I hope this chapter goes some way towards challenging such conceptions, and opens up an invitation to explore the potentials of working with CCTV technology in useful and promising ways in the future.

Notes

1 I here follow Grasseni's (2007a) argument that the concept 'observation' is too closely tied to the generic critique of looking.
2 The issue of the pertinent place of politics and values in research is not new. Certainly in sociology, it links to early commentaries, for example, by Gouldner (1962) and Becker (1967).
3 Coming from a conversation analytic perspective, Mondada (2006: 51) also coins this concept in her work.
4 *Domestic Kitchen Practices* was funded by the Economic and Social Research Council (UK) (code RES-000-22-0014) and I would like to thank the council for their support. The research team included Professor Sue Scott (co-applicant) and Dr Matt Watson (research associate). I am grateful to them for their input into this project. For a more comprehensive discussion of the research and its methodology, see the End of Award report (Martens and Scott, 2004).
5 When we shopped around for the CCTV technology, it became apparent that digital formats for recording were not yet sufficiently powerful. Working with VHS at this time was appropriate as it was a technology with which participants were familiar.

Bibliography

Anderson, J.B., Shuster, T.A., Hansen, K.E., Levy, A.S. and Volk, A. (2004) 'A camera's view of consumer food-handling behaviors', *Journal of the American Dietetics Association*, 104 (2): 186–91.

Arnout, R.H., Fischer, A., De Jong, E.I., Van Asselt, E.D., De Jonge, R., Frewer, L.J. and Nauta, M.J. (2007) 'Food safety in the domestic environment: an interdisciplinary investigation of microbial hazards during food preparation', *Risk Analysis*, 27 (4): 1065–82.

Becker, H. (1967) 'Whose side are we on?', *Social Problems*, 14 (3): 239–47.

Büscher, M. (2005) 'Social life under the microscope?', *Sociological Research Online*, 10 (1) (retrieved 22 December 2010 from: www.socresonline.org. uk/10/1/buscher.html).

Gouldner, A. (1962) 'Anti-minotaur: the myth of a value-free sociology', *Social Problems*, 9 (3): 199–213.

Grasseni, C. (2007a) 'Communities of practice and forms of life: towards a rehabilitation of vision?', in M. Harris (ed.), *Ways of Knowing: New approaches in the Anthropology of Experience and Learning*. Oxford: Berghahn Books. pp. 203–21.

Grasseni, C. (2007b) 'Introduction', in C. Grasseni (ed.), *Skilled Visions: Between Apprenticeship and Standards*. Oxford: Berghahn Books. pp. 1–19.

Grasseni, C. (2008) 'Learning to see: world-views, skilled visions, skilled practice', in N. Halstead, E. Hirsch and J. Okely (eds), *Knowing How to Know: Fieldwork and the Ethnographic Present*. Oxford: Berghahn Books. pp. 151–72.

Halkier, B. and Iben, J. (2011) 'Methodological challenges in using practice theory in consumption research: examples from a study on handling nutritional contestations of food consumption', *Journal of Consumer Culture*, 11 (1): 101–23.

Harris, M. (2007) 'Introduction: ways of knowing', in M. Harris (ed.), *Ways of Knowing: New Approaches in the Anthropology of Experience and Learning*. Oxford: Berghahn Books. pp. 1–24.

Heath, C., Hindmarsh, J. and Luff, P. (2010) *Video in Qualitative Research: Analysing Social Interaction in Everyday Life*. London: Sage.

Ingold, T. (1993) 'The art of translation in a continuous world', in G. Palsson (ed.), *Beyond Boundaries: Understanding, Translation and Anthropological Discourse*. London: Berg. pp. 210–30.

Jay, S.L., Comar, D. and Govenlock, L.D. (1999) 'A video study of Australian domestic food-handling practices', *Journal of Food Protection*, 62 (11): 1285–96.

Kindon, S. (2003) 'Participatory video in geographic research: a feminist practice of looking?', *Area*, 35 (2): 142–53.

Kindon, S., Pain, R. and Kesby, M. (eds) (2007) *Participatory Action Research Approaches and Methods: Connecting People, Participation and Place*. London: Routledge.

Knoblauch, H., Baer, A., Laurier, E., Petschke, S. and Schnettler, B. (eds) (2008) Special Issue on Visual Methods. *Forum: Qualitative Social Research*, 9 (3). Available at www.qualitative-research.net/index.php/fqs/issue/view/11 (accessed 6.2.12).

Laurier, E. and Philo, C. (2009) 'Natural problems of naturalistic video data', in H. Knoblauch, B. Schnettler, J. Raab and H.-G. Soeffner (eds), *Video Analysis: Methodology and Methods*. Frankfurt am Main: Peter Lang. pp. 183–92.

Lomax, H. and Casey, N. (1998) 'Recording social life: reflexivity and video methodology', *Sociological Research Online*, 3 (2): 1.1–8.5.

Lyon, D. (2002) 'Surveillance Studies: Understanding visibility, mobility and the phenetic fix', *Surveillance & Society*, 1 (1): 1–7.

Martens, L. (2010) 'Innovations in qualitative research in the UK', *The Language of Public Administration and Qualitative Research*, 1 (1): 49–71.

Martens, L. and Scott, S. (2004) 'Domestic kitchen practices: routine, reflexivity and risk', ESRC End of Award Report. pp. 21–52.

Mondada, L. (2006) 'Video recording as the reflexive preservation and configuration of phenomenal features for analysis', in H. Knoblauch, B. Schnettler, J. Raab and H.-G. Soeffner (eds), *Video Analysis: Methodology and Methods*. Frankfurt am Mein: Peter Lang. pp. 51–67.

Norris, C. and Armstrong, G. (1999) *The Maximum Surveillance Society: The Rise of CCTV*. Oxford: Berg.

Palmer, G. (ed.) (2008) *Exposing Lifestyle Television: The Big Reveal*. Aldershot: Ashgate.

Pantzar, M. (1997) 'Domestication of everyday life technology: dynamic views on social histories of arifacts', *Design Issues*, 13 (3): 52–65.

Pink, S. (2007) *Doing Visual Ethnography: Images, Media and Representation in Research* (2nd edn). London: Sage.

Pink, S. (2009) *Doing Sensory Ethnography*. London: Sage.

Reckwitz, A. (2002) 'Toward a theory of social practices: a development in culturalist theorizing', *European Journal of Social Theory*, 5 (2): 243–63.

Redmond, E.D., Christopher, J., Griffith, C.J., Slader, J. and Humphrey, T.J. (2004) 'Microbiological and observational analysis of cross contamination risks during domestic food preparation', *British Food Journal*, 106 (8): 581–97.

Røpke, I. (2009) 'Theories of practice – new inspiration for ecological economic studies on consumption', *Ecological Economics*, 68 (10): 2490–7.

Schaeffer, J.H. (1975) 'Videotape: new techniques of observation and analysis in anthropology', in P. Hockings (ed.), *Principles of Visual Anthropology*. New York: Mouton de Gruyter. pp. 253–82.

Schatzki, T. (1996) *Social Practices: A Wittgensteinian Approach to Human Activity and the Social*. Cambridge: Cambridge University Press.

Schatzki, T. (2002) *The Site of the Social: A Philosophical Account of the Constitution of Social Life and Change*. University Park, PA: Pennsylvania State University Press.

Schnettler, B. and Raab, J. (2008) 'Interpretative visual analysis: development, state of the arts and pending problems [45 paragraphs]', *Forum: Qualitative Social Research*, 9 (3): Art. 31 (retrieved 22 December 2010 from: www.qualitative-research.net/index.php/fqs/article/viewArticle/1149/2555).

Schubert, C. (2006) 'Video analysis of practice and the practice of video analysis: selecting field and focus in videography', in H. Knoblauch, B. Schnettler, J. Raab, H.-G. Soeffner (eds), *Video Analysis: Methodology and Methods*. Frankfurt am Mein: Peter Lang. pp. 115–26.

Shapiro, M.A., Porticella, N., Jiang, L.C. and Gravani, R.B. (2011) 'Predicting intentions to adopt safe home food handling practices. Applying the theory of planned behavior', *Appetite*, 56: 96–103.

Sutton, D. (2006) 'Cooking skill, the senses, and memory: the fate of practical knowledge', in E. Edwards, C. Gosden and R.B. Phillips (eds), *Sensible Objects*. Oxford: Berg. pp. 87–128.

Wenger, E. (1998) *Communities of Practice: Learning, Meaning and Identity*. Cambridge: Cambridge University Press.

4

VIDEO IN ANALYTIC PRACTICE

Jon Hindmarsh and Dylan Tutt

While the 'practice turn' in contemporary social science covers a broad range of definitions of, and approaches to, the study of 'practice', ethnomethodology (Garfinkel, 1984 [1967]) has indubitably had influence on its character and development. The ethnomethodological focus on practical action and practical reasoning, indeed its fundamental emphasis on the constitutive character of (interactional) practices, has a significant place in this field. Within the most influential collection on 'the practice turn' there are two articles from leading ethnomethodologists that outline its contributions to our understanding of practice (Coulter, 2001; Lynch, 2001). This influence is not, however, restricted to the theoretical or conceptual development of the field. For instance, the recent re-flourishing of 'practice-based approaches' to the study of work and organising (Corradi et al., 2010; Nicolini et al., 2003) makes frequent reference to a body of ethnomethodological work that draws on the study of situated work practices using naturalistic video recordings of organisational environments. These video-based studies of work practice (Hindmarsh and Heath, 2007) are advancing our understanding of the detailed accomplishment of work and the constitutive character of work and interactional practice.

The rewind button is critical to these video-based studies of work practice. This facility makes available to the analyst the rich and varied interactional resources that participants use in making sense of the conduct of others, in coordinating action with others and, indeed, in accomplishing work with others. Researchers are able to stop and restart recordings of workplace activities and transcribe them to chart and unpack their organisation in ways that are way beyond the perceptual capabilities of traditional participant observers. Advances in digital video enable analysts to inspect, zoom in, juxtapose, annotate and slow down audio-visual records to facilitate extraordinarily detailed inspection. Furthermore, the recording provides opportunities for colleagues to share and discuss data in rather distinctive ways for the social sciences. Indeed collaborative data analysis sessions, or 'data sessions', are now common working practices in ethnomethodological communities and beyond.

In this chapter, we aim to examine this visual methodology in various ways. On the one hand, we will introduce this approach to the study of work practice and some of the core methodological principles that guide it. However, we will also provide a brief analysis of work practices evident in 'data sessions'. That is to say, we will open up the black box of methodological texts through a partial analysis of the practices that constitute analytic work. It is extremely rare in texts on method and methodology to turn the analytic lens on the very analytic work that you are describing (for an alternative approach to exploring 'research as practice', see Martens, this volume). And yet this goes to the heart of the 'practice turn', moving from the level of the abstract to a serious consideration of what people do and how it is constitutive of broader, even 'macro-social' (Coulter, 2001), themes in social life. In general we aim to reveal how this particular 'visual' methodology enhances analytic potential in studying work practice by drawing on a brief analysis of the work of social scientists.

Video and the study of work practice

Video-based studies of work practice have come to prominence in a range of disciplines within and beyond the social sciences (see Heath et al., 2010). The proponents are specialists in ethnomethodology and conversation analysis, and yet they are applying their studies to a broad range of issues and concerns. Aside from the disciplines of sociology (Heath and Button, 2002) and organisational studies (Llewellyn and Hindmarsh, 2010), more applied studies of work practice have emerged over recent decades in education, health studies, consumer research and more. For example, one major home for these studies falls within the interdisciplinary fields of human–computer interaction (HCI) and computer-supported cooperative work (CSCW). The pioneering studies of Lucy Suchman (1987), in which she video-taped and analysed people using photocopiers, paved the way for a range of video-based studies of the workplace – studies that develop detailed descriptions of work practice to inform design projects, but also aim to re-specify core concepts in the design of collaborative systems, such as 'awareness', 'realism', 'user' and the like (e.g. Heath and Luff, 2000).

Despite the range of academic and applied audiences for this type of work, the studies are all underpinned by a core set of analytic commitments drawn from ethnomethodology (Garfinkel, 1984 [1967]). Ethnomethodology focuses attention on the production of social order in and through practical action. Within the context of work and organisation studies, video-based approaches in this field are concerned to unpack the artful interactional practices that underpin the accomplishment of work. To do this, they draw on a guiding principle from conversation analysis (CA) – a branch of ethnomethodology – that interaction is overwhelmingly, and inescapably, sequentially organised.

For researchers working in the various 'interpretive' traditions of social science, unpacking the context in which actions are produced, emerge and are understood is critical to analytic work, to understand the social and moral organisations of human life. Often researchers will consider a range of features of context that are treated as enclosing, even determining, observed behaviour, whether individual characteristics of the participant (race, gender, class, role, status, etc.) or aspects attributable to the setting (nation, culture, type of organisation, etc.). However, knowing which features are most relevant in the production of one action or another is highly problematic. In CA, an understanding of sequence delivers a radical alternative.

The concept of 'sequence', in straightforward terms, suggests that any turn at talk, or indeed any action in interaction, is oriented in relation to what comes immediately prior and what immediately follows. So, each action is shaped by immediate contexts of action, and it also re-shapes the context in which subsequent actions emerge (Heritage, 1984). The context in which an action is produced relates to the prior action, even when participants disattend the prior turn, participants will still make that visible in and through their conduct. So sequential context is always and inescapably relevant.

This leads to a particular treatment of evidence. Again, an enduring concern for qualitative social science has been to prioritise the participants' perspective. While many will explore this through different approaches to achieving analytic distance or immersion, sequential analysis suggests that if participants themselves attend to, or display, their understanding of prior actions in and through their own conduct, this should provide the evidence for claims made by analysts. Essentially analysts should attend to the ways in which participants themselves treat conduct in situ, rather than trying to abstract actions from their immediate sequential context. This stands in direct contrast to a great deal of more traditional approaches to the study of social interaction.

So the notion of sequence is absolutely fundamental to the work of conversation analysis, furnishing radical and distinct approaches to foundational aspects of qualitative inquiry, such as 'context' and 'evidence'. The rest of the chapter considers how a concern with 'sequence' is oriented to in interactional practices that underpin data sessions.

The data session: a general introduction

Participant observation often involves a lone researcher observing conduct that is fleeting and rendered into the form of fieldnotes either immediately or within a few hours. The data are then accounts of conduct produced by the researcher, rather than the conduct that underpins those accounts. Video on the other hand enables researchers to share the raw materials, the recorded events that form the basis for analysis. Thus the 'data session' has become a common practice in certain sub-disciplines of the social sciences, in which a number of researchers can view, discuss and collaboratively analyse video of social activities.

The data session facilitates collaborative interrogation of short stretches of recorded data (from a few seconds to a few minutes depending on approach and concerns). It enables participants to explore tentative formulations and analyses and to receive immediate comment, contribution and feedback from colleagues in relation to those data sources. Data sessions can involve larger or smaller groups of researchers analysing video data, in combination with transcripts (of talk and non-vocal conduct) and sometimes other data sources (see Figure 4.1).

It should be highlighted that these data sessions do not represent the final or even core work involved in data analysis. Rather, they provide opportunities to make preliminary observations, debate alternative characterisations of conduct and identify avenues for further inquiry. In many ways, they are about opening up rather than closing down the analysis. Speculative analytic claims are encouraged and then those claims can be interrogated further within the data session and pursued in later, more focused, analytic endeavours. The specific data session that we will consider involves discussion of one feature that might form the foundation to some broader analytic work.

The data session: a single case

To explore conduct in data sessions, we will to refer to a short video clip from one data session. The data are drawn from a broader research project concerned with the design of e-Social Science tools to support 'distributed' data sessions (see Fraser et al., 2006; Hindmarsh, 2008). As part of that project we

Figure 4.1   Images of data sessions

collected recordings of routine face-to-face data sessions as well as distributed data sessions using our prototype tools (Tutt et al., 2007; Tutt and Hindmarsh, 2011). Given the often sensitive nature of working with video data, we have been careful with our descriptions and depiction of the data corpus, and have ensured that participants are content with our use of the selected video images and our descriptions of their conduct. In addition to the use of pseudonyms throughout, we have used AKVIS software to transform raw video images to line drawings – this preserves the richness of the scene but also acts as a further shield for anonymity.

The clip we discuss here is located within a one-and-a-half hour data session involving two participants. It is led by Mark, who has put together a collection of video fragments to discuss with his colleague, Daniel. These fragments have been assembled to allow them to explore the theme of emotionality in interaction – Mark is particularly interested in ways in which emotion is experienced, displayed and performed in moments of interaction. The clips that they are discussing are all taken from a corpus of recordings of Mark and his young daughter, which was originally collected to explore aspects of child development.

As well as operating playback of the video, Mark has provided Daniel with a copy of a transcript, which charts the talk and some aspects of visual conduct. In introducing the clip, Mark (re)states its potential relevance to the study of emotion in interaction and also says that it includes a sequence in which his daughter does a 'curious thing'. He indicates roughly when this occurs in relation to the transcript but rather than moving straight to playing that segment, he states that 'you need to see a bit of it beforehand'. Of course, here we are doing a similar thing through our textual description, in that we are giving you some general context prior to focusing on the specific sequence of the data session that we wish to discuss.

Rendering visible 'sequence'

The extract is played until just after the 'curious thing' has been produced and responded to in the video. Mark then says 'now that strikes me as quite odd' and the extract is re-set to play again. Interactions are too rich and dense to catch the details of their organisation first time around. This richness of interactional detail available on the video record, coupled with an analytic commitment to sequential organisation, encourages a charting and recharting of verbal or visual conduct. This is a dominant activity in data sessions and the fragment below provides one such example. Before proceeding to a discussion of the fragment, it is worth noting a couple of brief points regarding the transcription conventions adopted. Firstly, a range of standards and symbols are used to indicate aspects of the temporal organisation and delivery of the talk (see Appendix). Secondly, three 'speakers' are indicated: Mark (M), Daniel (D), and also a voice on *their* video data – Mark's daughter (DV). In this extract, Mark and Daniel's attention is drawn to the moments that follow DV's utterance 'an' then:: (.) go:::' (which they had discussed in some detail earlier in the data session).

Fragment 1a: DS-14/07/06-42:00

```
 1   DV:    an' then:: (.) go:::
 2          (4.3)
 3   M:     then: you begin the look up^
 4          (1.5)
 5   M:     look dow:n. (.) look up
 6          (4.3)
 7   D:     .hhh .pt (.) she's wat:ching:.
 8   M:     yeah:^
 9          (1.5)
10   M:     looks agai:n^=
11   D:     =oh she- no sh- ah youf forgot the breathe
12          (.) .hhh-nhhh
13          (0.3)
14   M:     oh^ yeah:^
15          (1.8)
16   M:     >ah now- is it< why: did I turn around?
17          (.)
18   M:     wh-why [(did I-)
19   D:            [pr'bly co- I think because she went
20          .hhh-nhhh
21          (2.3)
22   M:     yeah::: that's true actually, it's probably
23          the sound of tha:t.
24          (1.4)
25   D:     and it's also a move:ment. the shoul:ders
26          move, the chest moves.
```

Some key features of this work should be evident immediately and would not escape a researcher relying solely on observations in the setting. For instance, the participants talk over, or commentate on, the emerging temporal organisation depicted in the video. It would be impossible for Mark and Daniel to mention all the actions of each participant visible on-screen, so this commentary starts to discriminate features of conduct they see as relevant to understanding the sequence. This attention to detail is not for detail's sake, but rather it goes to the heart of the conversation analytic project that we described earlier. The video recording is used as a resource to build up a map of the *temporal* associations between actions – what happens first, second, third and so forth. This then provides the basis for making judgments about the *sequential* relationships between aspects of conduct.

While an observer might note that commentary occurs, it would be impossible for them to capture its real-time organisation. Indeed any attempt to produce the detail evident in our transcript would be hopeless without the recording; access to this level of detail enables us to make a number of observations about the work at hand.

Mark's commentary not only highlights the features of visual conduct that he presents as significant or otherwise relevant, but also provides the framework within which Daniel is able to add to the commentary. So, for example, in line 7, Daniel re-characterises Mark's announcement 'look up' into a comment that the daughter is 'watching' her father. This starts to move beyond a potential behaviourist characterisation of the head movement ('look up') to explore descriptions of the daughter's conduct that begin to capture interactional qualities. So the 'look up' is re-characterised not as 'staring into the middle distance' or 'inspecting', but rather 'she's watching'.

The way in which Mark announces the series of events also makes 'missing' elements publicly recoverable. That is, in announcing the order, Daniel is able to challenge that order, by pointing out elements that should be included. In line 11, he says 'youf forgot the breathe'. Of course, Mark may well have heard the audible breathing, but he has not mentioned it in his account of the unfolding events. Thus, his commentary implicitly treats the breathing as irrelevant to the organisation of the father and daughter's conduct. However, having started to make his own announcement ('oh she-'), Daniel reformulates his turn to challenge Mark's suggestion that the next relevant action in the series is that she 'looks again' with 'no sh- youf forgot the breathe'. The 'breathe' rather than the look is presented by Daniel as the next in the series.

This conduct displays an orientation to the notion of sequence and in doing so provides an interactional practice that renders candidate sequence visible to both parties. The researchers are trying to piece together the orderliness of the conduct, and especially the sequential organisation of the conduct – how one action attends to the prior and is attended to in the next. The vocal rendering of the order of key elements provides the basis on which such analytic work can be collaboratively managed. Fundamentally, it enables the two participants to establish what the order of events is and then to explore the sequential relation-ships between those events.

As they are collaborating on the analysis of visible phenomena – namely, the embodied conduct of the father and daughter on-screen – much of their work is about debating and discussing its organisation. This demands that they make it visible to one another, but of course they cannot 'see' through the other's eyes. So the commentary is key in this regard. They announce the order of events along with the video playback and thereby discriminate between analytically relevant and non-relevant conduct. This, in turn, allows colleagues to assess the validity of the candidate order as it corresponds to the video playback. Establishing a 'shared seeing' entails not simply noticing (and having others notice) phenomena, but collaboratively piecing together and agreeing the order of analytically relevant conduct.

Interestingly, this work of announcing the order of relevant conduct is highly significant as a resource to address the analytical question then raised by Mark in line 16: 'why: did I turn around?'. He is referring to his own actions on the video; in other words, why did I (as the father on the video) turn to look at my daughter in that moment rather than others? Again, this is a common type of question in data sessions. It encourages participants to explore the sequential relationship between one action and the next. It may be that an action just happens to occur at that moment, but it might be produced with regard to another's actions. This is key to the sequential analysis of recorded materials.

Having established a revised order of relevant events, Daniel is in a position to proffer a tentative argument – that the daughter's audible breath attracted the father's attention. Indeed he reenacts the breathing '.hhh-nhhh' to animate his point. Mark then tentatively agrees in saying that 'yeah::: that's true actually, it's probably the sound of tha:t'. Again, in specifying the sound as most rel-evant, Daniel is in a position to refine the argument further, in suggesting that the sound is not in isolation, but that there are visible features of the conduct that may have contributed to attracting the on-screen father's attention – 'and it's also a move:ment. the shoul:ders move, the chest moves'.

Pursuing analytic claims

If we follow their discussion further (see Fragment 1b), we can see how Mark and Daniel develop and pursue the tentative proposal. Mark sets the video to replay the extract. It took nearly a minute for him to locate the appropriate starting point on the video and to create a beginning and end point that can be replayed with ease on subsequent occasions. Once the extract has played again, this is the talk that follows:

Fragment 1b: DS-14/07/06-42:00

```
        ((M Replays fragment))
27  D:  did yu- iss th- it's the in-drawn breath.
28      (.) [((sniff))   (0.7)   ((sniff)) ]
29  M:     [is it- (.) it's  so:  it's v]ery ti:ny:.
30      >I canna< y'know, we can't- >it's not very good<
31      recording, so I can't really hear it (.) rea:lly
32      [well.
33  D:  [ptt
34      (6.7) ((M Replays fragment))
35  M:  ah:: (0.5) is it two ((sniff))
36      (.)
37  M:  is it [ever slight snorty sound and .hh in-breath?
38  D:        [yeah ((sniff)) ((sniff))
39      (.)
40  M:  (how [        )
41  D:        [it's it's almo:st- it's almost like a crying
42      sound.
43      (7.0) ((M Replays fragment))
44  M:  yeah::. yeh. (.) and  I immediately turn and look
45      like tha:t.
```

In line 27, Daniel states much more strongly that the 'in-drawn breath' attracts Mark's gaze. This upgraded proposal immediately follows the re-viewing of the video. The context in which the upgrade is produced is important, because it links the re-viewing with the upgrade; it implies that Daniel has just seen further evidence in the video to support his proposal. However, Mark's response to the playback is more ambivalent. He does not explicitly deny the sequential relationship between in-breath and gaze shift, but rather he suggests that the video recording may not provide sufficient quality of evidence to support it. Indeed, the formulation of this utterance is rather complex and demonstrates the sensitivity in challenging a claim, especially as his colleague has just upgraded it. Even within the utterance, the challenge moves from 'it's very ti:ny:' to '>I canna< y'know, we can't-' to '>it's not very good< recording, so I can't really hear it (.) rea:lly well.' In the end Mark does not deny the existence or potential import of the in-breath, but questions whether it is sufficiently recoverable, by him or indeed Daniel, from the data at hand. Mark replays the extract to inspect it further (line 34).

Following playback, it is now Mark who displays hearing the 'in-breath' and refines its characterisation to 'ever slight snorty sound and .hh in-breath', which Daniel then refines further to 'it's almost like a crying sound'. Following this characterisation they replay it a further time to re-check their emerging refined observations. This time Mark provides further evidence for the claim when he says 'and I immediately turn and look like tha:t'. The immediacy of the response by the father on-screen (who is of course Mark himself) is used to strengthen the association between the two actions. The fact that the turn comes then and not moments later is used to make the argument for the sequential relationship stronger. Furthermore Mark reenacts the face the father pulled when he turned. The expressive quality of this face is presented as a visual 'comment' on something his daughter has just done. So, the treatment of the daughter's 'in-breath' is evidenced by Mark in the speed and nature of the response.

There are three elements that we would like to comment on here. Firstly, we see within this sequence how a tentative analytic claim emerges, is defined and refined. The early claims are tagged with 'probably' to mark their tentative status; we then see the claim upgraded by Daniel, delicately undermined by Mark, then agreed and confirmed. In the course of this short sequence the video is replayed four times to identify and check the claim. Indeed, part of the sense and significance of various claims are bound up with their position vis-à-vis the playback. The video is treated as a powerful source with which to assess, challenge or verify those claims. It is a rather immediate form of 'constant comparison' in the terminology of grounded theory (Strauss and Corbin, 1990).

Secondly, it is interesting to note that certain elements of the discussion and not others were recorded by Mark on his transcript during the data session (see Figure 4.2). Most notably, linked to line 70 there is 'tiny breath!!' written down, which in turn is linked to a further annotation, 'almost like a crying sound'. These refer to points made in the course of the data session and recorded on the transcript. It is not that they are now somehow 'fixed', but rather when Mark returns to work on this extract, they provide some basis to begin that work – either to challenge, refine, or agree the characterisations developed in this data session.

The third point is to note that, over the course of a minute or so, the characterisation of the daughter's action that is the focus of this sequence emerges and develops. Clearly, the verbal characterisation transforms ('the breathe', 'in-breath', 'a snorty sound', 'almost like a crying sound', etc.). However, these are accompanied by other forms of presentation of the on-screen action – reenactments. Reenactments (Sidnell, 2006) are embodied demonstrations of past events or scenes and are highly prevalent in data sessions (Tutt and Hindmarsh, 2011). Of course, reenactments are not a reproduction of the actions on-screen but rather a version of events that inevitably

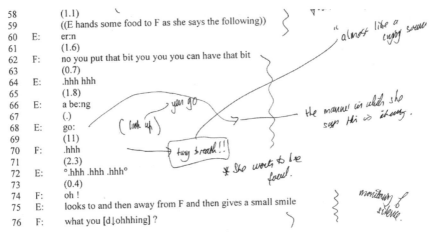

58   (1.1)
59   ((E hands some food to F as she says the following))
60   E: er:n
61   (1.6)
62   F: no you put that bit you you you can have that bit
63   (0.7)
64   E: .hhh hhh
65   (1.8)
66   E: a be:ng
67   (.)
68   E: go:
69   (11)
70   F: .hhh
71   (2.3)
72   E: °.hhh .hhh .hhh°
73   (0.4)
74   F: oh !
75   E: looks to and then away from F and then gives a small smile
76   F: what you [d↓ohhhing] ?

Figure 4.2   A section of Mark's annotated transcript

selects and often exaggerates certain features. In this case, both Daniel and
Mark produce versions of the 'in-breath' that capture aspects of the quality
and nature of its production.

Daniel's initial reenactments in lines 12 and 20 are much louder and more
pronounced than the later 'sniffing' sounds that are produced in lines 28,
35 and 38. The reenactments provide a resource through which emergent
analytic observations can be characterised and highlighted. During this
early stage of analysis, the phenomenon is yet to be formally described. The
reenactments thus provide a means through which phenomena can be highlighted for co-participants prior to formal, linguistic categorisation. Indeed, as
the reenactments refine, we can note how Daniel characterises the conduct as
'almost like a crying sound' – a characterisation that gets noted down by Mark
on his transcript. The reenactments, coupled with an emerging series of verbal
descriptions, help to achieve that characterisation. Indeed, it may be responsive
as much to the latest reenactment as to conduct revealed on the original data
record.

Video and the visible

Video-based studies of work practice are demonstrating and developing the
ways in which visible phenenomena – embodied conduct, tool use, interactive technologies, etc. – are fundamental to the organisation of collaborative
work. Hopefully, the importance of the visible will be clear from our discussion thus far. For instance, Mark and Daniel spend significant amounts of
time delineating and debating the relevance of visual aspects of the interaction
between the father and daughter on-screen. Similarly, here, the video record

makes available the visible conduct that underpins interaction in the course of Mark and Daniel's data session. Our visual record makes an in-depth analysis of gestural conduct (such as the reenactment) a feasible analytic activity, and elsewhere we have pursued this very interest (Tutt and Hindmarsh, 2011). However, more generally, the video record provides a means to explore how the verbal and the visual are interdependent resources for sense-making. Let's take a simple example to illustrate this.

Consider some of the visible conduct that surrounds lines 29–31 of the transcript. Figure 4.3 presents some images of conduct that emerge alongside points in the talk. Throughout the sequence, it is Mark talking.

During data sessions it is unsurprising to note that participants do not spend the whole time in a face-to-face orientation. Indeed, much of the time, participants are collaboratively viewing the screen. However, the movements towards and away from a face-to-face orientation can have sequential import. Here, just prior to this fragment of data, and as in many other points in the data session, Daniel delivers an analytic proposal as he turns to look at Mark. Mark has returned his gaze and watches Daniel reenact the in-drawn breath. However he then turns back to the screen as he says 'it's so' and by the time he begins to say 'I canna' not only is he looking at the screen but Daniel has returned his gaze to the screen also.

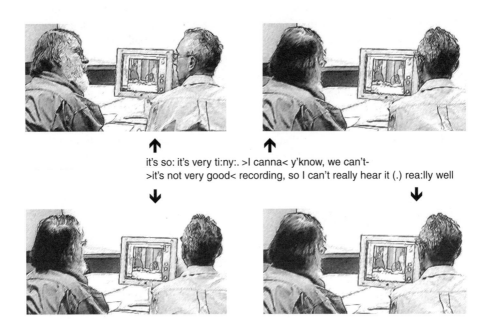

it's so: it's very ti:ny:. >I canna< y'know, we can't-
>it's not very good< recording, so I can't really hear it (.) rea:lly well

Figure 4.3   The interdependence of the verbal and the visible

What is interesting here is that they could have elaborated the analytic discussion based on Daniel's strong assertion that the daughter's 'in-drawn breath' has attracted the father's gaze. But they do not. In looking back at the screen and moving the computer mouse (during 'very ti:ny:.'), Mark's actions project the renewed relevance of the screen as the principal site of collaborative activity. His actions are not treated as a distraction or as rude, but Daniel treats them as projecting future action related to the computer screen.

Furthermore, during the section when Mark says 'it's not very good recording, so I can't really hear', the sound menu is visible at the top right hand side of their computer screen (although only just discernable on the rendered image that we are able to provide in Figure 4.3). Not only is the menu visible, but also Mark can be seen to turn up the volume on the computer by dragging the level icon upwards. This is not only visible to us as analysts but also available to Daniel in the data session. The video is, and can be seen as, being prepared for replay.

While the utterance marks a problem, his accompanying visual conduct embodies a potential solution – that if the sound is turned up it may compensate for the poor recording and the fact that Mark cannot hear the in-breath 'really well'. In making sense of Mark's utterance then, Daniel is able to draw on a range of visible resources that are not independent from, but thoroughly interwoven with, the talk. In understanding the interactional practices that underpin collaborative work, video makes visible and available a range of resources that are available to the participants themselves.

While video makes these elements visible to analysts and their colleagues, rendering these moments visible and available to readers of analytic work is far more problematic. Still images may work for aspects of gestural work, gross shifts in orientation and the like, but often actions can be so slight that even a series of images is not sufficient to highlight the relevant aspect of conduct. Thus, their textualization requires ethnographic description rather than visuals. One way forward is the digital publication where video extracts can be incorporated alongside analytic accounts (e.g. Brown, 2004; Büscher, 2005). However this demands a degree of ethical clearance that can be difficult to attain, particularly within workplace and organisational settings.

Closing remarks

The 'practice turn' in the social sciences includes a range of approaches to the analysis of social action. Often, however, 'practice' is glossed. Even rich and interesting ethnographic studies fail to fully engage the real-time production and organisation of social life. The type of video-based studies that we discuss here attempt to hone and specify our understanding of those production methods.

Unlike many branches of visual methodology, we are not interested in the visual record as a topic for study (in and of itself), but rather wish to consider the video as a resource to analyse the production of work (see also Martens, this volume). Digital video provides unprecedented access to details in the organisation of work, access that is otherwise unimaginable – not simply in terms of the opportunities for playback and sharing, but also because of the range of ways in which digital technologies can be used to interrogate the video record.

Interestingly, Schatzki (2001: 3) argues that 'practice approaches promulgate a distinct social ontology: the social is a field of embodied, materially interwoven practices centrally organized around shared practical understandings'. In specifying that position, we would argue that the kinds of video-based studies of work practice that we outline here demonstrate ways in which social interaction forms the principal vehicle through which specialised practices, procedures and routines emerge and are sustained. The video materials open up not only the verbal exchanges that are so central to many workplace activities, but also highlight the ways in which 'embodied, materially interwoven' – visible – phenomena are central to work practice.

In this chapter, we have turned the analytic lens on the work of analysts themselves. It is interesting to note that while textbooks on method and methodology routinely outline different perspectives on or approaches to data analysis, it is very rare to be instructed in the ways in which they relate to practice. In some ways such textbook accounts present characterisations of how studies *should* be done and how methods *should* be deployed. In describing the practical accomplishment of everyday research work, our study starts to consider how research *is* done and how methods *are* realised.

We have presented an example of the practical work of following through a particular methodological orientation to visual data at a particular stage of data analysis – a 'data session' at the early stages of work with fragments of video. These moments do not help us foresee the next stages of work on these data, or how analytic claims were subjected to further development. However, they do nicely reveal how classic concerns of qualitative sociologists – problems of meaning, interpretation, evidence, the participants' perspective and the rest – are managed and grappled with in real time and in relation to their video data. We have started to unpack various interactional practices used to attend to these matters. For instance, we have seen how the work of 'assembling order', to underscore a sequential analysis, is accomplished through live commentary and reenactment which render analytic observations available and open to agreement, challenge or refinement.

While in this chapter we explore but one episode of one type of work, research work, video has opened up opportunities to unpack the practical accomplishment of work in an extraordinary range of settings. In doing so it facilitates a distinctively ethnomethodological treatment of sociological concepts, whereby the concern is 'to make topics of sociological discussion visible in the witness-able daily life of the society' (Sharrock, 1989: 663), to respecify these topics of sociological discussion as practical matters for societal members. Even in the short analysis presented here, we can see how video makes available the complex resources, verbal, bodily, visible and material, that are interwoven in the ongoing accomplishment of working tasks. Thus, the affordances of digital video, coupled with the analytic sensitivities of ethnomethodology, deliver a novel contribution to the 'practice turn' in the social sciences and lead to quite innovative accounts of the real-time production of work and organisational practices.

Acknowledgements

This work has been supported by the MiMeG ESRC e-Social Science Research Node (Award No. RES-149-25-0033). We are deeply indebted to the research team featured in the data presented here for allowing us to record and share their social scientific work. We are also grateful to Sarah Pink, Christian Heath, as well as past and present members of the WIT Research Centre for their comments on, and contributions to, this work.

Appendix

A brief description of key symbols used in the transcript. For further details, see Heath et al. (2010).

(4.3)	A pause between or within utterances (in seconds)
(.)	A pause of less than 0.2 of a second
:	An elongation of the sound of a word or syllable
>I canna<	Words that are spoken more quickly than surrounding talk
why	Words that are spoken more loudly than surrounding talk
oh^	Rising intonation
.hhh	Audible in-breath
hhh	Audible out-breath
.pt	Lip smack
[	When square brackets are aligned, they mark overlapping utterances

References

Brown, B. (2004) 'The order of service: the practical management of customer interaction', *Sociological Research Online*, 9 (retrieved from: www.socresonline.org.uk/9/4/brown.htm on 1 November 2011).

Büscher, M. (2005) 'Social life under the microscope?', *Sociological Research Online*, 10 (retrieved from: www.socresonline.org.uk/10/1.html on 1 November 2011).

Corradi, G., Gherardi, S. and Verzelloni, L. (2010) 'Through the practice lens: where is the bandwagon of practice-based studies heading?', *Management Learning*, 41 (3): 265.

Coulter, J. (2001) 'Human practices and the observability of the "macro-social"', in T. Schatzki, K. Knorr-Cetina and E. von Savigny (eds), *The Practice Turn in Contemporary Theory*. London: Routledge. pp. 29–41.

Fraser, M., Hindmarsh, J., Best, K., Heath, C., Biegel, G., Greenhalgh, C. and Reeves, S. (2006) 'Remote collaboration over video data: towards real-time e-social science', *Computer Supported Cooperative Work*, 15 (4): 257–79.

Garfinkel, H. (1984 [1967]) *Studies in Ethnomethodology*. Cambridge: Polity.

Heath, C. and Button, G. (eds) (2002) 'Special issue on workplace studies', *British Journal of Sociology*, 53 (2).

Heath, C. and Luff, P. (2000) *Technology in Action*. Cambridge: Cambridge University Press.

Heath, C., Hindmarsh, J. and Luff, P. (2010) *Video in Qualitative Research*. London: Sage.

Heritage, J. (1984) *Garfinkel and Ethnomethodology*. Cambridge: Polity Press.

Hindmarsh, J. (2008) 'Distributed video analysis in social research', in N. Fielding, R.M. Lee and G. Blank (eds), *The Sage Handbook of Online Research Methods*. London: Sage. pp. 343–61.

Hindmarsh, J. and Heath, C. (2007) 'Video-based studies of work practice', *Sociology Compass*, 1 (1): 156–73.

Llewellyn, N. and Hindmarsh, J. (eds) (2010) *Organisation, Interaction and Practice: Studies in Ethnomethodology and Conversation Analysis*. Cambridge: Cambridge University Press.

Lynch, M. (2001) 'Ethnomethodology and the logic of practice', in T. Schatzki, K. Knorr-Cetina and E. von Savigny (eds), *The Practice Turn in Contemporary Theory*. London: Routledge. pp. 131–48.

Nicolini, D., Gherardi, S. and Yanow, D. (eds) (2003) *Knowing in Organizations: A Practice-Based Approach*. Armonk, NY: ME Sharpe.

Schatzki, T. (2001) 'Introduction', in T. Schatzki, K. Knorr-Cetina and E. von Savigny (eds), *The Practice Turn in Contemporary Theory*. London: Routledge. pp. 1–14.

Sharrock, W. (1989) 'Ethnomethodology', *The British Journal of Sociology*, 40 (4): 657–77.

Sidnell, J. (2006) 'Coordinating gesture, talk, and gaze in reenactments', *Research on Language and Social Interaction*, 39 (4): 377–409.

Strauss, A.L. and Corbin, J. (1990) *Basics of Qualitative Research: Grounded Theory Procedures and Techniques*. London: Sage.

Suchman, L. (1987) *Plans and Situated Actions*. Cambridge: Cambridge University Press.

Tutt, D. and Hindmarsh, J. (2011) 'Reenactments at work: demonstrating conduct in data sessions', *Research on Language and Social Interaction*, 44 (3): 211–36.

Tutt, D., Hindmarsh, J., Shaukat, M. and Fraser, M. (2007) 'The distributed work of local action: interaction amongst virtually collocated research teams', in *Proceedings of the European Conference on Computer-Supported Cooperative Work 2007*. Berlin: Springer. pp. 199–218.

5

VIRTUAL/VISUAL ETHNOGRAPHY
Methodological Crossroads at the Intersection of Visual and Internet Research

Elisenda Ardévol

Introduction

The use of the Internet in ethnographic fieldwork opens up many new avenues for exploration. It moreover poses some methodological questions similar to those faced by social researchers dealing with established and emerging audio-visual technologies. In this chapter I set out some methodological problems and challenges shared by virtual and visual ethnographers. In doing so I suggest how the opportunities that the Internet is opening up for research into people's visual practices are leading to advances in visual and virtual ethnographic methodologies.

Cross-references between the areas of visual and Internet ethnography are still minimal (Pink, 2007; Pauwels, 2008). Yet the methodological problems and challenges faced in both fields of study are more similar than one would expect. In what follows I explore how their intersections are leading to methodological development and innovation. My discussion is based on the empirical work of our *mediaccions* research group[1] and recent literature covering methodological issues relating to the use of Internet technologies and visual media. My starting point is the idea that the Internet, as well as visual media, can be understood from two different research perspectives: as a subject of study and as a research tool. Visual anthropologists, as well as many virtual ethnographers, have faced this question of the two-fold dimensions of the use of technological aids; visual media and the Internet are, at the same time, the object of research and the method for gathering data, not to mention that both media are also used for sharing the results. Visual objects and practices are the main object of study of visual researchers who also use visual technologies to produce data and to present their outcomes. Internet ethnographers are mainly interested in the Internet as a cultural artefact, and use Internet tools and online interaction to develop their fieldwork. While the camera mediates the visual ethnographer's experience in the field, online interaction is generally fundamental for gaining access to the field in the case of Internet research. In fact, Internet platforms such as web sites, virtual communities, electronic forums, online games and social networks are part of the ethnographer's field site. In both cases, fieldworkers try to conduct their research experience through a reflexive approach to the role of technological devices during fieldwork, therefore enhancing the scope of the ethnographic methodology. We could argue that the innovations these reflexive practices pose are not very different from those posed by the critical approach to the textual and narrative nature of the ethnographic work developed during the 1980s. Mediation is always present in any kind of social science research, but while the 'textual turn' was a reflection about writing, the 'mediation turn' is a question of how we integrate other representational tools and digital technologies in our daily fieldwork practices and knowledge production.

The Internet: object of study and methodological tool

During the 1990s, the first ethnographic studies of the Internet demonstrated that computer-mediated interactions were socially significant and were fully loaded with meaning for the participants (Hine, 2000). The first ethnographies of the Internet developed and used online methods to gain access to the issues researchers were studying, that is, how social interaction and cultural signifying practices were possible through computer-mediated communication (Baym, 1998; Paccagnella, 1997; Reid, 1994). This was a first step in legitimising the social and cultural study of the Internet, given that previous conceptions had considered that computer-mediated communication lacked social cues or believed it to be second-class communication. These ethnographic studies were based on the idea that social interaction in 'cyberspace' could be studied from the perspective of culture and characterised as a specific and relatively autonomous culture from the 'real' or physical world.

Daniel Miller and Don Slater's study of Internet use in Trinidad (2000) and Christine Hine's (2000) study of the case of Louise Woodward are both well known for following actors across their multiple activities in ways that bypass the division between online and offline ethnography. Hine reflexively brought to Internet studies the shift to understanding the constructed nature of the field site in anthropology (Amit, 2000; Gupta and Ferguson, 1997; Marcus, 1995), systematising her 'principles for virtual ethnography' through a multi-sited and connective notion of ethnography (Hine, 2000). Leander and McKim (2003) also pointed out that the online/offline dichotomy should not be the a-priori assumption of the ethnographer but is something that needs to be explained. What matters then is how participants create, bound and articulate different social spaces. This implies the development of combined online/offline methodologies (Dirksen et al., 2010) that blend research methods, as Mann and Stewart (2000) proposed. Simultaneously, and largely as a result of the process of methodological reflection and development undertaken by these authors, Internet technologies have become a research tool that social researchers from other areas have begun to use in their empirical work, the goals of which are not necessarily related with Internet studies. The net has become a research tool for many research purposes.

Annette Markham (2004) has analytically drawn on the duality of the Internet as a method: as just a research tool for collecting, analysing and presenting results; or as the field for conducting research – that is, the social context where the subjects and the researcher meet and interact. For researchers interested in the Internet as an object of study, the object, the tool and the research context collapse in many ways. Yet this analytical division can also be useful to those interested in incorporating the Internet into their field methods.

While the use of visual technologies has given rise to a whole new repertoire of research techniques and 'visual methods', the conversion of the Internet into a research tool has led to the creation of a collection of methods and research techniques based on the use of Internet technologies for data gathering, labelled as 'online research methods' (Mann and Stewart, 2000), 'Internet research methods' (Hewson et al., 2003), 'virtual methods' (Hine, 2005) or 'digital methods' (Rogers, 2009). These online methods include the adaptation and reformulation of conventional research techniques such as participant observation, interviews, focus groups and surveys, as well as innovative proposals based on the analysis of hyperlinks, such as 'web sphere analysis' (Foot et al., 2003) or 'web hyperlink research' (Woo, 2003). For instance, some authors have discussed the social dimension of hyperlinks (Beaulieu, 2005) and the need to include web analysis techniques in the ethnographic approach (Howard, 2002).

In many cases, it has been argued that the incorporation of the Internet in ethnographic fieldwork provides the conditions for studying collectives that would be practically inaccessible without the use of these technologies. Using the Internet in fieldwork may allow us to access geographically dispersed individuals, so we can construct geographically dispersed analysis units in a more radical way than that proposed by multi-situational ethnography (Marcus, 1995). For example, to research Ghanaians living in London, Burrell and Anderson (2008: 206) used the Internet, among other sources, to recruit informants, thus eluding both the 'ethnic neighbourhood' and the 'online community' as forms of study that identify the community itself as the object of analysis. The Internet is increasingly used to recruit informants, alongside more traditional techniques. For example, Angela Orend and Patricia Gagné (2009), when studying the popularity of corporate logo tattoos, placed flyers at local tattoo parlours, coffee shops, restaurants, stores and university bars, and posted a notice about the study on numerous Internet newsgroups, listservers and chat rooms. Sometimes using Internet technologies enables the development of strategies for gaining access to extremely elusive or especially sensitive groups, for example, medical patients (Illingworth, 2001; Orgad, 2005), neo-nazi groups (Kimmel, 2007), or people who are into extreme sexual practices (Pichardo, 2008).

The Internet offers social researchers many opportunities for primary data collection beyond recruiting participants or administering questionnaires, in that it is a source of textual and visual data for multiple research topics. For example, an increasing number of studies exploit the Internet as a repository about body, health or illness experiences, such as the study of the relatively hidden practice of self-injury (Adler and Adler, 2007) or the analysis of online stories of childbirth experiences to assess women's degrees of involvement in decision making (Bylund, 2005 in Seale et al., 2010). In these cases the Internet is not the focus of the research but part of the field for conducting research. Internet forums and communities allow researchers to approach participants gradually and to progressively construct a rapport, participating in a forum one step at a time, setting up a blog or creating a user profile account. Nicola Illingworth indicates how the Internet became her field site for the analysis of assisted reproduction techniques when it was impossible to gain access to participants directly from the hospital. Far from being a hindrance, using the Internet as the source for her empirical data had certain advantages. The anonymity of the interaction established over the Internet facilitated the participation of a large number of informants, many of whom recognised that they would not have agreed to a face-to-face meeting, especially if it had been in the hospital ward (Illingworth, 2001). José Ignacio Pichardo also believes that anonymity was a fundamental aspect in his research while studying the sexual practices of bondage and sadomasochism (Pichardo, 2008). A questionnaire administered on the Internet allowed him to obtain data from anonymous participants who would have been unwilling to participate in a face-to-face interview.

The Internet has therefore become one more means through which social scientists construct empirical knowledge. However, technologically mediated interaction profoundly changes the nature of the information collected through participant observation research or face-to-face interviews.

As Garcia et al. (2009: 62–3) noted, in face-to-face participant observation, ethnographers routinely experience and analyse participants' verbal utterances in conjunction with their facial expressions, tone of voice and body language, along with other sensory impressions of the environment. Instead, online ethnographers should take care to integrate visual aspects of the textual interactions into their observations and treat many visual data displayed by the Internet interface such as the use of emoticons, pictures, colors, page layout and graphic design of web sites as a key aspect of the online social interaction and context, as well as the technological script of the site. This will produce a great amount of visual and textual data that must be archived, classified and analysed. This may require developing a new set of skills and data-collection methods similar to those already used by visual anthropologists and sociologists.

Since the beginning of the 1980s, social scientists have explored the possibilities brought forth by computers, specialised software and computer applications for data storage and retrieval. The pioneering use of software for textual analysis (Podolefsky, 1987) has quickly led to the development of specific qualitative data-analysis programs (CAQDAS). The development of specialised programs has given rise to what some authors have termed 'computer-based methods' (Fischer, 2006), which, as well as qualitative data-analysis systems, include simulation and applications for analysing structural relationships (Lyon and Magliveras, 2006). Moreover, many of us who use digital cameras realise that digital technology is changing not only the way we take images, but also the way we see, store, analyse and show them (Parmeggiani, 2009). The ability to create interactive and multimedia representations (Biella, 1996) on CD-ROMs has been explored since the middle of the 1990s by various researchers, especially in the field of visual anthropology. This approach was later transferred to the Internet, at which point various forms of hypermedia representation were experimented with (Banks, 2001; Pink, 2004, 2007). In most cases, these ideas have focused on the use of digital technologies for analysis and knowledge representation.

Nowadays, the Internet is a powerful tool for sharing textual, visual, audio and audiovisual information, both in the social scientist's imagination and as part of contemporary global popular culture. In recent years, visual digital technologies have undergone an intense process of expansion in parallel to that of the Internet. Their proliferation has resulted in the use of webcams, CCTV cameras, digital cameras, multimedia mobile phones and tablets. All these technologies produce sounds, images and video, which circulate on the Internet and can be simultaneously viewed on the screens of portable multimedia players. Visual elements are increasingly used in telecommunications technologies and are ever-present in the daily lives of people and institutions. Contemporary visual practices are therefore marked by complex interactions between digital technologies and networked infrastructures.

Visual practices and the Internet

The Internet is becoming increasingly visual. Videos, photos and all kinds of graphic animations (from porn to scientific images, everyday snapshots, self-made videos and remixed films) circulate on the Internet and are produced and consumed in diverse social contexts. This proliferation of visual content is accompanied by the extension of digital photographic and video technologies that are commonly entangled with Internet and mobile devices. As different digital technologies and the Internet become increasingly interwoven, this blending has deep implications for all the domains of visual research.

The Internet opens up two new research fields for visual researchers. First, it provides them with a whole new raft of cultural practices mediated by visual and Internet technologies, through which the meaning and the significance of visual documents are very often redefined. Second, it provides access to an extensive amount of visual documents published on the Internet, a global archive of visual cultures. Today, many such records are easily accessible to researchers, whereas previously they could be accessed only in private contexts or by establishing a prior relationship with informants (for example, family photos and intimate photos). In sum, the analysis of online visual material is likely to be an important element for visual culture studies.

Photography as technology, object and practice is a research subject that overlaps visual and Internet studies. As a form of cultural production conveying a set of practices, material devices and narratives, it brings out new forms of sociality and identity formation through technologically mediated practices. For example, in online identity studies, the importance of the use of self-portraits by online participants was initially analysed as part of the technologies of self-presentation in personal webpages (Cheung, 2000) and later in social network profiles (boyd and Heer, 2006). For example, O'Riordan shows how photographs are part of online identity performance and contribute to the visual construction and intersection of race and desire (O'Riordan, 2007: 121); Nakamura is concerned with how self-images that people post on the Internet contrast with visual stereotypes of gender and race (Nakamura, 2008); and Piela (2010) explores photographic self-representation of Muslim women on the Internet. Power relationships are being explored through digital photo production and sharing; it is not only a question of performing online identity, but how online identity construction is intermingled with embodied daily life experience, political contestation and resistance (Hjorth, 2006; Lee, 2005).

The digital camera as a mass tool of representation is more than a vehicle for documenting one's conditions; it can be used for creating alternative representations of oneself (sex, class, age group, race, etc.) or for gaining power over one's image (Slater, 1995: 290). Digital photographs are also objects for sociality. There is a vast corpus of literature about photographic digital practices and the Internet, especially on youth and their use of camera phones for social bounding (Okada, 2005; Scifo, 2005; Tinkler, 2008). These studies show that the camera phone is more than a personal technology for subjectivity construction; it is a collective technology that mediates long-distance and face-to-face sociality within contexts of local interaction and within the group of peers (Scifo, 2005: 367).

Ethnographic methods have been used widely by social scientists to investigate social uses of photography. Writing about practices and flows of digital photography, Jonas Larsen takes a non-representational perspective to the ethnographic study of tourist digital-photography practices; that is, going beyond representation by focusing upon practices and not simply on what is produced (Larsen, 2008: 157). By understanding photography as a mobile practice, involving bodily doings and technical enactments, he follows networks, circulations, performances, objects and meanings of tourist photography (Larsen, 2008: 143). 'Mobile' ethnography does not distinguish between online and offline fieldwork. It is partly inspired in multi-sited ethnography and in visual ethnography, because it involves observing and recording visually the embodied, social and material practices, technologies and performances (Larsen, 2008: 155). Similarly, through a practice theoretical framework, Edgar Gómez-Cruz conducted ethnographic fieldwork among a group of amateur photographers, mostly located in Catalonia and organised through the photo-sharing site Flickr (Gómez-Cruz, 2009). Whereas early theorisations insisted on the delocalisation of virtual communities and characterised online identities as detached from the 'real' selves, his fieldwork shows that social network sites are based on personal rather than anonymous interaction, and use locality to increase and coordinate social interaction. His subjects do not limit their interactions to Flickr, but use many other devices (Facebook, email, Twitter, phones, etc.) as well as face-to-face encounters and meetings for collective photographic performances. As the digital camera becomes connected to the Internet, amateur photographers become more and more engaged in photographic practices and expand their pleasure as cultural producers, sharing tips and improving their skills collaboratively. In doing so, they create a collective sense of belonging and socialisation, which itself becomes the core of the group activity. Both ethnographers point to the 'newness' of digital photography as an everyday practice that has to do with how the digitalisation of images relates to media convergence and the performance of sociality.

One of the consequences of the proliferation of popular visual production is the breakdown of the cultural circuit dominated by mass media production, something that has been analysed in terms of participatory culture (Jenkins, 2004) or homecasting (van Dijck, 2007). The intermingling between amateur, commercial and institutional production has become more and more complex and has blurred the clearly defined roles of producers and audiences (Marshall, 2004). The study on the reception of media has attracted anthropologists since the middle of the last century, from the pioneering work of Margaret Mead and Roda Metraux to the creation of the subfield of media anthropology at the crossroads with visual anthropology, communication and media studies (Ginsburg et al., 2003; Rothenbuhler and Coman, 2005; Spitulnik, 1993).

Approaches based on the study of audiovisual materials, such as the work of Elizabeth Bird (2010), support the use of ethnographic studies focusing on media practices, in other words, the need to study those processes by which audiovisual narratives and models are incorporated into social life, going beyond reception and audiences' ethnographies. Expanding Couldry's (2004) imperative to seek 'what do people do with media?', visual and media ethnography now has to deal with how people creatively engage in media production.

In our work on popular self-representations of the Madrid Metro on YouTube, Gemma San Cornelio and I (Ardévol and San Cornelio, 2007) explored many aspects of people's video production. Users of the Metro create self-representations for a great variety of purposes and in genres that range from critical parodies of the Metro's institutional advertisements to remakes of film scenes, recreations of TV shows, and documentaries. Others include video snapshots capturing social interactions among young peers or 'funny' situations. We analyse those 'media moments' in which the subway (a non-place in terms of Marc Augé, 1992) is redefined as a living and signifying place by the producers and actors, but also the role that the Internet plays in these 'media rituals'. Most of these productions cannot be fully understood without taking into consideration that they do not fit the category of 'home videos'. Rather, they are more like 'media products', in that their producers were already thinking about uploading them for an Internet audience at the very moment of shooting them. The youth we studied record videos on the subway and upload them to YouTube for the purpose of making fun of their intended Internet audience, and the whole video production context is defined by this last objective. This means that the content of the video itself has to be understood in the context of the Internet. Moreover, the videos that circulate on the Internet have inscriptions (titles, comments, tags, rankings) that the producers explore and exploit, and which transform the audiovisual experience in shaping the materiality of the visual object itself. The Internet and its particular technologies – in this case YouTube – mediate the production of the visual object, the kind of content recorded, the circulation of the image and its consumption. When Internet practices and infrastructures mediate the visual object in this way, all the dimensions of the visual analysis must be rethought.

For both Internet researchers and visual scholars the Internet represents an opportunity to access a vast field of visual data that reflects an equally large variety of visual practices and social phenomena. Thus visual and Internet methods merge further. From an ethnographic perspective, the interpretation of images and visual practices are concerned with the production context, the object of the photograph, the context of consumption, and the materiality of the images themselves (Banks, 2001; Pink, 2007). Recording videos in the subway or uploading a photo of oneself every day in a blog are practices that need to be understood in relation to their publication in YouTube, Flickr or Photolog. These social networks play a multiple role in shaping the circulatory images. The Internet is more than a context that helps to explain the meaning of the images; it shapes the images in determinate ways, because the technology contributes significantly in how the visual object is created, manipulated and shared.

When analysing the data in a film, it should to be placed in its production and exhibition context; we need to bear in mind, as Worth states, 'how the films were made, under what cultural rules, by what groups and for what purpose' (1995: 212); otherwise any conclusions will be difficult to substantiate. When applying this notion to visual elements on the Internet, the researcher who wishes to collect data from the Internet must determine, depending on the object of the study and its analytical units, to what degree specific data is conditioned by the particular context of the Internet (Pauwels, 2008). As such, regarding the Internet as a simple repository of visual data for the analysis of any subject of study may not always be possible. In many cases, isolating the data from their technological inscriptions would lead to a loss of the meaning of the same subject we are trying to study.

Mediated experience in ethnographic fieldwork

Because online ethnographers are not necessarily physically co-present with their research subjects, they must conduct participant observation through computer-mediated interaction and develop the technological, social and cultural competencies necessary to fully participate in online settings, as well as improve their skills in the analysis of textual and visual data. Garcia et al. (2009) remark that in online methods the nature of the participant observation changes because what we observe are mainly visual and textual arrangements, and participation is mostly based on textual and visual interchanges with the participants of our research. Technologically mediated fieldwork raises a whole set of questions that virtual and visual ethnographers share. In fact, research experience is an intensively mediated experience, both for 'visual' and 'virtual' ethnographers: the camera, like any Internet technology, is central to the social relations and events the ethnographer is involved in.

One of the main methodological and epistemological questions posed by visual ethnography refers to the implications of the use of cameras in the field: what are the consequences of using a camera in fieldwork for the subjects, for the data and the knowledge produced? The answer largely depends on the epistemological framework and how the camera is used in the field, including the conceptualisation of the technology by the researchers and participants.

For scholars who view ethnography as naturalistic research, the camera is often perceived as a disrupting element that alters the behaviour of subjects in the field, leading them to question data authenticity. The methodological correlate is the reluctance to use the camera, or to ensure that it is almost invisible to the social actors. Such approaches are usually accompanied by an understanding of the technology as a recording tool that does not interfere with the ethnographic field (Heider, 2006). From other positions closer to phenomenology, ethnographic film is the product of an encounter between the researcher and the subjects, and audiovisual data is the result of a co-production that occurs during fieldwork (McDougall, 2006). The ethnography is considered to be intersubjective and the camera is a social actor that gives access to the flow of shared experiences. In other words, the use of the camera during fieldwork does not only have expected consequences for the type of data constructed, but it is also a key element for the field experience itself. Thus, the ethnographer is not trying to prevent the camera from intruding, but rather she is prompted to accept its presence as part of the field relationships. Sarah Pink, for example, has stated that the camera was helpful and relevant in the construction of her identity during her fieldwork on the bullfighting culture in the south of Spain (Pink, 2007); and, as I have discussed elsewhere (Ardévol, 2006), the camera is a theoretical tool that interplays with the gaze of the researcher and her data to envisage new theoretical horizons.

Parallel to the claim that cameras may distort natural behaviour, Internet researchers are faced with the extended belief that online interactions are not 'real' or are less authentic than face-to-face encounters (Kendall, 2004). People may lie to the researcher and online behaviour and identity may not correspond to a 'real' identity and 'real' life behaviour. In both cases, the use of technology has been seen as interfering between the ethnographer and the subjects during participant observation, posing questions of authenticity and data validity. Moreover, the technology contributes to shaping the context of research and the mode of interaction and relationship of the participants. Hine discusses the question of authenticity in online social interaction as something that is negotiated and sustained by the social actors themselves. Thus the researcher does not always need to clear up the 'actual' identity of the online actors to give them credibility, but to analyse how they manage authenticity for their claims (Hine, 2000). Instead of considering the presence of technology in fieldwork as a 'distortion', many visual and virtual ethnographers consider it an 'opportunity' to rethink ethnographic methodological assumptions and to reformulate some of their knowledge practices. The solution is not to banish technology from our methods, but to incorporate it reflexively. Visual and virtual ethnographers have had to deal with reflexivity in relation to the technologies they use (Hine, 2000; Ruby, 1980); the quality of the data they manage; how it contributes to their theoretical perspectives (Loizos, 2000; Seale et al., 2010); and how technological mediation participates in defining the very context of research and limits of their field site (Burrell, 2009; Pink, 2007).

The notion of technological mediation allows us to decentralise methodological problems from a specific research practice linked to a particular technology, whether it is the camera or the Internet, and to situate in the same epistemic scenario diverse methodological practices and technologies. In doing so, the methodological questions faced by visual and virtual researchers enhance, reformulate and renew each other.

The incorporation of the Internet as part of the ethnographic field has a two-fold dimension: first, it is a strategy to participate in the same setting as the participants, to establish rapport and share interactions, and second, it is an opportunity to reflexively interrogate the technological artifacts that take part in the very social interactions and practices the ethnographer is involved in. For studying blogging practices, Estalella (2008) created his own blog and for studying self-produced videos, in my own work (Ardévol and San Cornelio, 2007) I had to open a YouTube account and upload my own videos, as did Michael Wesch in his proposal to introduce YouTube for teaching ethnography (www.youtube.com/user/mwesch). Others, like Taylor (2002) and Boellstorff (2008), created their avatars to fully participate in the virtual worlds they study. As Taylor puts it:

> Presence is one of the most elusive and evocative aspects of virtual systems – and yet it forms the very foundation on which immersion is built. It goes to the heart of what feels 'real' and creates the quality of experience that signals to us 'I am here' (Taylor, 2002: 42)

For Estalella, to open a blog was, on the one hand, a strategy of co-presence with his subjects of study, enabling them to interact with him through the same blogging practices he was studying; on the other hand, it gave him first-hand experience of the backstage and onstage contexts of the blogging practices he was interested in. However, it cannot substitute the 'field diary' to annotate observations and impressions; it is the point of reference of the researcher in the field. The 'fieldblog' guided the researcher's experience, provided him credibility and rapport, and allowed him to inform bloggers about his research, thus responding to elementary ethical concerns (Estalella and Ardévol, 2007: 52). There, the field was constructed through networking, since the blogosphere is not like a virtual world with delimited boundaries that can be accessed through a click. Blogging appears to be mainly a writing and reading practice, or at least, that is what we usually think when thinking about blogs. Yet it goes beyond this. In their daily practice, the bloggers brought into play many other devices apart from the blog, such as image and video services and repositories of favorite links. They also have formal and informal meetings where taking photos, chatting or conferencing about blogs are part of their activity. There are many blogging-related practices that do not take part in front of the screen and that the ethnographer recalls by interviews, field notes, photos and videos (Estalella, 2008). So, the result is a heterogeneous collection of visual and textual data, most of it produced in online interactions, some of it emanating from the bloggers' self-productions which circulate through different Internet platforms, and other data which is produced by the ethnographer.

.Internet data is easy to record, using screen capture programs or by saving naturally occurring conversation in instant messaging or webcam conferences. An online ethnographer can digitally record her or his visit to a website and replay it at will, stopping, starting and moving around the data as needed (Garcia et al., 2009: 64), creating 'movies' of his or her interaction with the website or recording online interviews with a webcam.

The camera registers sound and image, but as visual ethnographers are aware, our data is more than the audiovisual record. On the one hand, what happens in the field exceeds the recorded piece, and, on the other hand, what we have selected to film carries the theoretical charge of the researcher's interpretation. Therefore, we keep taking notes about information and impressions that images cannot capture. Internet data is easy to record and archive; we can capture records on screen that are the exact products of textual interaction and no transcription is needed. However, what is happening is more than what is on the screen, and the task of the virtual ethnographer is to provide context to the online interaction and the captured data. Sometimes, the process of analysing them is similar to what in visual ethnography has been called 'differed observation' (de France, 1989).

As in the case of visual ethnography, the virtual researcher's and participants' online interaction is registered technologically – textual interactions, comments or photos can be captured by specific tools, but generally they are kept in the blog archives, can be retrieved by the researcher and the participants, and sometimes are open and accessible to anyone. Thus, although they are textual and visual records, the nature of online interaction registers differ, posing considerable ethical problems that are difficult to solve. Ethical problems of Internet researchers relate to image rights (Gross et al., 1991, 2003), as well as considerations about anonymity and privacy regarding the traces that fieldwork may leave on the Internet archives (Bakardjieva and Feenberg, 2001).

Pushing the limits: expanding methods, enhancing theories

On the one hand, the Internet offers methodological challenges and opportunities to visual ethnographers, as an object of study and as a field of research. On the other, virtual methods require visual analysis. That said, to enhance the field of visual methods to include Internet practices means reformulating the dimensions of visual research and expanding fieldwork from face-to-face encounters to virtual social contexts. Moreover, Internet technologies offer the opportunity to incorporate new methodologies and tools for visual data-gathering and analysis, such as image-searching tools, graph programs or geo-mapping.

While visual ethnographers use photos and video in fieldwork, the Internet ethnographer, using chat, following links, capturing screens, writing a blog or reading what others have written, also engages various types of technology. In all these cases, we need to reflect on the experience of using these technologies. While in some cases visual technologies will mediate the researcher's fieldwork experience, in others, it will be Internet technologies, including data-handling and audiovisual production. In these situations, the incorporation of technology into fieldwork impels us to profoundly reconsider the consequences it will have on the production of knowledge and on our ethical concerns.

Visual and virtual methods add to the available array of ethnographic methodologies but also challenge our epistemic practices. As Sarah Pink (Chapter 7) notes in this volume, it's not only a question of method, but the theoretical framework that it brings to us. For her, engaging visual ethnography online poses theories of place and visuality (and sensoriality) in the foreground and demonstrates how this is useful for understanding her object of study: how Cittaslow towns constitute themselves as Cittaslow places, and the role of visual and digital media in these processes.

Virtual and visual ethnographers cope with the same problems as any pedestrian ethnographer: the tendency to privilege verbal or textual aspects of social interaction and to dismiss the material, visual, aural and kinetic components of human activity. In the case of visual methods, researchers must account for how camera mediation carries with it, among other things, the need to rethink what we see and the location of the senses and the corporeal in social theorisation, including aesthetic expression or even the recognition and cultivation of ethnographic sensibilities. In the case of Internet methods, ethnographers face the need to rethink locality, the materiality of social interaction and the role of the technology in the conception of nature and culture.

In both, technological mediation is key to knowledge production. In other words, ethnographic practices entail mediation technologies that transform experience into knowledge, and the nature of the knowledge we produce depends on how we transform technology into meaningful experience. If mediation is the recognition of a relationship of distance, the question then is not only the recognition of agency in our 'mediators', but also the need to understand mediation and immediacy in the everyday life of the people we study.

Acknowledgements

I want to express my gratitude to Sarah Pink, Luis Pérez-Tolón and to Francisco Osorio for their suggestions and comments in the revision of this text. This chapter also acknowledges the work of the *mediaccions* research group at the Universitat Oberta de Catalunya in the framework of the research project *Creative practices and participation in new media* (HAR2010-18982) funded by the Spanish Ministry of Science and Innovation.

Note

1 This chapter discusses some of the ideas developed in Ardévol and Estalella (2009) and Estalella and Ardévol (2010).

Bibliography

Adler, P. and Adler, P. (2007) 'The demedicalization of self-injury: from psychopathology to sociological deviance', *Journal of Contemporary Ethnography*, 36 (5): 537–70.

Amit, V. (2000) *Constructing the Field: Ethnographic Fieldwork in the Contemporary World*. London: Routledge.

Ardévol, E. (2006) *La búsqueda de una mirada: antropología visual y cine etnográfico*. Barcelona: UOC ed.

Ardévol, E. and Estalella, A. (2009) 'From virtual ethnography to visual ethnography', paper presented at the Internet Research and Visual Methods

Panel in the 1st International Visual Methods Conference, University of Leeds, September.

Ardévol, E. and San Cornelio, G. (2007) 'Si quieres vernos en acción: YouTube.com Prácticas mediáticas y autoproducción en Internet', *Revista Chilena de Antropología Visual*, 10: 1–29.

Augé, M. (1992) *Non-lieux: introduction á une anthropologie de la surmodenité*. Paris: Edition de Seuil.

Bakardjieva, M. and Feenberg, A. (2001) 'Involving the virtual subject: conceptual, methodological and ethical dimensions', *Journal of Ethics and Information Technology*, 2 (4): 233–40.

Banks, M. (2001) *Visual Methods in Social Research*. London: Sage.

Baym, N.K. (1998) 'The emergence of on-line community', in S.G. Jones (ed.), *Cybersociety 2.0. Revisiting Computer Mediated Communications and Community*. Thousand Oaks, CA: Sage. pp. 35–68.

Beaulieu, A. (2005) 'Sociable hyperlinks: an ethnographic approach to connectivity', in C. Berg (ed.), *Virtual Methods: Issues in Social Research on the Internet*. Oxford: Berg. pp. 183–97.

Biella, P. (1996) 'Interactive media in anthropology: seed and earth – promise of rain', *American Anthropologist*, 98: 595–616.

Bird, E. (2010) 'From fan practice to mediated moments: the value of practice theory in the understanding of media audiences', in B. Bräuchler and J. Postill (eds), *Theorising Media and Practice*. New York/Oxford: Berghahn Books. pp. 85–104.

Boellstorff, T. (2008) *Coming of Age in Second Life: An Anthropologist Explores the Virtually Human*. Princeton, NJ: Princeton University Press.

boyd, d. and Heer, J. (2006) 'Profiles as conversation: networked identity performance on Friendster', proceedings of the Hawai'i International Conference on System Sciences (HICSS-39), Persistent Conversation Track. Kauai, HI: IEEE Computer Society. January. pp. 4–7.

Burrell, J. (2009) 'The field site as a network: a strategy for locating ethnographic research', *Field Methods*, 21: 181–99.

Burrell, J. and Anderson, K. (2008) '"I have great desires to look beyond my world": trajectories of information and communication technology use among Ghanaians living abroad', *New Media & Society*, 10 (2): 203–24.

Cheung, C. (2000) 'A home on the web: the presentation of self on personal homepages', in D. Gauntlett (ed.), *Web.studies: Rewiring Media Studies for the Digital Age*. London: Arnold. pp. 43–51.

Couldry, N. (2004) 'Theorising media as practice', *Social Semiotics*, 14 (2): 115–32.

de France, C. (1989) *Cinéma et anthropologie*. Paris: Foundation de la Maison des Sciences.

Dirksen, V., Huizing, A. and Smit, B. (2010) '"Piling on layers of understanding": the use of connective ethnography for the study of (online) work practices', *New Media & Society*, 12 (7): 1045–63.

Estalella, A. (2008) 'Blogging as fieldwork: more than producing knowledge, performing reality in ethnography', paper presented at the 'In the Game' preconference, 9ª conference, AoIR, Copenhagen.

Estalella, A. and Ardévol, E. (2007) 'Ética de campo: hacia una ética situada para la investigación etnográfica de Internet', *Forum Qualitative Social Research*, 8 (3). Available at: www.qualitative-research.net/index.php/fqs/article/view/277/609 (retrieved: 12/10/2011).

Estalella, A. and Ardévol, E. (2010) 'Internet: instrumento de investigación y campo de estudio para la antropología visual', *Revista Chilena de Antropología Visual*, 15: 1–21.

Fischer, M.D. (2006) 'Introduction: configuring anthropology', *Social Science Computer Review*, 24 (3): 3–14.

Foot, K.A., Schneider, S.M., Dougherty, M., Xenos, M. and Larsen, E. (2003) 'Analyzing linking practices: candidate sites in the 2002 US electoral web sphere', *Journal of Computer-Mediated Communication*, 8 (4). Available at http://jcmc.indiana.edu/vol8/issue4/foot.html (retrieved: 24/11/2011).

Garcia, A.C., Standlee, A.I., Bechkoff, J. and Cui, Y. (2009) 'Ethnographic approaches to the Internet and computer-mediated communication', *Journal of Contemporary Ethnography*, 38 (1): 52–84.

Ginsburg, F., Abu-lughod, L. and Larkin, B. (2003) *Media Worlds: Anthropology in New Terrain*. Berkeley, CA: University of California Press.

Gómez-Cruz, E. (2009) 'The fractures of photography: following the relationship between technology practices, sociality and identity formation in digital culture', paper presented at the Digital Culture and Communication Workshop, ECREA, Berlin.

Gross, L.P., Katz, J.S. and Ruby, J. (1991) *Image Ethics: The Moral Rights of Subjects in Photographs, Film, and Television*. New York: Oxford University Press.

Gross, L.P., Katz, J.S. and Ruby, J. (2003) *Image Ethics in the Digital Age*. Minneapolis, MN: University of Minnesota Press.

Gupta, A. and Ferguson, J. (1997) *Culture, Power, Place: Explorations in Critical Anthropology*. Durham, NC: Duke University Press.

Heider, K.G. (2006) *Ethnographic Film*. Austin, TX: University of Texas Press.

Hewson, C., Yule, P., Laurent, D. and Vogel, C. (2003) *Internet Research Methods*. London: Sage.

Hine, C. (2000) *Virtual Ethnography*. London: Sage.

Hine, C. (ed.) (2005) *Virtual Methods: Issues in Social Research on the Internet*. Oxford: Berg.

Hjorth, L. (2006) 'Snapshots of almost contact: gendered camera phone practices and a case study in Seoul, Korea', *Cultural Space and Public Sphere in Asia*, 15–16 March.

Howard, P. (2002) 'Network ethnography and the hypermedia organization: new organizations, new media, new methods', *New Media and Society*, 4: 551–75.

Illingworth, N. (2001) 'The Internet matters: exploring the use of the Internet as a research tool', *Sociological Research Online*, 6 (2) (retrieved from: www.socresonline.org.uk/6/2/illingworth.html).

Jenkins, H. (2004) 'The cultural logic of media convergence', *International Journal of Cultural Studies*, 7 (1): 33–43.

Kendall, L. (2004) 'Participants and observers in online ethnography: five stories about identity', in M.D. Johns, S.-L.S. Chen and G.J. Hall (eds), *Online Social Research: Methods, Issues, & Ethics*. New York: Peter Lang. pp. 125–40.

Kimmel, M. (2007) 'Racism as adolescent male rite of passage: ex-Nazis in Scandinavia', *Journal of Contemporary Ethnography*, 36 (2): 202–18.

Larsen, J. (2008) 'Practices and flows of digital photography: an ethnographic framework', *Mobilities*, 3 (1): 141–60.

Leander, K. and McKim, K. (2003) 'Tracing the everyday "sitings" of adolescents on the Internet: a strategic adaptation of ethnography across online and offline spaces', *Education, Communication & Information*, 3 (2): 211–40.

Lee, D. (2005) 'Women's creation of camera phone culture', *Fibreculture Journal*, 6 (retrieved from: http://six.fibreculturejournal.org/fcj-038-womens-creation-of-camera-phone-culture/).

Loizos, P. (2000) 'Video, film and photographs as research documents', in M.W. Bauer and G. Gaskell (eds), *Qualitative Researching with Text, Image and Sound*. London: Sage. pp. 93–107.

Lyon, M. and Magliveras, S.S. (2006) 'Kinship, computing, and anthropology', *Social Science Computer Review*, 2006: 24–30.

Lyon, S.M. and Simeon, M.S. (2006) 'Kinship, computing, and anthropology', *Social Science Computer Review*, 24 (1): 30–42.

Mann, C. and Stewart, F. (2000) *Internet Communication and Qualitative Research: A Handbook for Researching Online*. London: Routledge.

Marcus, G.E. (1995) 'Ethnography in/of the world system: the emergence of multi-sited ethnography', *Annual Review of Anthropology*, 24: 95–117.

Markham, A.N. (1998) *Life Online: Researching Real Experience in Virtual Space*. London: Altamira Press.

Markham, A.N. (2004) 'Internet communication as a tool for qualitative research', in D. Silverman (ed.), *Qualitative Research: Theory, Methods, and Practice*. London: Sage. pp. 95–124.

Marshall, D.P. (2004) *New Media Cultures*. London: Arnold.

McDougall, D. (2006) *The Corporeal Image: Film, Ethnography, and the Senses*. Princeton, NJ: Princeton University Press.

Mead, M. and Metraux, R. (2000) *The Study of Culture at a Distance*. Oxford/New York: Berghahn Books.

Miller, D. and Slater, D. (2000) *The Internet: An Ethnographic Approach*. Oxford: Berg.

Nakamura, L. (2008) *Digitizing Race: Visual Cultures of the Internet*. Minneapolis, MN: University of Minneapolis Press.

Okada, T. (2005) 'Youth culture and the shaping of Japanese mobile media: personalization and the Keitai Internet as multimedia', in M. Ito, D. Okabe and M. Matsuda (eds), *Personal, Portable, Pedestrian: Mobile Phones in Japanese Life*. Cambridge, MA: MIT Press. pp. 41–60.

Oksman, V. (2006) 'Mobile visuality and everyday life in Finland: an ethnographic approach to social uses of mobile images', in J. Höfflich and M. Hartmann (eds), *Mobile Communication in Everyday Life: Ethnographic Views, Observations and Reflections*. Berlin: Frank and Timm. pp. 103–19.

Orend, A. and Gagné, P. (2009) 'Corporate logo tattoos and the commodification of the body', *Journal of Contemporary Ethnography*, 38 (4): 493–517.

Orgad, S. (2005) 'From online to offline and back: moving from online to offline relationships with research informants', in C. Hine (ed.), *Virtual Methods: Issues in Social Research on the Internet*. Oxford: Berg. pp. 51–65.

O'Riordan, K. (2007) 'Queer theories and cybersubjetcs: intersecting figures', in K. O'Riordan and D.J. Phillips *Queer Online: Media Technology and Sexuality* (Vol. 40). London: Peter Lang. pp. 13–30.

O'Riordan, K. and Phillips, D.J. (2007) *Queer Online: Media Technology and Sexuality* (Vol. 40). London: Peter Lang.

Paccagnella, L. (1997) 'Getting the seats of your pants dirty: strategies for ethnographic research on virtual communities', *Journal of Computer Mediated Communication*, 3 (1) (retrieved from: http://jcmc.indiana.edu/vol3/issue1/paccagnella.html).

Parmeggiani, P. (2009) 'Going digital: using new technologies in visual sociology', *Visual Studies*, 24 (1): 71–6.

Pauwels, L. (2008) 'A private visual practice going public? Social functions and sociological research opportunities of web-based family photography', *Visual Studies*, 32 (1): 34–49.

Pichardo, J.I. (2008) 'Etnografía y nuevas tecnologías: reflexiones desde el terreno', in E. Ardévol, A. Estalella and D. Domínguez (eds), *La mediación tecnológica en la práctica etnográfica. Actas del XI congreso de antropología de la FAAEE*. pp. 133–50.

Piela, A. (2010) 'Challenging stereotypes: Muslim women's photographic self-representations on the Internet', *Online – Heidelberg Journal of Religions on the Internet*, 41 (retrieved from: www.online.uni-hd.de/).

Pink, S. (2000) '"Informants" who come "home"', in V. Amit (ed.), *Constructing the Field: Ethnographic Fieldwork in the Contemporary World*. London: Routledge. pp. 96–119.

Pink, S. (2004) 'Making links: on situating a new web site', *Cambridge Journal of Education*, 34: 211–22.

Pink, S. (2007) *Doing Visual Ethnography: Images, Media and Representation in Research* (2nd edn). London: Sage.

Podolefsky, A. (1987) 'New tools for old jobs: computers in the analysis of field notes', *Anthropology Today*, 3 (5): 14–16.

Reid, E.M. (1994) 'Virtual worlds: culture and imagination', in E.G. Jones (ed.), *CyberSociety: Computer-Mediated Communication and Community*. Thousand Oaks, CA: Sage. pp. 164–83.

Rogers, R. (2009) *The End of the Virtual: Digital Methods*. Amsterdam: Amsterdam University Press.

Rothenbuhler, E.W. and Coman, M. (eds) (2005) *Media Anthropology*. Thousand Oaks, CA: Sage.

Ruby, J. (1980) 'Exposing yourself: reflexivity, anthropology, and film', *Semiotica*, 30 (1/2): 153–79.

Scifo, B. (2005) 'The domestication of camera-phone and MMS communication: the early experiences of young Italians', in K. Nyíri (ed.), *A Sense of Place: The Global and the Local in Mobile Communication*. Vienna: Passagen Verlag. pp. 363–74.

Seale, C., Charteris-Black, J., MacFarlane, A. and McPherson, A. (2010) 'Interviews and Internet forums: a comparison of two sources of qualitative data', *Qualitative Health Research*, 20 (5): 595–606.

Slater, D. (1995) 'Domestic photography and digital culture', in M. Lister (ed.), *The Photographic Image in Digital Culture*. London: Routledge. pp. 129–46.

Spitulnik, D. (1993) 'Anthropology and mass media', *Annual Review of Anthropology*, 22: 293–315.

Taylor T.L. (2002) 'Living digitally: embodiment in virtual worlds', in R. Schroeder (ed.), *The Social Life of Avatars: Presence and Interaction in Shared Virtual Environments*. London: Springer-Verlag. pp. 40–62.

Tinkler, P. (2008) 'A fragmented picture: reflections on the photographic practices of young people', *Visual Studies*, 23 (3): 255–66.

van Dijck, J. (2007) 'Television 2.0: YouTube and the emergence of homecasting', paper presented to the Creativity, Ownership and Collaboration in the Digital Age. Cambridge: Massachusetts Institute of Technology. Available at http://web.mit.edu/commforum/mit5/papers/vanDijck_Television2.0.article (retrieved: 21/03/2010).

Woo, H. (2003) 'Hyperlink network analysis: a new method for the study of social structure on the web', *Connections*, 25 (1): 49–61.

Worth, S. (1995) 'Hacia una semiótica del cine etnográfico', in E. Ardévol and L. Pérez-Tolón (eds), *Imagen y Cultura: perspectivas del cine etnográfico*. Granada: Biblioteca de Etnología, Nº 3. Ediciones de la Diputación Provincial de Granada. pp. 203–20.

PART 3
NEW VISUAL SPATIALITIES

The 'spatial turn' in the social sciences and humanities has created new questions and new opportunities for thinking about how we might conceptualise the wider ecologies in which we practise visual research, and how we might understand the configurations of place that other people experience. The three chapters in this Part explore the development of visual methodologies in the context of questions about how people perceive, create and map their material localities and web platforms, and how they live the worlds that bridge these online/offline contexts. This Part also continues themes relating to visual practices, the politics of looking, and the senses initiated in Part 2. Indeed, place might be understood as both a way of situating practices within a wider ecology of things and processes, and/or also as a product of practice. The three chapters in Part 3 explore how spatialities are being reconceptualised in ways that advance visual methodology, through three themes.

First, visual mapping is a historically embedded visual practice. It is a means of defining or objectifying place that has been associated critically with the flattening or slicing through of a world that is lived and in progress. Yet, alternative forms of mapping are becoming increasingly important in the ways that people constitute lived places. In Chapter 6, Cristina Grasseni focuses on how engaging community mapping as a research method can enable the collective production of place. In this project, mapping, and annotating maps, made the map as an object much more than a flat surface, but rather a tool through which to locate memories, historical processes and more. Thus community mapping can be seen as a type of mapping that contests the visual objectification of conventional mapping to introduce multiple practices of looking and visioning and this, like the visual practices discussed by Martens in Chapter 3, involves a politics of looking. In Chapter 8, Francesco Lapenta also discusses new digital mapping practices in relation to changing geo-locational technologies, which also offer opportunities for volunteered information tagged in online maps which may be available publicly or private. As we see, both old and new media afford opportunities for forms of mapping that are collective, participatory and processual which can bring new visual and experiential perspectives to ethnographic and other types of qualitative research.

Grasseni's chapter discusses a context where the web has a limited presence in both the participants' lives and in the research process. In contrast, the chapters by Pink (Chapter 7) and Lapenta (Chapter 8) engage with social and technological contexts where the web is an ever-present dimension and indeed part of the visual practices that they discuss. Pink is concerned with how we might conceptualise the online/offline ecologies that make up the sites of visual Internet ethnography. Following some of the broader insights and points made by Ardévol in Chapter 5, she focuses in on the question of how spatial theory and notions of visuality have been applied in Internet ethnography. She proposes that the contemporary technological context and recent theories of place demand a rethinking of how we might understand visual images and processes – as part of an ecology of place that encompasses online and offline contexts, and as dispersed, rather than bounded within one locality. In Chapter 8, Lapenta approaches time and space through a discussion of recent literatures, and technological developments concerning the new location-based technologies that he calls 'geomedia'. In terms of (visual) ethnographic research practice, these new technologies and the 'hidden' algorithmic and visualisation processes that compose them create both contexts of and opportunities for what Lapenta describes as 'new forms of representation and visualisation of communications and social interaction'.

Together these three chapters therefore advance the ways we think about space, place, the image and the map in visual research by emphasising how participant-generated knowledge, new mapping and visualisation techniques, and engagements with media are developing in tandem with alternative ways of theorising space and place. The outcome is to invite visual researchers to take revised approaches to the ways they engage theoretically and practically with people, places and maps.

6

COMMUNITY MAPPING AS AUTO-ETHNO-CARTOGRAPHY

Cristina Grasseni

Many disciplines call for a wider appreciation of multi-sensory perception across cultures. For instance, the issues of place-identity and of belonging are increasingly associated with practice-based representations of locality. Nevertheless, a number of methodological issues arise when trying to render a visual representation of a 'sense of place'. This chapter proposes how this might be achieved through community mapping – a research-based methodology that is well rooted in the history of visual anthropology but also spans geographical and digital-media practice.

My critical reflections follow a recently concluded community-mapping project in an Italian alpine valley (2007–2008). The project was part of a funded 'Observatory of landscape transformations' within the Ecomuseum of Val Taleggio (http://ecomuseovaltaleggio.it/). The chapter sketches out the methods used and the critical issues encountered: from citizen participation; to the role of visual inscription vis-à-vis textual narration; and the role of the anthropologist as a mediator of the many layers and phases of representation involved.

Community maps are introduced and discussed, as a creative and heterogeneous means to gather and analyse a diverse range of 'skilled visions' (Grasseni, 2007) with a potential for generating practical effects towards sustainable development and community awareness. In particular, I discuss how ethnography and participatory cartography can and must go hand in hand to produce a meaningful exercise of collective self-representation. In the discussion of the specific methods employed in this case study, I shall draw on my further commitment to cultural mapping as an ethnographic way to explore landscapes of skill and memory (or sense-scapes, see Grasseni, 2009a). The idea of a sense-scape is tied to the fact that what we *see* in a place is at once a tacit moral order, made of aesthetic and moral assumptions, as well as a 'taskscape' (Ingold, 1993), which is the result of an 'education of attention', namely cognitive and bodily strategies directing our attention in the environment in a disciplined way. Focussing on the actual practices that construct a locality, I used the notion of 'skilled landscapes' (Grasseni, 2004) to express culturally and historically situated modes of inhabiting the land, of interpreting and moving in the landscape. 'Sense-scapes' aim at acknowledging the result of collective practices of signification. I deliberately play on the double meaning of 'sense' (evoking the senses but also a 'sense' of place) to stress that sense of place is not just a phenomenological experience, but it is also imbued with symbolic meaning, through memory and through the actual practices of locality that allow us to share a space socially, as a *place* (Grasseni, 2009a). Such sense-scapes require new reflections on the power of ethnographic representation. In particular, which type of visual inscriptions are apt at rendering tacit knowledge and sense of place? My proposal here is to evaluate community maps as a form of 'auto-ethno-cartography', namely as a visual-research method with the ambition to provide thick *inscriptions* of place-based knowledge. The pun contrasting with Geertz's well-known method of thick *description* is deliberate: in a thick inscription, textual and visual information should be made available through a form of collective representation that would otherwise be delegated to individual representations or to oral narratives.

Community maps and ecomuseums: a common ground?

Place perception and collectively held 'senses of place' are inextricably linked to life histories and social scenarios. In contemporary anthropology and in social theory, new and more flexible modes of representation are required by the increasingly changing and complex social identities that are pinned onto the social uses of space. The relationship between territory, cultural tradition and collective identities is neither unambiguous nor devoid of political and economic meaning (Bravo, 2006). This is why new methods for representing place span scholarly and applied concerns. Anthropologists and social scientists increasingly take part in projects and social experiments that express and develop collective meanings, critical points and patrimony.

Furthermore, different 'professional visions' (Goodwin, 1994) embody different 'taskscapes' (Ingold, 1993) on place experience. A plurality of visions and competences are exercised in the same place, and thus render local self-representation at once familiar and potentially conflicting, specifically in the case of local attempts to represent one's own territory (Grasseni, 2003a: 223). I would like to focus on community mapping as precisely one such practice of ethnographic self-representation, namely as a form of 'auto-ethno-cartography'.

In ethnography, knowing is intimately connected with doing and with being there – even more so is 'auto-ethnography' (Reed-Danahay, 1997). Community mapping requires the inhabitants' involvement in the representation of a certain place, in their capacity as residents and holders of specific forms of local knowledge that derive from being acquainted with the territory. As such, it aims at being a form of 'counter-mapping' (St. Martin, 2009) from the bottom up. Its main philosophy was developed by Sue Clifford and the association Common Ground in the late 1980s as one of fostering the conservation of 'the Commonplace, the Local, the Vernacular and the Distinctive' in particular landscapes (see Clifford and King, 2006).

I first became personally involved in a community-mapping project in Val Taleggio (800 inhabitants, spread over two municipalities) which I knew well from previous fieldwork (see Grasseni, 2009b), then in a more ambitious and still work-in-progress project of a participatory cultural map of Val San Martino (ca. 33,000 inhabitants over nine municipalities).

Community maps are used in development projects to enhance communication and participation, aiming for a higher cohesion and social consensus. It is often understood that these tools are used to support sustainable projects and that they should bring to the surface existent situated knowledge leading to ongoing consultation and democratic decision making about the patrimonialization of heritage, new regional economic vocations and social innovation (Fahy and Ó Cinnéide, 2009; Healey, 2001; Newman and McLean, 1998).

Community mapping should not be primarily about achieving a *representation* of a landscape, a community or a territory. It should rather be a *process* during which material culture, intangible cultural heritage, seasonality and sociability come to the fore according to their proper local expressions, rooted in convention, routines, social environments and rituals. Participatory policy-making and sustainable governance should be the medium-term effects.

This has particular sense within the context of social and institutional innovation represented in ecomuseums, at least according to the intentions of their founders. Hugues de Varine in particular underlines the interactive and innovative approach of a notion – the community museum or *musée de societé* – a concept of the French *nouvelle museologie*[1] based on the idea of popular participation in the conservation and reproduction of immaterial heritage (de Varine, 2005). President of the International Council of Museums between 1962 and 1974 and founder of the first French ecomuseum, *Le Creusot* in Bourgogne in 1972, de Varine states that:

> the ecomuseum is an institution that manages, studies, uses the heritage (*patrimoine*) of a community for scientific, educational and cultural purposes – including the natural and cultural environment of that society. The ecomuseum is thus a tool for community development and for the people's participation in the

management of their territory. In order to do so, it should use all the tools and methods available to enable the community to grasp, analyse, critique and govern the issues it faces in concrete everyday life, freely and responsibly. It is above all a deliberate factor of change. (de Varine, 2005: 273; my translation)

These sketchy premises simply aim at showing how two very different notions and tools have belatedly met in the theory and practice of ecomuseology in Italy, coming together via convergent but distinct cultural routes. The community map was an invention of the 1980s English-speaking urban studies, critiquing the hyper-specialisation of cartography and architecture as a symptom of a crisis of representation, and opposing them to the lived experience of the landscape conveyed in qualitative, artistic and creative modes of representation (Clifford and King, 1993). Community maps sometimes are not even 'maps' in the strict sense of the term: they may be paintings, mosaics, films, knit-work or other types of local artwork striving to represent a collective perception of a locale's distinguishing features (positive or negative). The ecomuseum was a dynamic concept born out of the 1960s French revolutionary rethinking of museums as western cultural institutions and their social role, suggesting the local community to be an inescapable interlocutor in the recasting of cultural and natural environment as 'heritage', and further, as a collective patrimony (Davis, 1999; de Varine, 1988). From the late 1990s onwards, community mapping has become a popular tool in nascent ecomuseums, especially in Italy, to chart a locale's intangible cultural heritage and to find social cohesion and fresh agendas in the exercise of representation (Clifford et al., 2006).

Mapping and re-mapping Val Taleggio

The community map of Val Taleggio was promoted by the two municipalities of the valley which invested in the project of establishing the Ecomuseum Val Taleggio. Their request was to provide professional help in producing a captivating representation of the immaterial landscape of the valley. This initial request oriented the choice of type of artefact that we would produce. It was clear in this case that the community map would be part of a larger observatory of the landscape of Val Taleggio, hence it was ideal to cross-reference qualitative and subjective data (oral history, subjective perceptions, historical visual documentation) with other data already inscribed in cartography (aerial views, satellite photographs, soil use and land register).

Furthermore, over time, Val Taleggio had displayed a collective vocation for self-representation, for instance, through local historical research, in a number of local publications by resident historians and naturalists, as well as through the valley parish newsletters and photographic exhibitions, often including local artists or archive materials such as period postcards. This spontaneous and voluntary vocation to collective self-presentation was nevertheless fragmented and ephemeral – not even the local library kept track of the photographic exhibitions and of the plethora of local publications on the art, history and natural history of the valley.

The administrators' will was clearly also one of seeking a higher profile for publicity reasons, their interpretation of the ecomuseum being largely that of an open-air museum or theme park, hopefully attracting cultural tourism and encouraging the sustainable development of local entrepreneurship based on local arts and crafts and especially the production and sale of local mountain cheese. They intended the community map to be a sort of address card, a collective self-representation offered to potential tourists. My own agenda was to use the community-map project to bring to light the bulk of materials and attempts at self-representation that different groups and individuals had already showed over time, with great vitality. Above all though, we agreed on the idea that something more than the natural and architectural landscape had to be represented and valued in Val Taleggio. An intangible landscape of memory, practices and values wove together a multifaceted but coherent form of life, embedded in the lived environment. The community map aimed at somehow casting all this into a visual inscription that should be representative of local forms of life. Without aiming at exhaustiveness, the idea was to provide a start-up archive that could be accessible in terms of technical requirement and open to integrations over time.

Considering the wish to cross-reference the cultural map with other types of maps, I proposed a standard form of cartographic representation, namely a geographical map, CTR (*carta tecnica regionale*) upon which one could literally inscribe annotations about cultural life and values that would be cross-referenced to archive materials (bibliographies, texts, photographs, and where possible, video). Group-work annotations were carried out in a very low-tech way to facilitate access to all ages (Val Taleggio being inhabited by a high rate of retired and over-60s residents) and to encourage face-to-face interaction. The actual act of inscription was literally left to putting pencil to paper, as I describe in detail below and in the figures. Later, the job of cultural inscription was transposed onto an aerial view and this was layered with other information such as place names and paths, but also made available in the digital archive of the project so that the other maps of the landscape observatory would be annotated on the same cartographic basis. This way, within ample margins of error considering the manual annotation of the cultural map, this nevertheless shared the same cartographic basis as all the other two-dimensional representations of the same territory: CTR, land register, soil use, geology, satellite view, etc.

During previous fieldwork, I had taken part in a local voluntary mapping group. This was a precious starting point for the community-map project, allowing me to build on experience and relationships that had proven existent and vital in the valley. Also, knowing that providing a map of Val Taleggio was an authentic *bottom up* collective agenda even before the ecomuseum was set up was important to me. It justified the rationale of the project which did not appear as a development strategy designed and imposed from above.

I have described elsewhere my participation in a voluntary group that redrew the map of the hiking paths of the valley in 1999 (Grasseni, 2004). The objective of the 1999 work group was to make a larger set of information available about local paths and the history of the territory. The work group published a map drawn by local cartographer Stefano Torriani on the basis of the standard geo-referenced map CTR (henceforth, I shall refer to this as the Torriani map). Also, an accompanying booklet edited by the local mayor and group coordinator described the itineraries and gave a summary of local knowledge about the history, function and naturalistic significance of the places reached by the paths (Arrigoni, 1999). I have argued that the individual life histories and apprenticeship into different communities of practice gave to the participants of the Torriani map work group significantly different outlooks on their shared landscape. The Torriani map was thus already an attempt at inscribing different 'skilled landscapes' in standard cartography (Grasseni, 2004).

The Torriani map focussed on place names in the local Bergamasque dialect, the Venice/Milan 15th-century boundary stones dotting the valley (locally known as *termenù*)[2] and the many springs and torrents to which Val Taleggio owes its local celebrity as a valley rich in water. Later, the community-mapping project documented live knowledge of trout-fishing; memory of shrimp-picking and frog-hunting; and current leisure activities involving the valley's rivers and cascades such as diving, fishing and hiking to the river Enna's spring. Memories of the places used for fishing had been conserved, even after a number of floods has recently changed the course of the river and ruined some of the previous generations' favourite ponds.

It was essential, for the sake of the community-mapping project, to acknowledge this previous collective work and to make judicious use of it (with the authors' permission) to create a further participatory representation of the valley's landscape. A free training course for volunteers wishing to become the valley's ecomuseum operators seemed to be the most logical place to start from. About 20 participants, almost all born in and residents in the valley, or in any case working or married in the valley, aged between 20 and 70 and with an education ranging from university degrees to secondary schools, attended the course. The first phase of data collection consisted of a two-step collective annotation of the Torriani map, which was made available to the group as a ground layer, in a black-and-white photocopy in the original scale of 1:20,000. Two simple questions were posed to the two 10-person groups in which the course had been split: which are the most important places in the valley and why? Two research assistants moderated the group work and channelled it towards constructive annotations, especially the construction of a legend for each group, whilst I filmed and audio-recorded the entire session.[3]

The details of the two annotated maps that were thus produced demonstrate the density of the inscription, the diversity of the types of knowledge involved and its vitality: devotional chapels, festive processions associated with particular sanctuaries and natural resources both present and past (quarries, woods used to make charcoal, pastures with watering places, etc.). This exercise in auto-ethno-cartography identified floorless buildings straddling streams in the woods, which were used to store and mature cheese in ideal temperature and humidity conditions, as well as to keep fresh fish in running water; the exercise also identified more commonly significant buildings such as churches, mills, electric dams, private residences, etc. The historical memory of the valley included *lieux de memoire* associated with violent episodes during the civil war in the Second World War (caves where bodies of dead partisans were found, a partisan mountain refuge that was attacked and burnt with much bloodshed in the winter of 1944, and a private house where gunshots were aimed at the inhabitants to force them to reveal troop movements in the area; see Figures 6.1 and 6.2).

Figures 6.1 and 6.2   Annotating the Torriani map

This was just a starting point, requiring a lot of subsequent work to decipher, classify and transcribe these first traces, with the help both of research assistants and of additional informants in the valley. Ethnography met cartography with in-depth interviews and on-site visits, which were carried out to better ground some of the information that had just been sketched on the map or mentioned in the working groups. At the same time, the qualitatively annotated maps had to be *translated* into geographical information that could be transferred onto standard cartography. This was done by carrying out follow-up interviews with the workshop participants, asking them to decipher everything that had been annotated on each of the two group maps. The transcripts of the interviews were used to list and classify each place, festivity, saying or historical fact mentioned and annotated. These were then systematised into one legend which included:

1   places of cultural, historical or architectural interest;
2   places associated with festivities and community events;
3   sites of economic and functional interest, particularly:

   (i) mills and
   (ii) streams, springs, pastures' watering places and anything associated with the 'valley of the water';

4   natural and environmental resources;
5   significant paths, and nodes in significant paths;
6   the valley's boundaries as perceived and annotated by the inhabitants;
7   *lieux de mémoire* and legends, proverbs and beliefs associated with particular sites;
8   ecomuseum sites and;
9   sites of interest according to the children of the valley.

In total, 53 significant sites were singled out and each was represented in a simple descriptive *fiche*, including text – mostly written by local residents – photographs and bibliographic references. The references were aimed at acknowledging the vast amount of materials and publications already existing in the forms of private photographic archives, newsletters, local publications, etc. All the photographs used in the community-map projects were either produced in situ by ecomuseum operators or came from local private archives and in very few cases from referenced published materials. These fiches would be difficult to visualise here as the images they contain were reduced to thumbnail size, whilst the text would be unreadable as well as the icons and sidebar. They can be downloaded from appropriate hyperlinks (www.osservatoriovaltaleggio.it) or reached from the community-map link (www.ecomuseovaltaleggio.it).

That it was possible to create a *fiche* entirely dedicated, for instance, to the sports ground of the village of Vedeseta – its history, photographs of the first football teams and references to local publications about it – witnesses the vast amount of detailed information gathered and made available by public and private sources. The choice was to make a *compendium* of local knowledge about each place available through such a simple collage of text, visuals and archive information in a word document. A blank format is downloadable from the project web site and anyone can propose additional *fiches*. Each *fiche* is linked to icons placed on an aerial view of the valley, composed with Arcview software. The different place-values listed above are summarised in a legend and each *fiche* usually bears more than one associated place-value. Each icon on the online map represents a place-value and most of them are active links to one of the 53 *fiches*. As in a hypertext, some *fiches* are interlinked with each other. The density of icons on the map represents the enormous amount of diffused knowledge about the territory.

A prototype of the aerial view layout, with icons relative to just one central fragment of the valley, was publicly presented and discussed in October 2007 at the valley's *Festa del Ritorno*, which celebrates the end of the *alpage* season with the return of cattle herds from the high pastures and a cattle fair. A complete version was presented and discussed in a focus group with the children and parents of the local primary school in December 2007. On that occasion the 18 schoolchildren of the valley produced drawings and selected places relevant to their own perception and activities, during a theme week that was coordinated with the school teacher and which resulted in the last of the place-values in the map legend: 'the valley of the children' (see Figure 6.3).

What should be clear at this stage is that this particular project was an example of a visual research method, not only and not predominantly because of the techniques of visual production employed (which were, overall, quite basic and certainly not cutting-edge in technological terms), but rather because of its ambition to provide a visually oriented archive of place-based knowledge that would make available a vast amount of textual and visual information otherwise circulated as single publications or in narrative form. In fact, it would have been possible already in 2007 to opt for a geo-blog type of interface (such as Google Maps) and for more advanced techniques of self-tracking through mobile geo-positioning systems. Francesco Lapenta (Chapter 8 in this volume) elaborates on the epistemological consequences of such choices. For Val Taleggio, this was a choice largely dictated by the will to make information available via the web, but to a community that mostly used the PC for word processing and emailing, with a majority of retired and older age operators in the group. It was not the case of preferring traditional means of inscription to more 'reprehensible' means of automatic recordings – a distinction which Lydia Martens (Chapter 3 in this volume) deconstructs.

Figure 6.3   Discussing and correcting the prototype on paper with school children and their parents

Furthermore, the objective wasn't cartographic accuracy (providing longitude and latitude of the last existing traces of a *casello* for instance), but rather to provide a coherent overview of existing sources and live knowledge about the existence and function of *caselli* in the valley's landscape and economy.[4] Therefore, a large part of the visual-research practice involved in the ethnographic process was largely kept invisible for the wider aim of using a simple cartographic tool and an even simpler document set-up, in order to visualise the still vast and vital practical and historical knowledge of the landscape of Val Taleggio. Thus filming was largely done for revisitation purposes (as Claudine de France suggests, classically: de France, 1979), while archive photographs were sought and quoted but also used in interview elicitation. We strove to gather our own view of the landscape as it is today, thus providing at least two photographs (in the past and in the present) for each locality. Doing visual ethnography was in this case more a matter of *visualising* an all-round sensory practice than one of *documenting a visual practice* (see Pink, 2007, 2009). There could not fail to be several critical points in one such project, dealing at once with the representation of individuals and of collective memory, the association of specific places with social practice and the historical and economic traces inscribed in the landscape. In the following and concluding section I wish to elaborate on these points, within a methodological and epistemological perspective.

Critical views

My critical reflections refer in particular to the notions of community, memory and landscape, as well as to the time constraints vis-à-vis the ambition and potentials of community-mapping projects. Tools for research-action such as community mapping are hailed by the most optimistic operators as seeds of new citizenship, initiating participatory processes that help local communities to re-situate and reappropriate their cultural heritage (de Varine, 1988). The communitarian premise of such a conviction is that sense of place is a symptom of a virtuous relationship with one's territory and that belonging is a premise for participation. This is true in particular of the ecomuseum context, in which Hugues de Varine underlines the distinction between community-driven projects and mere conservation projects that are part of top-down agendas targeting the environmental patrimony (2005).

Linking empowerment to a notion of community is not always devoid of ambivalences, however. A social critique to an obsolete notion of community as being small, bounded and homogeneous is often already present in the theoretical background of some community-mapping projects (which also explains the variety of alternative designation used to name such projects: cultural mapping, parish maps, community mapping, perceptive maps, mental maps, participatory cartography, etc.). Anthropology at least has amply deconstructed the notion of the small-scale community as a natural enclosure in social, symbolic and relational terms. Christian Bromberger reminds us that:

> the community and the common can become attractive fields of investigation because of their coherence and relative functional simplicity (which abstract conditions need to be verified case by case). Complexity is disarming for anthropologists especially when working individually and especially when not limiting themselves to gather objects or beliefs, techniques or rituals which are easily singled out of their own contexts. It is nevertheless such complex context that attributes actual significance to those objects. (Bromberger, 1987: 68; my translation)

In Val Taleggio for instance, the Venetian–Milanese medieval state border still represents a fresh cultural boundary dividing and distinguishing the eastern and the western municipalities. Even in focus groups with a dozen people, a dialectic relationship was easy to detect, resulting in reciprocal suspicions that one side could be over-represented in respect to the other, etc. To straddle that boundary meant negotiating choices between the materials gathered and making sure that the visual outcome would not look unbalanced, both in terms of the number of icons placed on the valley's aerial view and in terms of the choice of place-values and *fiches*. Once again, then, mapping Val Taleggio proved its multivocality (Rodman, 1992) which in turn not only presented strictly cartographic challenges and methodological choices about visual tools, but also raised the issue of *representation* both in political and epistemological terms. The idea of a monolithic and coherent community backing the project was unacceptably nostalgic, and the actual research practice favoured an interpretation of the 'community' mandate in terms of a plurality of communities of practice and a diversity of practices of locality, each putting forward its own 'skilled vision' (Grasseni, 2004).

Another critical point inevitably regards the clash of timing between funded schedules, which expect deliverables within reasonable times, and the participatory nature of community mappings. The latter include downtimes and longer perspectives, whilst the former require final reports and artefacts for dissemination within and outside the community. Community-mapping projects may oscillate between a communication purpose (congenial to the former perspective) and a participatory mandate (less easy to adapt to fixed schedules and deliverables). In the latter viewpoint, processes and relationships are more important than final artefacts, but this generates a number of coordination problems. When is the project actually finished? Should it be left open-ended? How to ensure that someone within the community will take it upon themselves to continue it? As I anticipated above, in this particular case the need to leave the project potentially open to future accretions meant a precise choice in the medium and formats of representation. Their quasi-artisanal technical quality was also meant to facilitate a handover of competences to the ecomuseum operators who had been the protagonists of the first focus groups. Rather than an external incentive to self-representation – a capacity which is not lacking in the valley as testified by the numerous publications and archives – it was meant as a framework and an archive of existent competences, materials and skills.

Moreover, this particular community-mapping project found its rationale within a wider project, the observatory of the landscape of Val Taleggio, part of an Agenda 21 measure aimed at documenting and fostering the knowledge of local resources for more sustainable livelihoods. Thanks to this, visualising a territory was never understood as merely a cartographic exercise but as a social process. The community map was never considered as a tool to initiate a development plan (since the ecomuseum project was already existing and moving ahead). Nor was it a cultural initiative in a territory lacking the ambition of self-representation, whether in the form of auto-ethnography (as in the many local history publications) or of auto-cartography (as in the Torriani map). On the contrary, the map served as a process to catalyse the training and cohesion of a group of local operators, and both their previous knowledge of the territory and mine were crucial assets in its development.

Consistently with this, the community map was never an 'address card' for the valley. It is far too rich and complex a document to be adaptable to the simple messages of tourist publicity. Nevertheless, the inhabitants themselves shared the view that Val Taleggio was worth displaying and even 'packaging' for tourist purposes – as the following successful development of the Ecomuseum Val Taleggio proves, and as the vocation of the valley as a dairy producer in a sense already required (see Grasseni, 2003b). Val Taleggio has recently become the setting for some innovative formats of tourist guiding based on street-theatre techniques and multimedia installations. Rather than setting up an orthodox ethnographic museum about cheese-making and folk life in the mountains, the ecomuseum has invested in 'soft' activities, including the reenactment of some local crafts by professional actors (but not by local crafts-men) and sensory workshops accompanying cheese-tasting sessions.

In the absence of an actual ethnographic collection gathering objects, mem-oirs, oral testimonies or photographic collections of a form of life that is in many senses still alive – an absence which was my main criticism of the eco-museum's development plan – the community map of Val Taleggio lacks root-ing on the one hand, but on the other, it provides a collection of facets of a single place as it is interpreted and transformed. Precisely because it aims at voicing and empowering collective representations of place, however, commu-nity mapping does not escape a measure of performative ideology, in that, as with any map, its final *mise en forme* contains hegemonic elements of *mise en ordre* and a cognitive and emotional 'erasure of the muddling' (Turnbull, 2007) that characterises identity claims. In fact, one of the advancements hoped for in visual methodology that this chapter would aim to contribute to is precisely the awareness of the ambivalence and 'symbolic violence' (Rabinow, 1977: 129–30) that even the most interactive and participatory form of fieldwork, through multimedia and multidisciplinary engagement, concedes to experiment with.

Certainly in this case, the local bounds of sense did not coincide with the valley's geographical boundaries. Nor did mapping prove more spontaneous or less constructed thanks to its participatory, interactive and visual methodology. In fact, this is something that any critical analysis of visual research methods should disband: the presumption or sometimes the hope that an increase in multi-mediality and multi-vocality may result in a more transparent and even mechanical act of inscription. In fact, the advancements in visual methods and the interdisciplinary collaborations with IT specialties and cartography proves how the ethnographic object becomes epistemologically complex and ethically nuanced, every time we try to chart it.

Notes

1 At the 1972 ICOM conference of Santiago in Chile the *Nouvelle Museologie* established a new paradigm of cultural conservation based on the principles of participation and inclusion, of interaction and of a social redefinition of humankind's cultural expressions.

2 This is a peculiarity of Val Taleggio and of neighbouring valleys that were crossed by a state boundary from 1428 until 1797, dividing the Republic of Venice on the east from the Dukedom of Milan on the west. In Val Taleggio, only one of the two municipalities, Taleggio, was faithful to the Venetian state whilst Vedeseta was part of the Milanese feud, which sparked quarrels and bloodshed throughout the Middle Ages and the Renaissance (Arrigoni, 2007).

3 Val Taleggio's community map (online at www.osservatoriovaltaleggio.it), acknowledges the essential contribution of research assistants and local informants, historians and operators. By a conscious recognition of equality between researchers and informants, they are all listed in alphabetical order. Nevertheless, the initial phase of data gathering through focus groups and on-site interviews was carried out by Lia Zola and Chiara Brambilla, whilst the second phase (deciphering, classifying and transcribing the Torriani maps), with additional follow-up interviews and data gathering, was carried out by local operators, notably Erika Arrigoni, Barbara Pesenti Bolò and Osvalda Quarenghi, and by a research assistant, Roberta Capretti. The cartographic and IT realisation was achieved in cooperation with other researchers and professionals within the wider frame of the landscape observatory of Val Taleggio, notably Moris Lorenzi and Grazia Morelli (of Terraria srl).

4 A *casello* is a traditional floorless building, usually constructed in such as way as to straddle a natural stream, in order to exploit its humidity to maintain fresh fish or to mature cheese, as it would be in an underground cellar, without the aid of refrigeration systems.

References

Arrigoni, A. (1999) *Tra storia e natura: Valle Taleggio.* Clusone (BG): Ferrari Grafiche.

Arrigoni, A. (ed.) (2007) *Cenni ed osservazioni sulla Vallata di Taleggio: Manoscritto del 1823 di Locatelli Giuseppe.* Città di Castello: Geam.

Bravo, G. (2006) *La complessità della tradizione.* Milano: Franco Angeli.

Bromberger, C. (1987) 'Du grand au petit: variation des échelles et objets d'analyse dans l'histoire récente de l'ethnologie de la France', in I. Chiva and U. Jeggle (eds), *Ethnologie en miroir.* Paris: Edition de la Maison des Sciences de l'Homme. pp. 67–94.

Clifford, S. and King, A. (eds) (1993) *Local Distinctiveness: Place, Particularity and Identity*. London: Common Ground.

Clifford, S. and King, A. (2006) *England in Particular: A Celebration of the Commonplace, the Local, the Vernacular and the Distinctive*. London: Hodder & Stoughton.

Clifford, S., Maggi, M. and Murtas, D. (2006) *Genius loci. Perché, quando e come realizzare una mappa di comunità*. Torino: IRES Piemonte.

Davis, P. (1999) *Ecomuseums: A Sense of Place*. London and New York: Leicester University Press.

de France, C. (1979) *Pour une anthropologie de la visuelle*. Paris/Le Haye/New York: Mouton Publishers.

de Varine, H. (1988) 'Rethinking the museum concept', in J.A. Gjestrum and M. Maure (eds), *Økomuseumsboka – identitet, økologi, deltakelse*. Tromsø: ICOM. pp. 33–40.

de Varine, H. (2005) *Le radici del futuro. Il patrimonio locale al servizio dello sviluppo locale*. Bologna: CLUEB.

Fahy, F. and Ó Cinnéide, M. (2009) 'Re-constructing the urban landscape through community mapping: an attractive prospect for sustainability?', *Area*, 41 (2): 167–75.

Goodwin, C. (1994) 'Professional vision', *American Anthropologist*, 96 (3): 606–33.

Grasseni, C. (2003a) *Lo sguardo della mano. Pratiche della località e antropologia della visione in una comunità montana lombarda*. Bergamo: Bergamo University Press.

Grasseni, C. (2003b) 'Packaging skills: calibrating Italian cheese to the global market', in S. Strasser (ed.), *Commodifying Everything: Relationships of the Market*. New York: Routledge. pp. 341–81.

Grasseni, C. (2004) 'Skilled landscapes: mapping practices of locality', *Environment and Planning D: Society and Space*, 22 (5): 699–717.

Grasseni, C. (ed.) (2007) *Skilled Visions: Between Apprenticeship and Standards*. Oxford: Berghahn.

Grasseni, C. (2009a) *Luoghi comuni. Antropologia dei luoghi e pratiche della visione*. Bergamo: Lubrina Editore.

Grasseni, C. (2009b) *Developing Skill, Developing Vision: Practices of Locality in an Alpine Community*. Oxford: Berghahn.

Healey, P. (2001) 'Place, identity and governance: transforming discourses and practices', in J. Hillier and E. Rooksby (eds), *Habitus: A Sense of Place*. Aldershot: Ashgate. pp. 173–202.

Ingold, T. (1993) 'The temporality of the landscape', *World Archaeology*, 25 (2): 152–74.

Newman, A. and McLean, F. (1998) 'Heritage builds communities: the application of heritage resources to the problems of social exclusion', *International Journal of Heritage Studies*, 4 (3&4): 143–53.

Pink, S. (2007) *Doing Visual Ethnography: Images, Media and Representation in Research* (2nd edn). London: Sage.

Pink, S. (2009) *Doing Sensory Ethnography*. London: Sage.

Rabinow, P. (1977) *Reflections on Fieldwork in Morocco*. Berkely, CA: University of California Press.

Reed-Danahay, D. (ed.) (1997) *Auto/Ethnography: Rewriting the Self and the Social*. New York and Oxford: Berg.

Rodman, M. (1992) 'Empowering place: multilocality and multivocality', *American Anthropologist*, 94 (3): 640–56.

St. Martin, K. (2009) 'Toward a cartography of the commons: constituting the political and economic possibilities of place', *The Professional Geographer*, 61 (4): 493–507.

Turnbull, D. (2007) 'Maps and plans in "Learning to See": the London Underground and Chartres Cathedral as examples of performing design', in C. Grasseni (ed.), *Skilled Visions: Between Apprenticeship and Standards*. Oxford: Berghahn. pp. 125–43.

7

VISUAL ETHNOGRAPHY AND THE INTERNET
Visuality, Virtuality and the Spatial Turn

Sarah Pink

Introduction

Both visual and virtual ethnography have their origins in the late 1990s, and became further established as we moved through the first decade of the 21st century. They are now firmly situated within a range of contemporary research techniques. However, even in the short number of years since these ethnographic practices began to be documented and critically reflected on there have been significant changes in the theoretical and methodological underpinnings of ethnographic practice and the ways it might be understood. Elisenda Ardévol (this volume) has highlighted that the Internet brings new challenges and opportunities to visual researchers, and these include those that invite us to develop new methodologies. In this chapter I respond to such an invitation by examining the implications of recent shifts towards phenomenological and multi-sensory approaches, and critical theories of place for the (re)conceptualisation of doing visual Internet ethnography.

In doing so I develop two themes: the question of how visual Internet ethnography might be conceptualised through a theory of place; and how the concept of multi-sensoriality might enable us to better understand visuality in Internet ethnography. I build on two examples of existing work: Christine Hine's (2000) *Virtual Ethnography*, and Tom Boellstorff's (2008) *Coming of Age in Second Life*, in which concepts of place and understandings of the visual have been mobilised to discuss Internet environments. Departing from these works, I then draw on a sensory ethnography approach (Pink, 2009) that is rooted in recent conceptualisations of place, movement and knowing in the work of Tim Ingold (2007, 2008), Mark Harris (2007) and Doreen Massey (2005). To demonstrate this, I discuss my experiences of extending my existing research about the visual culture of a Cittaslow (Slow City) town in the UK to engage with its increasing Internet presence. In what follows, I propose an advance in visual methodology through a paradigm for understanding visual Internet ethnography that is coherent with recent developments in sensory, phenomenological and spatial theory across the humanities and social sciences. Yet I also suggest that with the increasing proliferation of web-based practices amongst participants in research, in ways that are relevant to our research questions, we might rethink the status of doing visual ethnography on the Internet. The Internet is becoming not something we engage with by doing a special kind of online visual ethnography, but a part of the 'ethnographic places' (Pink, 2009) in which we become implicated as visual ethnographers.

The emergence of the visual and the virtual in 21st-century ethnographic practice

Since the year 2000, there has been a dramatic increase in the methodological literature concerned with the visual and virtual aspects of ethnographic practice. Amongst the first contributions to this wave of publications was Christine Hine's (2000) *Virtual Ethnography*, published shortly before the first edition of my book, *Doing Visual Ethnography* (Pink, 2007 [2001]). Some reflections on these earlier moments provide an interesting starting point for considering the intellectual trajectories of these methodological developments and their contemporary implications.

In some ways Hine's (2000) and my own (Pink, 2007 [2001]) texts pursued different directions, since they explored rather contrasting contexts for ethnographic practice. Yet an analysis of their common heritage offers some interesting insights. Even though each book had its principal origin in a different discipline (Hine's in sociology and my own representing an interdisciplinary approach rooted in anthropology), both volumes ring clearly of a set of theoretical and methodological strands that emerged in the 1990s: like me, Hine was concerned with the 'writing culture debate' that continued to range into that period, through discussions of the authority of the ethnographer's authenticity and reflexivity as developed by Clifford and Marcus (1986). In fact I believe it was partly the new openness to doing, or at least writing about, ethnography in different ways, the invitations to subjectivity and the possibilities for experimentation that were created through those moments in the 1990s, that made it possible for formulations of ethnography as being *virtual* or *visual* to take a place amongst standard ethnographic methods. In the period that built up to these two publications, understandings of ethnographic practice, what it entailed and where it was done had been through a period of change inspired by the 'writing culture' debates (e.g. Clifford and Marcus, 1986, and see James et al., 1997). Indeed, during this period ethnography had also been recognised as being gendered (Bell et al., 1993); multi-sited (Marcus, 1995); intimate and sexual (Kulick and Willson, 1995); and embodied (Coffey, 1999). It comes as little surprise that it could also be virtual (Hine, 2000) and visual (Pink, 2007 [2001]) – or that I might also later understand it as sensory (Pink, 2006, 2009). These understandings also contributed to the emerging ideas of virtual and visual ethnography. Therefore, for instance, for Hine, the point that culture could be disassociated from places (e.g. Gupta and Ferguson, 1997), and that ethnography was no longer located in one locality but could be multi-sited (e.g. Marcus, 1995), was very compatible with the idea of doing ethnography online. As she puts it:

> ... if culture and community are not self-evidently located in place, then neither is ethnography. The object of ethnographic enquiry can usefully be reshaped by concentrating on flow and connectivity rather than location and boundary as the organizing principle. (Hine, 2000: 64)

For the question of doing visual ethnography, the implications of working with new technologies did not initially raise similar questions about place and locality. Visual ethnography was done in the same contexts as 'ordinary' ethnography. Thus the need to consider the role of new technologies in fieldwork took a different direction. In visual ethnography, the relationship between the technology and the embodied and gendered self of the researcher came to the fore, as a means of reflexively understanding the processes through which ethnographic knowledge is produced (Pink, 2007 [2001]). However, now, 10 years later, both the spatial and phenomenological elements of fieldwork practice become particularly salient when discussing the idea of visual Internet ethnography. In the first part of this chapter, I contextualise my argument by outlining how spatial concepts and phenomenological approaches have been used in existing approaches to understanding the visual dimension of Internet ethnography. I then suggest how understanding visual Internet ethnography through phenomenological and spatial approaches invites new ways of appreciating the multi-sensoriality of visual Internet ethnography and its relationality to material realities.

A critical perspective on virtual places

Although Hine's (2000) *Virtual Ethnography* is firmly situated in the context of late 20th-century debates about ethnographic practice, it is simultaneously a particularly contemporary text in that she is concerned with notions of space, place, flow and movement. In this section I develop a critical discussion of existing uses of these concepts and the ways they have been related to visual images and experience in Internet ethnography in two texts. First, I outline Hine's development of the discussion about space, place and flows and how this relates to her discussion of visual images in a web 1.0 context. Then I turn to the contrasting example of Boellstorff's (2008) more recent monograph, where he has used concepts of place and the visual to frame his ethnography of a 3D web site.

Hine was concerned with the spatial terms upon which culture has been understood and with how in anthropology the idea of cultures being bounded had been deconstructed (Hine, 2000: 58). It is the latter of these debates that I am most interested in here. Following this strand in anthropological methodology, Hine's approach departs from what she refers to as 'the tendency to treat the field site as a place which one goes to and dwells within', which, as she puts it, 'reinforces an idea of culture as something which exists in and is bounded by physical space' (2000: 58). Her own approach for studying the Internet moves 'away from holism and towards connectivity as an organizing principle' (2000: 60). Following the ideas of Olwig and Hastrup (1997) and Marcus (1995), she outlines how: 'Ethnographers might start from a particular place, but would be encouraged to follow connections which were made meaningful from that setting' (2000: 60). And of particular relevance to the discussion here, Hine suggests: 'The ethnographic sensitivity would focus on the ways in which particular places were made meaningful and visible' (2000: 60).

To deal with this context, Hine harnesses Manuel Castells' (1996) notion of the 'space of flows' to understand online ethnography. As she describes it:

> In the space of flows, the emphasis is on connection rather than location. Flows of money, people, objects and communication travel around the world, and connectivity becomes the vital factor that structures inclusion. Much social experience is still tied to place, but the space of flows provides an alternative way of conducting social relations that is increasingly the site of the exercise of power by the elite. (Hine, 2000: 84–5)

Significantly, within this framework Hine cites Castells' point that 'relations between place and flows are possible, but are "not predetermined" (Castells 1996a: 423)' (Hine, 2000: 85). Thus, Hine suggests that: 'As a way of connecting distant places, the Internet seems an ideal medium for the space of flows' (2000: 85). She proposes that this raises specific questions for the ethnographer including: 'How do people negotiate a path through [the] timeless time [of the "space of flows"] and the [chronological] time of place' (2000: 85). I return to Hine's ideas below.

In his recent monograph, *Coming of Age in Second Life* (2008), Tom Boellstorff takes a rather different approach to place. Although Boellstorff's work might be seen as primarily ethnographic, it is worth considering his theoretical and methodological approach. The differences with Hine's (2000) argument might in part be attributed to the point that his research, a decade later, was done on a rather different Internet to that inhabited by Hine, as he writes: "'a shift from the 2D web to the 3D web" is really the shift from network to place, or, more accurately, the addition of online places, since networks will continue to exist' (Boellstorff, 2008: 91–2).

More specifically, though, it seems that in the eight years between Hine's (2000) and Boellstorff's (2008) monographs there have been shifts in the possible ways of both conceptualising and experiencing the Internet. In their respective contexts and projects, Hine and Boellstorff were able to inhabit and experience the Internet in different ways. They subsequently fit different theoretical perspectives to their ethnographies. As referenced above, Boellstorff suggests that networks still exist, but that there is now something more in that one is able to feel what he describes as 'a sense of place' (2008: 91) online. Indeed, Boellstorff claims that there are 'online places' (2008: 92) which I read to refer to being akin to the idea that there are online localities in that he writes:

> We all shared an understanding of a virtual world with land that could be bought and sold and built upon, proximity, area, residency, buildings, a community in the vicinity of a building, indeed a neighborhood, a neighborhood in which people live, into which they put effort so that it looks nice. (Boellstorff, 2008: 92)

In this sense, Boellstorff's rendition of places has in common with Hine's that they both claim something experiential. But, crucially for Boellstorff, there can be 'places' online precisely because, siding with existing 'philosophical and empirical work, [that] however, has shown the salience of place and sensory experience online, including in virtual worlds,' he argues that since 'virtual worlds are places' this means 'they can be fieldsites: it makes an ethnographic approach conceivable' (2008: 90). Boellstorff does not elaborate his theoretical commitments further in this direction. Yet the impression his discussion gives is that he is arguing that because we can have sensory experiences in/ of online 'worlds' then they must be places, because sensoriality is a quality of place (2008: 91), as is sociality (2008: 92). This would seem to suggest that an online place is an online locality. Of particular interest for the question of the relationship between visual and virtual ethnography is that he goes on to discuss the sensoriality of online places specifically in terms of their visuality and in relation to concepts of landscape.

For Boellstorff, vision plays a central role in Second Life, especially during the historical period in which he did his research (and given the fast-changing nature of web platforms it is appropriate to situate such recent change as historical in this context). He takes vision as the starting point for his discussion of place (2008: 92). In contrast to earlier forms of online engagement, he associates place with vision and landscape (2008: 92–3), proposing that:

> A broad cultural shift during the time of my fieldwork was that the notion of 'virtual world' increasingly presupposed three-dimensional visuality: a defining characteristic of a virtual world (versus a blog or website) was that it was a place in which you could look around. (2008: 92)

Therefore, for both Hine and Boellstorf, place is an important element of the experience of the Internet, and Boellstorf stresses the visuality of place. In what follows, I build on this by asking how we might rethink visual Internet ethnography through an alternative theory of place and multi-sensoriality. Boellstroff's rendering of networks and places does not make a firm distinction between ideas of locality, landscape, a sense of place and theoretical understandings of place. I have argued elsewhere (Pink, 2009, 2012), that if place is to be used as an analytical concept then a clear definition of it is required and that it should be used as distinct from locality. Thus, following my existing methodological work (Pink, 2009), I propose using place as a theoretical concept, whereby it is better understood as an abstract means of understanding configurations of things and the processes through which they are formed or change. Such a definition of place, which is drawn from the work of theorists such as Ingold (2007, 2008) and Massey (2005), conceptualises place as 'open' (Massey) and 'unbounded' (Ingold). However, if the term 'place' is used simultaneously to a bounded locality or to a visible landscape then there is potential for slippage between the different levels of analysis – from theory to lay concepts – which actually refer to quite different things and processes (Pink, 2012). Therefore, for the task of understanding how places and networks might be implicated in the doing of visual Internet ethnography a firm distinction should be made between the levels of ethnographic and theoretical analysis. This means distinguishing between, on the one hand, network theory in contrast to the feeling that one is part of a network in which one is connected to others; and on the other, between a theory of place in contrast to the sense of place that one might have in relation to a particular locality and the sensoriality and socialities associated with it. In the next section, I outline how a theory of place as open and unbounded enables us to understand the Internet as part of a multi-sensory environment where we might participate as visual ethnographers.

Place and the Internet

When understanding the use of the Internet we need to consider how such an activity is rooted both in the everyday materiality that we inhabit in our physical environments and what have come to be called virtual worlds. Of course these are in fact both part of one and the same world, but any discussion of them is haunted by the legacy of the notion that there was a virtual world that one could go to online that was part of a different reality. Qualitative Internet researchers have generally now accounted for this question (see Markham and Baym, 2009). Moreover, some media scholars have already begun to work with spatial theory to bring these domains together. For instance, Nick Couldry and Anna McCarthy propose the concept of 'MediaSpace'. This is 'a dialectical concept, encompassing both the kinds of spaces created by media, and the effects that existing spatial arrangements have on media forms as they materialise in everyday life' (2004: 2). To understand the practice of doing visual Internet ethnography, we need to both account for the relationality and continuities between digital and material elements of places and their visuality *and* account reflexively for how the ethnographer is situated at this interface.

In *Doing Sensory Ethnography* (Pink, 2009), I have conceptualised the ethnographic process through a theory of place. I suggest that researchers are always emplaced and moreover make 'ethnographic places' in the process of doing ethnography. Later, in *Situating Everyday Life* (Pink, 2012), I propose that contemporary Internet use, platforms, practices and their relationships to offline materialities, sensations and socialities can likewise be understood through a theory of place. Therefore, following this approach, ethnographers should not be seeking to find places online, or to determine that these are places by measuring them against certain sets of qualities and possibilities for visual experience that places are deemed to hold. Rather, the visual Internet ethnographer should attend to how the (audio)visuality of the material offline and digital online localities become interwoven in everyday and research narratives. To outline the theoretical foundations of these ideas I now reiterate arguments made in my existing publications with particular reference to the visual. For a fuller development readers should refer to Chapter 2 of *Doing Sensory Ethnography* (Pink, 2009) and Chapter 2 of *Situating Everyday Life* (Pink, 2012). The understanding that informs this approach is rooted in recent work seeing place as 'open' (Massey, 2005) and 'unbounded' (Ingold, 2008). While Massey and Ingold are opposed in some elements of their definitions of place and space, it is where they coincide that is most interesting for the framing I develop here. Theorists of place tend to be interested in the question of how sets of diverse things come together, become entangled and interwoven with each other, and in doing so become part of the creation of new (but always changing) configurations of things or ecologies. While they are not necessarily primarily interested in the visuality of place, it is possible to understand how processes involving visual practices, productions and representations are part of these configurations of place. In this way of thinking place becomes an abstract term for discussing what Massey calls 'constellations of processes' (2005) or what Ingold calls a 'meshwork' of lines (2008). The focus in these approaches is on relatedness, and this is developed in such a way that enables us to think of how things are interwoven or entangled with each other and the continuities this involves, rather than in thinking of how they are separate but connected. In this line of thinking the idea of relatedness is distinguished from the model of a network. As I have argued elsewhere (Pink, 2012), Massey's notion of place as 'open to the externally relational' (2005: 183) is particularly interesting for understanding environments where we are engaged in using online digital technologies. She argues for 'an understanding of the world in terms of relationality, and world in which the local and global really are "mutually constituted"'. In this conceptualization, 'The "lived reality of our everyday lives" is utterly dispersed, unlocalised, in its sources and in its repercussions. The degree of dispersion, the stretching, may vary dramatically between social groups, *but the point is that the geography will not be simply territorial*' (Massey, 2005: 184; my italics). Following Massey's points we can understand place as based not in locality, not as simply the immediate visual landscape that we can sense when participating in a virtual reality platform, and not as a node of closely clustered pages in a network of electronic materials. Rather, it invites us to understand the Internet as a field of potential forms of relatedness. Direct relationships between different elements of the Internet might not necessarily be activated. Yet they always have the potential to be interwoven into particular intensities of place that also involve persons, interactivity, material localities and technologies.

To take this discussion further, to understand how we experience and 'navigate' when doing visual Internet ethnography, in the next section I incorporate two further concepts – movement and multi-sensoriality – both of which also form the basis of other publications and arguments in this area (Pink, 2009; Pink, 2012).

The multi-sensory Internet

The idea of multi-sensoriality proposes that our sensory experiences, rather than being separated out into the modern western categories of sight, sound, touch, taste and smell, are part of a more complex system of human sensory perception in which they cannot necessarily be separated. As detailed elsewhere (e.g. Pink, 2009, 2011), these ideas emerge from both neurological studies and from the phenomenological approaches influenced by the work of Maurice Merleau-Ponty, which are becoming increasingly influential in social, visual and sensory ethnography (e.g. Geurts, 2003; Grasseni, 2007; Ingold, 2000; MacDougall, 1998). This approach establishes that the modern western sensory categories cited above are culturally constructed. They are as such the categories that we, as researchers participating in what scholarship has become in modernity, use to research and represent sensory experience. Importantly, as Ingold demonstrates, this means that we should not consider vision as *the* dominant sense in any essential way, but rather it is the category of vision that has been understood as dominating in modern western culture (Ingold, 2000). The implication for the visual Internet ethnographer is that we need to understand the visuality of web-based phenomena and the ways we look at them – what Grasseni (2007) calls our 'skilled vision' – in terms of their interrelationships with other dimensions of sensory experience.

When we use desktop monitors, laptops and mobile devices to access the Internet, we are always participating in a multi-sensory environment. Our visual practices are inevitably part of this, in that they are implicated in the way we experience and navigate the screen, touch-pad, keyboard, and the physical localities we participate in. Indeed, the idea of the visual Internet ethnographer as someone who sits at a desk gazing into a monitor is becoming increasingly redundant in a world where the Internet is so often accessed through mobile devices and in contexts of changing social and material composition. In this sense, the web pages, platforms and other applications ethnographers might engage with online are not simply bounded visual landscapes that can be sensed as virtual places. Rather, they are experienced inevitably as part of places that straddle the different environments we engage in and perceive multi-sensorially and memorially. Therefore, I understand places in visual Internet ethnography as constituted by intensities of flows that converge, become interwoven or entangled, and in which the visual ethnographer her- or himself becomes implicated. In a visual ethnography, particular attention will be paid to the images and visual practices that form part of these places. Yet this must be qualified by situating the visual as part of multi-sensory experience in screen-related ethnography.

There are important experiential (and practical) differences between navigating from one visual/textual page to another in a web 1.0 environment, moving in the visual landscapes of a web 2.0 virtual world, and engaging with digital texts as discussed below. Yet the idea that we are moving *through* the Internet rather than moving *from* one connected locality *to* another offers us the opportunity to understand the ethnographer's attentive engagement with the social, material and visual/sensory dimensions of the environment she or he experiences in alternative ways. Many web elements are inter-platform (often audio-visually) interdependent with what is happening offline, and interlinked with others in ways that are better thought of as relational than as simply connected to each other. Navigating this relationality itself should, I propose, be seen as a multi-sensory experience.

The visuality of the Internet can therefore be experienced in different ways. This varies between the kinds on online activity and engagements described respectively by Hine and Boellstorff and the web 2.0 contexts I discuss below. Visual experience of the Internet might be understood as part of the multi-sensory process of moving through and learning as one moves digitally in ways that are inextricable from the material world and its own visuality. By the latter I refer not simply to the immediate physical environment that the Internet user is part of, but also, as in the cases discussed below, the physical localities and persons that Internet content represents, and the ways the body is engaged in imagining and remembering them. Understanding the visuality of the Internet this way enables us to move beyond the notion of 'looking at' images on a screen, to conceptualise our emplaced experience as one of moving through a digital environment while rooted in the materiality of our immediate circumstances and engaging embodied memories and imaginations of past and possible future experiences.

The visual ethnographer goes online

I now draw on my research about the Cittaslow (Slow City) movement in the UK. I explore the implications of the methodological approach outlined above for understanding what happens when both the visual practices of research participants and the research of the visual ethnographer shift to the Internet. I have deliberately chosen to examine an example in which the online component of the research develops as a continuation of face-to-face and other mediated encounters, in order to provide a contrast to approaches that understand online ethnography as something that takes the Internet as its starting point. Between 2005 and 2007 I did ethnographic research about the Cittaslow movement, focusing on its development in the UK, along a range of themes connecting with well-being, sustainability, the senses and consumption. My visual and sensory ethnography research methodologies are discussed elsewhere (e.g. Pink, 2007, 2009); they involved eating with people, walking video tours, interviews, photography, and the analysis of the existing visual culture of the towns I was researching. At the time, Cittaslow had an Internet presence: UK and International websites, as well as other national websites. However, by 2010, its web presence had grown, along with web 2.0, and I began to ask myself how this could be understood in relation to changing digital technologies and the development of the movement. As part of this next stage of the research process I undertook an analysis of the Cittaslow International web presence, encompassing its Facebook activity, YouTube channel, blog and website (Pink, 2012). The analysis was framed by the theoretical principles of place outlined above, and attended to how a digital Cittaslow could be understood in relation to activist practices. In this study I was able to understand Cittaslow's web 2.0 presence as part of a place that incorporated localities but was not essentially based in a bounded geographical unit.

The next stage of my research turned to the question of how the Cittaslow activists of towns where I had done fieldwork during 2005–2007 were now using the Internet as *part of* their self-production as Cittaslow members. As I noted above, as part of my earlier fieldwork I had focused on how these towns used photography, video and other media as ways of representing and indeed constituting themselves as Cittaslow (Pink, 2008, 2011, 2012). To investigate this question anew in an online visual ethnography, I began to explore how the Internet is being engaged in similar ways. My focus is on Diss, a town in South Norfolk, UK. The town and its Cittaslow identity already had an Internet presence during my earlier research, and this has continued to develop. Below I discuss how I encountered two online visual representations, which I suggest form part of the visual ethnographic field – or 'ethnographic place' – in which I am researching. Moreover, both have strong continuities with the earlier visual research I undertook in the town. The first is a digital map that represents a Cittaslow walk around the town, and the second a locally made video documentary that was used to represent the town at a Cittaslow International Conference. These are very different Internet contexts to those described by Hine (2000) and Boellstorff (2008). Yet, as I will argue, the framing of visual Internet ethnography and its relationship to physical environments through a theory of place is equally relevant whether it refers to ethnography done in a virtual reality site or if it is practised at the interface between online and offline experiences as is the case for this example.

To consider how Cittaslow in Diss was produced audiovisually, I returned to an earlier article where I examined 'how routes and mobilities are represented in local visual culture' through a focus on photography, documentary film and video in Diss, one of the Cittaslow towns (Pink, 2008). This town has an interesting history of visual representation. It is featured in a (now) historical television film, *Something About Diss* (1964), which involves a tour of the town by its director, the Poet Laureate John Betjeman. Routes around the town have also been represented photographically by a local group campaigning about disabled-access issues, as well as pictorially in local maps and illustrated walking guides around the town. Therefore the town already had a rich local visual culture, much of which seemed to involve the making of routes around or touring the town.

The Snail Trail

Drawing on this local visual culture, as well as my own existing visual ethnographies that have used walking and touring methods (Pink, 2004, 2007), during the fieldwork period in Diss I took a series of established walks around the town, including a video walk led by the local historian, Bas. I viewed existing (audio)visual photographic and video texts produced by research participants and in one case including a historical documentary film, which took as their narratives mobile routes through the town. I ended an article in which I discussed these routes and walks in relation to each other (2008) noting how by then, the new tour of the town that I discuss here was being produced:

> In the summer of 2007, once the Cittaslow Centre was opened, Cynthia (the Cittaslow Co-ordinator) told me that as part of their activities a group of Cittaslow leaders, in collaboration with an agency they had commissioned, was designing a new route through the town that tourists and locals alike would be able to follow. This was being tentatively called the 'Snail Trail' and would be a Cittaslow tour of the town. It would possibly incorporate local-produce eating places, areas of historical interest, and other things of Cittaslow value. Thus a Cittaslow tour of the town, similar to that I had envisaged as a research exercise [but that I did not have the opportunity to create], was to be created by the Cittaslow committee members as something that would be meaningful and useful to *them*. (Pink, 2008: 27)

The Diss Snail Trail was, at the time of writing this chapter, available online as an interactive map (www.farrowsweb.com/diss/snailtrail.php) as part of the Cittaslow Diss website. Such digital presence starts to give new meanings to the idea of participant-produced media in visual ethnography. Whereas the predominant method in the past has been to *invite* participants to produce materials, in this case there was an interesting convergence between visual ethnography and local visual practices. The map could be downloaded and printed, and also be used online. As it said on the website, 'The Snail Trail is unique in that it incorporates wildlife, history, shops and restaurants.' By clicking on the appropriate textual link the viewer was taken across the hand-drawn map to the spot where the particular element of the town selected was indicated. Below the map appeared written information about the particular item. In this sense, the online map served as a straightforward guide to what was visualised on it and what one might find if walking the route that it proposed. Maps are flat, yet the interactive map took one deeper than the surface of the map because it linked each point with a written description. It highlighted local food and crafts (markets, shops and cafes), local history (the museum), the local landscape and materiality (the Mere, the Cathedral and Mount Street), as well as independent traders. All of these are very relevant to the local sustainability agenda of Cittaslow and they moreover invite sensory experiences of the town that reinforce the Cittaslow principles. While the map looked at the town from above, the Snail Trail should be appreciated from within; and because it involved a walk around the town, which engaged, for example, with its locally sourced food, its views, its surfaces underfoot and the sociality of its markets and independent trading shops, it invited its users to a multi-sensory experience of the town.

There are some resonances between the digital Snail Trail map and the project of community mapping discussed by Grasseni in Chapter 6, and by Lapenta in Chapter 8 (although the types of digital map discussed in each chapter are rather different). As I pointed out in my earlier article (2008), this digital (and printable) map emerged from local practices rather than a research exercise. The Snail Trail was designed by a committee of local people and based on established local narrative and embodied knowledge. In this sense, it engaged the viewer and potential walker with a series of sites that recur in the routes and tours I discussed in my 2008 article, for example, the Mere (the town's rather unusual historic lake) and the Corn Hall. Yet it also engaged the International Cittaslow discourse that both argues for, and, to some extent, frames the local uniqueness the map promoted. This indeed is reflected in the representation of the Mere and the Corn Hall but also in the farmers' market and food places it includes. In achieving this, the map invited online users to engage with the town through a series of images and texts. If actually in the town, it invited people to experience the town's physical environment, through a certain narrative. The narrative it followed also had a commitment to generating a specific set of sensory experiences, or sensory 'pleasures', that were *part of* the agenda of Cittaslow and at the same time specific to the embodied experience of the town as a physical locality and to local discourses on its history and features that precede Cittaslow.

From the above discussion, it is easy to start to understand how as a visual Internet representation, the Snail Trail Map was in fact part of a place that can be seen to traverse online and offline worlds. It brought together locality as it is experienced and locality as it is digitally mediated. It also intertwined the local and the global as it combined the town's historical narratives and local produce with the discourses of Cittaslow. The extension of the town's visual self-representation onto the Internet invited the visual ethnographer to also extend what I have elsewhere called the 'ethnographic place' to encompass this Internet context. Yet, as I have suggested, to engage with the Internet map I needed to also draw on my own sensory embodied experience of being in the town, and on 'old' media representations of the town that I had previously analysed. Visual Internet ethnography itself involves engaging with the ecologies of media and historical layers of representations that are inextricable from the online presence that one is attending to.

Diss – a Cittaslow Town: a YouTube video representation

When seeking to continue my Cittaslow fieldwork online I encountered a new video – www.youtube.com/watch?v=HtMbHzGbXig. As I noted above, participant-produced videos that represented the issues I was concerned with had already existed prior to my fieldwork in Diss. Extending my ethnographic research to the Internet added a new dimension. While conventionally visual ethnographers have asked or invited participants to produce videos about their own lives, experiences or localities, I found that materials were now being produced and posted online. This in itself presents an interesting shift in the way that we might conceptualise the visuality of ethnographic places, in that they are increasingly becoming contexts where the processes, practices, socialities and representations that constitute them also interwine online and offline contexts. Thus, for the visual Internet ethnographer, the visuality of place is not necessarily concerned only with the idea of experiencing a visual landscape while interacting online. Rather, it is concerned with the very relationality of the visuality of Internet representations, other visual media and the way that vision is part of the multi-sensory and embodied experience of being part of a material locality. This suggests that the experience of place, as it is constituted through the interweaving of online and offline experiences and components, is likewise multi-sensory.

Visual Internet ethnography can involve using a range of web platforms. It also means moving not only through different parts of the Internet, but between written and audio/visual texts too. In addition it is illustrative of how, although it is not as 'new' as social media platforms such as Twitter and Facebook, email plays an important role in the interpersonal communications of digital ethnography. I emailed Tony Palmer, an ex-Mayor and ex-Cittaslow Chairman in Diss, who is still on the Cittaslow committee, to ask about the origins of the Cittaslow video. Tony, who I had already met several times as part of my research in the town, emailed back to tell me that the video was made for him and his colleague Jane Trippet-Jones, who has taken over as the Chair of the committee to take to the International Cittaslow Conference in Korea. I moved again to a different type of file, to read the online report on their trip, which can be accessed through its link (www.disscouncil.com/cittaslow.php). In the report, Jane Trippet-Jones describes how:

> On the first day we gave our presentation which was a fantastic opportunity to promote Diss in front of an international audience. It is always daunting standing up in front of people and this was no exception especially as the stage was very large! Tony introduced me as the 'new' face of Cittaslow Diss before I continued with the presentation, which was based on a film that had been made for us by Toby Foster, a Diss 6th former.

Thus I followed further the town's Cittaslow progress online. Yet this was not detached from the fieldwork I had done in the town. Like the Snail Trail map, the video resonates in a number of ways with existing documentaries and walking tours of the town. It represents, for example, the Mere, the auction rooms, the markets and the independent shops along with familiar routes I had traversed on foot. Encountering the video online and following up its status allowed me to understand how it had represented both the town's local knowledge narratives and the Cittaslow movement's values back to the wider members of the movement at its international conference. It thus feeds into my wider research agenda that seeks to understand how Cittaslow towns constitute themselves as Cittaslow places, and the role of visual and digital media in these processes (Pink, 2011).

Taking these points back to the theoretical approach I outlined above, referring to place, the senses and movement, there is an essential point to be made. The examples of the Cittaslow Diss Snail Trail and video show how in doing visual ethnography online, we do not need to necessarily seek out research topics and questions that are specifically about new types of social media or novel cultural configurations such as virtual reality worlds. Rather, the move of visual ethnography onto the Internet will more often than not be part of the ways in which the sorts of areas we were already working on begin themselves to engage with the visuality of the Internet in new ways. As Ardévol (this volume) shows, in some cases this can invite the production of new methods. Yet, it often, as for the two examples discussed here, means following the visual and textual practices of research participants as they go on the Internet. My point is that doing Internet ethnography does not have to mean inventing new visual methods. It *does* nevertheless involve working with a methodological approach that can encompass visualities, visions and ways of looking that are both online and offline. As I have argued, a theory of place and attention to multi-sensoriality offer a route to such an analysis.

Conclusion

The existing Internet ethnography literature has engaged with notions of place and visuality. In this chapter I have argued however that its rendering of these concepts is limited. Instead I have suggested framing our understanding of visual Internet ethnography through theories of place, movement and multi-sensoriality. Based on this argument, I propose a set of methodological principles for doing visual Internet ethnography:

The relationship between offline and online visual ethnography practices is integral to how ethnographers encounter the intensities of interrelated things and processes that become ethnographic places.

Different digital (visual) and mobile technologies have a range of roles to play in these practices, and in creating relations between online and offline materialities, visualities and research practices.

The visuality of the Internet is experienced at an interface between everyday materialities, the technologies through which we access the Internet and the place of the visual in the multi-sensory experience of the screen.

Our experience of the Internet is multi-sensory; therefore vision, visual experience and images should be situated as part of the multi-sensoriality of human experience – not simply as representing the dominant sense.

A theory of place enables us to abstract both the subject matter and the process of doing visual Internet ethnography. It allows us to understand what we are researching as a constantly shifting configuration – or ecology of things – that encompasses web-based and material/local contexts. It moreover enables us to understand the practice of doing (visual) ethnography as one that creates 'ethnographic places' by bringing together things and processes analytically.

Bibliography

Bell, D., Caplan, P. and Jahan Karim, W. (1993) *Gendered Fields: Women, Men and Ethnography.* London: Routledge.

Boellstorff, T. (2008) *Coming of Age in Second Life: An Anthropologist Explores the Virtually Human.* Princeton, NJ: Princeton University Press.

boyd, d. (2008) 'Can social network sites enable political action?', in A. Fine, M. Sifry, A. Rasiej and J. Levy (eds), *Rebooting America.* Creative Commons. pp. 112–16 (retrieved 2 September 2010 from: www.danah.org/papers/Rebooting_America.pdf).

Bräuchler, B. and Postill, J. (eds) (2010) *Theorising Media and Practice*. Oxford and New York: Berghahn.

Castells, M. (1996) *The Rise of the Network Society*. Cambridge, MA: Blackwell.

Clifford, J. and Marcus, G. (1986) *Writing Culture: The Poetics and Politics of Ethnography*. Berkeley, CA: University of California Press.

Coffey, A. (1999) *The Ethnographic Self: Fieldwork and the Representation of Identity*. London: Sage.

Couldry, N. and A. McCarthy (2004) 'Orientations: mapping MediaSpace', in N. Couldry and A. McCarthy (eds), *MediaSpace: Place, Scale, and Culture in a Media Age*. London: Routledge.

Downey, G. (2007) 'Seeing with a "sideways glance": visuomotor "knowing" and the plasticity of perception', in M. Harris (ed.), *Ways of Knowing: New Approaches in the Anthropology of Experience and Learning*. Oxford: Berghahn.

Geurts, K.L. (2003) *Culture and the Senses: Bodily Ways of Knowing in an African Community*. Berkely/Los Angeles/London: University of California Press.

Grasseni, C. (2007) 'Communities of practice and forms of life: towards a rehabilitation of vision', in M. Harris (ed.), *Ways of Knowing: New Approaches in the Anthropology of Experience and Learning*. Oxford: Berghahn.

Gupta, A. and Ferguson, J. (1997) *Culture, Power, Place: Explorations in Critical Anthropology*. Durham, NC and London: Duke University Press.

Harris, M. (2007) 'Introduction: ways of knowing', in M. Harris (ed.), *Ways of Knowing: New Approaches in the Anthropology of Experience and Learning*. Oxford: Berghahn.

Hine, C. (2000) *Virtual Ethnography*. London: Sage.

Ingold, T. (2000) *The Perception of the Environment*. London: Routledge.

Ingold, T. (2007) *Lines: A Brief History*. London: Routledge.

Ingold, T. (2008) 'Bindings against boundaries: entanglements of life in an open world', *Environment and Planning A*, 40 (8): 1796–810.

James, A., Hockey, J. and Dawson, A. (1997) *After Writing Culture: Epistemology and Praxis in Contemporary Anthropology*. London: Routledge.

Kulick, D. and Willson, M. (eds) (1995) *Taboo: Sex, Identity and Erotic Subjectivity in Anthropological Fieldwork*. London: Routledge.

Lee, J. and Ingold, T. (2006) 'Fieldwork on foot: perceiving, routing, socializing', in S. Coleman and P. Collins (eds), *Locating the Field: Space, Place and Context in Anthropology*. Oxford: Berg. pp. 67–86.

MacDougall, D. (1998) *Transcultural Cinema*. Princeton, NJ: Princeton University Press.

MacDougall, D. (2005) *The Corporeal Image: Film, Ethnography, and the Senses*. Princeton, NJ: Princeton University Press.

Marcus, G.E. (1995) 'Ethnography in/of the world system: the emergence of multi-sited ethnography', *Annual Review of Anthropology*, 24: 95–117.

Markham, A.N. and Baym, N.K. (eds) (2009) *Internet Inquiry: Conversations About Method.* Thousand Oaks, CA: Sage.

Marks, L. (2000) *The Skin of the Film.* Durham, NC and London: Duke University Press.

Massey, D. (2005) *For Space.* London: Sage.

Olwig, K.F. and Hastrup, K. (1997) *Siting Culture: The Shifting Anthropological Object.* London: Routledge.

O'Reilly, K. (2009) *Key Concepts in Ethnography.* London: Sage.

Pink, S. (2004) *Home Truths.* Oxford: Berg.

Pink, S. (2006) *The Future of Visual Anthropology.* London: Routledge.

Pink, S. (2007 [2001]) *Doing Visual Ethnography.* London: Sage.

Pink, S. (2008) 'Mobilising visual ethnography: making routes, making place and making images', in *Forum: Qualitative Research (FQS)*, online at www.qualitative-research.net/fqs/fqs-eng.htm.

Pink, S. (2009) *Doing Sensory Ethnography.* London: Sage.

Pink, S. (2011) 'Sensory digital photography: re-thinking "moving" and the image', in *Visual Studies*, 26 (1): 4–13.

Pink, S. (2012) *Situating Everyday Life: Practices and Places.* London: Sage.

GEOMEDIA-BASED METHODS AND VISUAL RESEARCH

Exploring the Theoretical Tenets of the Localization and Visualization of Mediated Social Relations with Direct Visualization Techniques

Francesco Lapenta

Introduction

The adoption of smart phones and portable computers has increased in recent years, reaching 3.3 billion worldwide subscribers in 2007 (ITU), with a projected figure of 5.3 billion subscribers by the end of 2013. This is all the more significant when compared to the 2007 figure of 1.5 billion worldwide registered Internet users (ITU). This is a shared market and there is a popular belief that a big driver of the current mobile industry expansion has been the integration of GPS tools and multimedia functionalities with the characteristic portability of mobile phones. It is moreover predicted that the growth of new features, software and applications will guarantee the growing popularity and increased adoption of smart phones and other portable devices in the next few years. The introduction of the iPhone in 2007 and the iPad in 2010 constituted a cultural and technological shift that imprinted a decisive market move towards a novel interpretation of mobile computing based on increased power, functionality and the constant development of new technical features and their integration with other existing devices and applications. Mobile phones especially have quickly moved from being simple voice-calling devices to flexible and integrated portable devices. They offer scanning, multimedia, imaging, location and other data-capture capabilities within a ubiquitous and flexible computing device that is always available at the fingertips of a mobile user.

These technological shifts not only have implications for the ways we experience and research mediated social relations but also how they are theorized. In the past it was claimed that modern-age communication technologies and media platforms promoted a polarization between two main modes of social interaction (Giddens, 1990). One, face-to-face, is 'context bound' and dominated by 'presence' and 'localized' communications and exchanges; the other, fostered by analogue communication technologies, is independent of space and local contexts and characterized by 'relations between absent others' (Giddens, 1990: 18). Giddens argued that this early stage, technologically induced, evolution of personal communications fundamentally transformed social interaction, creating a characteristically *de-localized* and increasingly *mediated* and globalized society. Giddens's work described the modern shift towards an increasing dominance of mediated and distant social interactions characterized by a 'distanciation of the time and space' (Giddens, 1990: 18) of personal communications. This concept was later embraced by scholars who saw the Internet as a further evolution of spaceless and timeless forms of communication (Fuchs, 2008: 243), interpreting the Internet as a system that 'negates geometry' (Mitchell, 1996: 8) and establishes the 'death of distance' (Cairncross, 1997).

In this chapter, alongside other scholars (Goodchild et al., 2000, 2007; Hine, 2000; Lapenta, 2011; Pink, 2011; Steinberg and Steinberg, 2005; Uricchio, 2011), I critique this de-localized paradigm. I discuss how this contemporary shift towards patterns of relocalization of mediated interactions and the emergence of new heterogeneous time and space dimensions are constructed by and intertwined with new location-based communications technologies. In doing so, I examine how these shifts imply new contexts, new topics, and themes of investigation in, and subsequently advances in, research methodologies for contemporary visual researchers. My central focus is on digital mapping and the electronic and technological bases through which these visualization systems are engaged – which are usually overlooked in the visual methods literature. I will suggest that these new electronic architectures and visualization software and applications frame a context where both new topics and techniques of (visual) sociological research are emerging. On the one hand, because these developments are emergent at the time of writing, this chapter is intended to be speculative, and to open up an *invitation* to readers to participate in the production of this future. On the other hand, I examine some concrete developments and possibilities for visual research in this context, along with a discussion of recent work in this field.

Volunteered geographic information and the geospatial web

While the centrality of space and place has always been taken for granted in geography and regional sciences, as Goodchild and colleagues comment, 'in contrast, in the mainstream of the social sciences, attention to the spatial (and space-time) dimension of phenomena is much less apparent' (Goodchild et al., 2000: 140). This is especially true for the study of new social phenomena developing through the now extended use of Internet-based interactions. Initially, the ubiquitous nature, redefinition of space and fragmentation of time that characterized the Internet (after all, most of what made the Internet unique was based on its unique ability to challenge modern definitions of time, space and identity) might seem to justify claims of 'death of distance' and 'negation of geometry'. However, Goodchild et al. (2000), Goodchild and Donald (2003), Hine (2000), and many other geographers have already called for increased attention in the social sciences for the evaluation of the 'contexts' of what appeared context-less mediated interactions. Goodchild and colleagues' critique (Goodchild et al., 2000; Goodchild and Donald, 2003) remind us that *context* and *location* are fundamental dimensions of sociological research, and that social action, regardless of how abstract or universal in its scope, finds its roots in socio-historical (time and) contexts. Likewise, Hine (2000) was well aware that these preconditions meant that even Internet-based mediated communications and interactions rooted their meanings and contents in established contexts of production and experience. The contemporary context has further implications for these debates in that it is characterized by a fast-paced evolution and adoption of modern location-based technologies, and associated graphic software. These are becoming increasingly embedded in our everyday lives, mediated communications and interactions. In this context, a redefinition of the agenda of media scholars is emerging, which has put such new renewed questions about space, time and context of interaction at the forefront of mainstream scholarly agendas.

Elsewhere I have argued that the contemporary evolution of location-based communication (Lapenta, 2011: 14–22) is two-fold. On the one hand, there is the increasing availability of global positioning systems and augmented reality applications that have opened the way for a new generation of location-based digital communications and mediated interactions. On the other, is the development and emergence of new digital forms of visualization of information and data – the virtual maps of applications such as Google Earth (2005) and Google My Maps (2007), which advance a new geolocational agenda. This, along with a redefinition of the time and space of mediated interactions, is creating a profound renegotiation of the social value and perception of the image, and its function in contemporary mediated exchanges and interactions (Lapenta, 2008, 2011; Uricchio, 2011). This evolution poses a question of method and purpose. It both invites a new theme for social science analysis and also creates a context to which researchers need to adapt their methods and research tools for working in a new social environment in order to take advantage of the possibilities that this evolution offers.

In this chapter, I focus my attention on the visual dimension of this shift to explore the theoretical and methodological implications of these new forms of representation and visualization of communications and social interaction. New location-based communication technologies offer, because of their wide availability, richness of data and inherently visual nature, an unprecedented opportunity for the elaboration of new sociological and 'ethnographic' methods, which go beyond existing approaches to 'netnography' (Kozinets, 1998); 'virtual ethnography' (Hine, 2000); or 'digital ethnography' (Masten and Plowman, 2003) that have hitherto set the agenda. This shift involves engaging with information visualization techniques ('InfoVis' and 'direct visualisation', Manovich, 2011), both to study social realities and to investigate the emerging social practices and social values and norms that their contemporary media-based interactions have come to embody. These new research practices are made possible by recent developments in mobile communications technologies, geolocational tools, and Web 2.0 platforms and social practices that have recently sustained the increasing availability of 'volunteered geographic information' (VGI) (Goodchild, 2007).

Contemporary location-based communication technologies are fostering the exponential growth and availability of VGI. This means the proliferation of the texts, images and sounds recorded and provided voluntarily by users of Web 2.0 applications that geotag and merge such data on live, virtual and navigable maps or augmented reality interfaces. These shared information and contents constitute the building blocks of new geographic information systems (GIS) that utilize 'a system of hardware, software, data, people, organizations, and institutional arrangements' (Dueker and Kjerne, 1989: 8–9) to collect, analyse, compile and distribute data elaborated in the forms established by different geolocational platforms and applications (Wikimapia, OpenStreetMap, Google Earth, Google Maps, Google Places, Google Latitude, Foursquare, Gowalla, Flickr, Facebook Places, MyMaps, etc.). The constant growth of these geomedia-based applications and information represents in many ways a simple evolution of Web 2.0 media users' interest in using the Web to create, assemble and share personal information with peers or the public. Although in some respects they are still emergent, these new Web 2.0 applications might be said to be defining a new geospatial turn and new visual trajectory for the Web. In this late evolution the virtual aspects of individuals' Web 2.0 online interactions, identities and communications are localized and visually merged on a virtual map with the real spaces of users' existence. This offers unprecedented opportunities for the advancement of visual methods, and the development of digital ethnographic approaches, that engage and explore in innovative ways individuals' social realities and their mediated social performances (Hine, 2000).

These opportunities are *embodied* by the virtual map in which these communications and exchanges are visually foregrounded and organized (the 'utopian' map that represents all 'heterotopian' (Foucault, 1967, in Mirzoeff, 2002) virtual maps). In this new *representational* and *projective* space, virtual identities, social networks and interpersonal communications can now be investigated in ways that take advantage of the eminently visual, 'ready made' and organized nature of such representations. By exploring these volunteered geographic information, new digital ethnographic methods can take advantage of new information visualization techniques, 'InfoVis' (Manovich, 2011), to interactively study the data for emerging social patterns and cultural practices. Moreover, these visualization techniques might be used, at a later stage, to display, organize and publish the results of these investigations in forms that might better represent and visualize these new hybrid social spaces, their social interactions and cultural artifacts.

For over two decades, visual scholars have interrogated the heuristic potential of mediated representations as both tools for social inquiry and means for the publication and visualization of the research results. Such emergent methods build on this tradition of sociological and ethnographic methodologies in developing innovative qualitative methods to explore individuals' mediated and social realities.

Volunteered geographic information and the digital visualization of identity

The evolution of mobile phones into integrated multimedia and data-storage devices has further enhanced users' 'emotional attachment' (Vincent, 2006: 117) to mobile phones which are perceived as personalized communications tools used to achieve 'continuous connectivity' to personal and business networks while engendering a feeling of intimacy by being permanently connected with friends and family (Vincent, 2006: 117). A significant element of the personalization of mobile communications involved the transfer of established Web 2.0 and social networking applications to mobile technologies. For instance, email accounts, Facebook profiles, Twitter accounts, online banking, YouTube profiles, Skype accounts and Google's services accounts are but a few of the personalized applications that have moved from the limited mobility of localized computing to the ubiquitous and continuous connectivity of mobile computing. This therefore potentially transforms the mobile into the epicentre of the individual's online existence. This transition, linked with the newly acquired geolocational, imaging and data-acquisition capabilities of smart phones, is pioneering an increase in the production and distribution of volunteered geographic information favoured by the development of new geographic information systems that shape and support existing and new Web 2.0 applications such as Wikimapia, OpenStreetMap, Google Earth or Google Latitude, Google Places, Foursquare, Gowalla, Facebook Places, and countless others.

Goodchild sees the new generation of GPS-enabled computing devices as the interfaces that transform mobile and geomedia users into 'augmented', 'intelligent, mobile sensors' (Goodchild, 2007: 24). Such 'sensors' collectively possess an incredible ability to gather a uniquely rich amount of knowledge and information about the 'surface of the Earth and its properties' (Goodchild, 2007: 24). At the core of this evolution Goodchild identified the evolution of Web 2.0 behaviours and collective projects such as Wikipedia or Google Earth. These projects inspired collective 'meshups', mapping projects like Wikimapia and OpenStreetMap or Google My Maps, that, similarly to Wikipedia, rely on volunteer work and volunteered geographic information to fulfill their aim to map the entire world.

As I have argued elsewhere (Lapenta, 2011), the new virtual map deserves further scrutiny because of the complex social dynamics and developing social functions that it engenders, and because of the significant technological and cultural developments it represents in terms of the representation and visualization of the world.

The virtual map's origin and basic function lies in its capacity to facilitate and organize Geomedia users' collective production and exchange of images, sounds and texts. It does so by visualizing information by means of elaborated 'algorithms' (Uricchio, 2011) that transform bits and pieces of information into a unified image of evolving representations of the world. This visual transformation, or 'algorithmic turn' (Uricchio, 2011: 25), of the representation of the world is leading and is representative of a momentous cultural and technological evolution in which the 'virtual map' embodies a historical function in the re-negotiation of the cultural value and perception of the image (Lapenta, 2011: 14–22; Uricchio, 2011: 25–34). However, the virtual map has further qualities – it moreover may be conceived as a complex, evolving, interactive and live visualization of the social identities, social relations and social interactions of the users that contribute to its composition. The digital symbolic system of the virtual map, the puzzle of countless photographic images, signs, texts and sounds produced and volunteered by geomedia users, represents an intrinsically new social phenomenon. This builds on sociocultural aspects that have been developing throughout the history of the Internet and are finally maturing in geomedia-based Web 2.0 social performances and dynamics. These dynamics have individual and collective significance. Once a disconnected collection of images, data and texts, in the virtual map this wealth of collectively produced information is now readily synthesized, organized in a network of social interactions and exchanges that are finally connected by geomedia technologies to what cannot be disconnected anymore, the individual's physical reality and digital identity.

As a *collective phenomenon* the virtual map has a projective social significance (Lapenta, 2011: 16, 18). In 1967, Debord already described modernity as an immense accumulation of 'spectacles' (Debord, 1983 [1967]: 2), an immense collection of images of every aspect of life that fused in a common stream to create 'a pseudo-world apart'. He characterized the society of the 'spectacle' not as a society simply 'collecting images', but as a system of 'social relations among people, mediated by images' (Debord, 1983 [1967]: §4). In 1991, Jameson described cognitive mapping as the coordination of existential data, the empirical position of the subject, with an abstract conception of an 'unrepresentable' socio-geographic totality (Jameson, 1991: 52). If framed within these theoretical perspectives, the virtual map can be interpreted as a utopian projection, or heterotopian realization, of this unrepresentable socio-geographic totality. More than a mere collection of representations of the world, the virtual map can be interpreted as *a new social space,* a visible articulation of the individual and social mediations of the once disconnected 'world of autonomous images' (Debord, 1983 [1967]) with the 'real' (Poster, 1988), 'cognitive' (Jameson, 1991) and social worlds of their producers. The virtual map can be interpreted as a *projective tool* that transforms our 'cognitive mapping' of the world, from a subject's abstract cognitive projection of an 'unrepresentable' geographic totality, to a collectively produced representation of individuals' merged images, texts and sounds. Thus it becomes the virtual map of a socio-geographic totality that visualizes our individual and collective mediated conditions of existence. As an *identity marker* instead, I suggest (Lapenta, 2011) the virtual map can be critically contextualized as part of a general development in information communications technologies. Synthetically, ICTs have gone through two phases normally referred to (somewhat problematically) as Web 1.0 and Web 2.0. If Web 1.0 can be seen as the initial move towards the simple transfer of content (image, text, sound) to a new digital medium and delivery system (digital information, the computer and the Internet), then Web 2.0 can be interpreted as the reorganization of such distribution of content on the basis of existing and developing social networks. In this new ecosystem, social identity and social interactions have been transformed into data, and data have become part and parcel of online personal identity and mediated social interaction. Age, location, interests, photos and videos, comments and replies, links, friends' lists and groups have all become, according to Sundén (Sundén, 2003), information used in social networking sites (SNS) and online social platforms to 'type oneself into being' (Sundén, 2003: 3). These data serve as exchanged 'identity markers' (West and Turner, 2008: 389) in SNS and are used by users to perform identity and to develop a sense of 'imagined community' (Anderson, 1991). What makes Web 2.0 platforms different from pre-existing forms of mediated-communication is, according to boyd and Ellison, that they 'enable users to articulate and make visible' their social identity and 'social networks' (boyd and Ellison, 2007). The process of production and consumption of images, sounds and texts in SNS can then be interpreted as part of a process of identity elaboration, impression management and self-presentation (Donath and boyd, 2004: 71–82). It is how people maintain relationships, and continuously perform and construct their online social identity and make it visible.

From these interrelated perspectives it is then easy to understand how it was only a question of time (and technological development) before the body, and its location, would become a system of reference used to organize the collective information flows that converge and constitute the virtual map. Geomedia and associated photographic applications, such as Photosynth and Google Earth, seem to represent a first response to this need to organize information in a way that makes it relevant to the body. It is also a way to technologically engage with a multi-sensorial organization of the increasingly multimodal and hybridized (part nature, part information) space of the individual media user (see also Pink, 2011 and in this volume).

The geomedia-based virtual map can therefore be theorized as a mediating space. It is a projective tool, in which two entities and identities converge and merge: the *geosphere*, the sphere of the body and the object, the physical and social environments in which media users communicate and live; and the 'infosphere' (Toffler, 1984), the bits of information, the photographic, iconic or symbolic representations of these physical environments, which media users produce and share (Lapenta, 2011).

Geomedia transform the geo-location of their users, their geosphere, into data, and connect these data to existing information that describe the user's online activities and identity (and his/her infosphere). By means of software applications (Foursquare, Bliin.comx, Google Latitude, Photosynth, QuickTime VR, Places iPhoto 2009, Layar, Ekin.net), geomedia platforms connect and merge, on a live navigable virtual map (Google Earth, Google Maps, Live Maps, etc), the user's physical location and the ever-increasing wealth of information that they produce as part of their online social interactions. Once a disconnected collection of images, data and texts, the infosphere is now readily synthesized on the virtual map, organized in a network of social interactions and exchanges and connected by geomedia technologies to one's individual physical reality and one's own digital identity.

Geomedia become then a tool used by subjects to navigate their social worlds, to organize their local social relations, and to maintain their networked 'latent ties' (boyd and Ellison, 2007). The photographic virtual map becomes the tool used to project, organize and make visible these social performances, personal mediated identities, and 'imagined' communities. As such, the new virtual map can also be interpreted as a new social space in which social interactions and communications and their multimedia forms of representation are readily organized for observation. Such vast amounts of data and social and cultural significations, often public and readily volunteered by media users, constitute a social world that could appropriately be explored by new forms of ethnographic and sociological methods. Such methods would be designed to investigate the social systems and social worlds represented by these new hybrid, interconnected, social spaces as well as the new forms of cultural production, value elaboration, mediated social interactions, communications, and exchanges among individuals and entire communities.

Opening up new methods in visual research: the algorithmic turn and the digital visualization of information

Above I have described the new virtual map as a projective visualization of the collective and social identities and social interactions of the users that contribute to its formation. Such developments invite new topics for, and methods of, visual qualitative research. Yet in what follows I go beyond the usual discussions of how technologies may be used in research methods. In doing so, I examine the implications of the *technological basis* of these potential digital research tools for their use in new forms of visual research.

The virtual map is evidence of another technological change, which is linked to the development of new software and hardware platforms designed to handle and reassemble this wealth of data and information. This software, which relies on the ever-increasing computing power of mobiles and portable devices, uses mathematical equations and designed algorithms and criteria to compare, combine and represent images (texts and sounds) in simulated 2D or 3D renditions of available information and data. These algorithms are the building tools that construct the virtual maps of the world, designed and developed to manage vast quantities of information, and assemble them according to specified tasks and criteria. In the case of visual mapping of multimedia data and information, well-known examples of these software applications are Google Maps, Google Street Views or Photosynth, in which composite photographic images are merged to display photographic renditions of physical environments and specific locations, or augmented reality (AR) applications such as Layer or Wikitude that 'overlay existing physical reality with an additional (augmented) layer, making visible information that can only be seen through a lens or on a screen' (Uricchio, 2011: 31).

Photosynth, an application developed by Microsoft Live Labs in collaboration with the University of Washington, generates a navigable three-dimensional model of a series of photographs taken in the same area. The software works in two steps. Multiple images taken in the same area are processed and analysed using interest-point detection and matching algorithms. Once the images' matching points have been captured, the software generates a points cloud that generates a 3D map of the positions and angles of each picture. The Photosynth viewer then uses this points cloud to created a navigable 3D rendition of the photographs that allows the user to seamlessly 'move' among the overlaid and juxtaposed pictures. Very similarly to Photosynth, Google Maps and Google Street View use custom-made photographs of physical spaces and locations to generate a seamless 2D or 3D navigable composite image of contiguous locations. In the case of Google Street View, the images are generated by an 11-lens camera called 'Dodeca 2360'. The camera, patented by Immersive Media, captures very high resolution, 360-degree video and geodata from a unified camera system configured according to a dodecahedral sphere (a 12-sided sphere). The video is then post-processed to select a number of (360 degree) frames that are then linearly arranged according to a 2D points cloud to provide the illusion of seamless 3D linear movement in space in a fashion very similar to the one used in Photosynth.

On the opposite side of the spectrum, there are applications that take advantage of the scanning, multimedia, imaging, location and other data-capture capabilities integrated in smart phones to use the physical space as the activating background of a new projected layer of information generated by users and designers. Such augmented reality applications, Uricchio explains, currently use three established systems 'to link the real and the virtual'. One system, the most primitive of the three, uses 'fiduciary markers' or 'coded tags that are physically attached to the object for which an overlay is sought' (Uricchio, 2011: 31). The second and currently dominating method uses a triangulation among 'geo-positioned data, GPS (Global Positioning Systems), a compass and an accelerometer' to provide geographically relevant information. The last and more interesting of the three finally uses 'nature feature tracking' (Uricchio, 2011: 31). This represents a fast-emerging system that is particularly interesting for its similitudes with the previous geo-mapping applications (Google Maps, Google Street View, Photosynth):

> *Natural feature tracking* systems represent a fast-emerging image technology that assigns data to location by making visual correlations between physical places (i.e. 'recognising' them) and the information to be appended. An image-recognition system, it

requires the user to position sights within a viewfinder, which the algorithms then process to find any correlations with the stored database. The system's search for unique identity points is conceptually related to Photosynth, except that in this case, the user is in the physical world attempting to correlate real and virtual data in order to trigger a virtual graphic overlay. (Uricchio, 2011: 31–2)

Such software applications represent instances of what Uricchio calls the 'algorithmic turn' (Uricchio, 2011: 25), and I define, paraphrasing Baudrillard, as the fifth 'geolocational' order of the simulacrum (Lapenta, 2011: 17–18), an evolution of graphic forms and photographic representations that are transforming the once binary relation of the image with its objects of reference into a multitude of algorithmic geo-reinterpretations. The algorithmic turn is characterized according to Uricchio by different forms of 'algorithmic intervention' and the emergence of new 'algorithmic regimes' (Uricchio, 2011: 31), such as the ones constructed by different software and applications like Google Street View, Photosynth or Layers, 'that now stand between the object and its representation' (Uricchio, 2011: 31) and are based on a different interpretation of location and space as the unifying and organizing principle (Lapenta, 2011).

Uricchio follows Culler's (1990) postmodern critique of the concept of 'authentic' as 'something unmarked or undifferentiated' (Uricchio, 2011: 34) to interpret authenticity as a 'sign relation' (Uricchio, 2011: 34) that, as Culler writes, prevents 'one from thinking of signs and sign relations as corruptions of what ought to be a direct experience of reality' (Culler, 1990: 9, in Uricchio, 2011: 34), but rather demonstrates 'that salient features of the social and natural world are articulated by what Percy calls "symbolic complexes" which are revelation of "the structural incompleteness of experience" and "its dependency on markers"' (Uricchio, 2011: 9). According to this interpretation, a rhetorical concept, that of 'the map of the empire' (the signifying system, the map, that wants to replace its system of reference, reality), can be transformed and interpreted as a social and experiential phenomenon, 'the virtual map', that composed by algorithmic representations (new digital signs and markers) interacts with, rather than replaces (or assumes the existence of an unmarked) reality.

The logic that informs the interpretation of the algorithmic turn has long-reaching consequences. Some refer to the epistemological value of the evolving relations between the object and its representation and the function of the specific algorithm designed for their representations. Others refer to the socio-cultural consequences of these different emerging 'algorithmic regimes' and their social functions. It is at the intersection of these two dimensions of the visual algorithmic turn that we can speculate about the heuristic potential of these algorithmic visualizations, and how they can be used or framed in new or old methods and theories of (visual) sociology (Goodchild and Donald, 2003; Steinberg and Steinberg, 2005) or ethnography relating to 'netnography' (Kozinets, 1997); 'virtual ethnography' (Hine, 2000) or 'digital ethnography' (Masten and Plowman, 2003); or GIS-based ethnography (Brennan-Horley et al., 2010; Matthews et al., 2005). This would involve not only studying the social and cultural effects of this evolution, but also elaborating on the heuristic potential of these new forms of algorithmic visualization, and exploring the methodological potential of new data and information visualization techniques for social research and publication.

The algorithmic as a cognitive projective tool: direct visualizations as a research method

Manovich's discussion of the heuristic potential of the contemporary transformation of information visualization (InfoVis) into what he calls 'direct visualization' of information (Manovich, 2011: 36) provides a starting point for considering how new forms of visualization might be engaged in research. Although it is not easy to define what exactly InfoVis may be today, Manovich uses a provisional definition that describes modern InfoVis 'as a mapping between discrete data and a visual representation' (Manovich, 2011: 37) that 'utilizes computer graphics and interaction to assist humans in solving problems' (Purchase, 2008: 46–64, in Manovich, 2011). At the core of information visualization, Thomas and Cook (2005) state, there is the assumption that 'visual representations and interaction techniques take advantage of the human eye's broad bandwidth pathway into the mind to allow users to see, explore, and understand large amounts of information at once' (Thomas and Cook, 2005: 30).

From its inception nearly 300 years ago, one of the defining characteristics of InfoVis has been its *reduction* of large amounts of data and information to graphic signifiers. Here 'reduction' is not intended as 'resampling', as when a full-resolution image is reduced to a smaller image, but as a reduction of the data to a different signifying, graphical element. Old forms of information visualization use graphic 'reductions' for the sake of data's cognitive significance and intellectual maneuverability (as in the case of original information visualization techniques that use 'line graphs', 'bar charts', 'pie charts' and 'circle graphs' to reduce data to significant and graphically described quantities and relations, or the analogue maps that reduce the world to graphic essentials for the sake of cognitive synthesis). Because of the computational power of contemporary graphic devices, for the first time in the history of InfoVis, scholars and designers are able to use data in its multimodal 'original' form (be it text, audio, photo or video). A full multimedia dataset can be used and graphically represented in interactive visual representations, which faithfully to the original heuristic intention of InfoVis, can help researchers to observe the data while changing their interrelations according to variable parameters (or algorithms) and forms of visualization. Manovich refers to this method as 'direct visualization', or 'visualization without reduction'. Direct visualization, Manovich states, does not 'substitute media objects with new objects (i.e. graphical primitives …) which only communicate selected properties', but preserves the 'much richer set of properties' of the original data objects to demonstrate 'that in order to highlight patterns in the data we don't have to reduce it by representing data objects via abstract graphical elements' (Manovich, 2011: 41). Indeed, Manovich is well aware of the research potential of such direct visualization techniques; he proposes:

> If scholars of the humanities start systematically using visualization for research, teaching and public presentation of cultural artifacts and processes, the ability to show the artifacts in full detail is crucial. Displaying the actual visual media as opposed to representing it by graphical primitives helps the researcher to understand meaning and/or cause behind the pattern she may observe, as well as discover additional patterns. (Manovich, 2011: 48)

And:

> Therefore creating visualization out of media is not just a nod to humanities tradition – it is an approach to visualization which is perfectly suited to particular methods and data of the humanities – i.e. cultural artifacts, and, more recently, people's communication and social activities related to these artifacts which happen on social networks. (Manovich, 2010: 8)

I agree with Manovich and others (Card et al., 1999; Kerren et al., 2008) that the social sciences and humanities should take advantage of the opportunities presented by contemporary visualization technologies, and direct visualization techniques, to study society, its relations and cultural artifacts. Moreover, it is in this context that I suggest that geolocational data, the virtual maps, the visualization software and the applications that use multimedia volunteered geographic information should be interpreted as one, albeit very significant, form of such direct visualization. It is a matter of simple theoretical repositioning to understand the modern digital virtual map as one of such forms of direct visualization, and a matter of methodological evolution and theoretical elaboration to describe different geolocational algorithms and mapping applications as alternative organizing principles (Lapenta, 2011), and visualization tools, that allow the investigation of a (multimedia) dataset according to different cognitive scopes, interpretative schemes and research-designed tasks.

Manovich's *Cinema Redux* (Dawes, 2004), *Preservation of Selected Traces* (Fry, 2009) and *Listening Post* (Rubin and Hansen, 2001) (in Manovich, 2011: 41) provide examples of modern direct visualization projects that manipulated their unreduced data for meaningful intellectual re-elaboration. Likewise, I suggest that Google Street View, Layer, Photosynth, Google My Maps and other visualization applications, faithful to InfoVis's original cognitive function, provide access to a visually synthesized, hence intellectually accessible, socio-geographic totality (Jameson, 1991) that should be utilized by researchers to correlate, visualize and investigate individual relations and social networks, meanings and cultural relations, or any other set of theoretical hypotheses.

Google My Maps: a case for the utilization of Participatory Geographic Information Systems (PGIS) for the development of new direct visualization methods and research

We are at an early stage in the adoption of direct visualization of geomedia-based data for research. Yet this area of research practice is likely to expand as researchers engage with the increasing availability of volunteered geographic information (VGI), the cheap or free availability of geographic information systems (GIS) and the continuous development of software and applications (like Photosynth or Google My Maps) that enable the visual correlation, merging and manipulation of geolocational multimedia information. As the tools expand, so will debate about the possibilities of new location-based, direct visualization-based methods for cultural and social research. This chapter therefore does not aim to offer a comprehensive overview of the software applications, nor evolving methods or projects, that use volunteered geographic information and new location-based direct visualization techniques. Rather, in order to reflect on an actual research application of location-based technologies and virtual maps based on Google My Maps, I discuss one recent project that utilizes virtual mapping, 'The new cartographers: crisis map mashups and the emergence of neogeographic practice' by Liu and Palen (Liu and Palen, 2010). First I situate new forms of virtual mapping within the context of the use of mapping as a visual research technique.

A number of tools are already available for the researcher, including applications such as Photosynth (described above) and 'Google My Maps' – a personal-mapping application feature of Google Maps that lets users create and share personalized, annotated maps of their world. This application, which requires basic computer skills, allows users to create a personalized map that visually overlays a standard Google Earth or Google Maps with locations and/ or areas of interest that are tagged and coded. These points or areas of interest can be enriched with metadata that embeds personal texts (Google Docs database, pdf or simple texts), images, videos and hyperlinks on the Google Earth map, which already offers a rich browsing experience including 3D terrain and buildings and various content layers. The personalized map can be made 'public' or be 'unlisted'. Public maps are fully integrated and searchable via Google search tools. Maps are also 'sharable' with a designated group of collaborators who have full access to the personalized map created by the initial user. The new personalized map will also download as a KML file onto a computer, which allows a user to view the map, email it, or post it on a website or make it available for anyone to download.

Applications like Google My Maps can be contextualized within the historical development and function of 'participatory mapping' (Chambers, 2006, 2008) and its late evolution into PGIS (Participatory Geographic Information Systems) and maps mashups (Liu and Palen, 2010). The systematic creation of participatory maps started in the late 1980s, developed by rural appraisal practitioners (Rambaldi et al., 2004, 2006) using participatory methods to 'elicit indigenous knowledge' and 'local community dynamics' (Rambaldi et al., 2006: 1) while facilitating communications between community members and researchers. While the practice of drawing maps by local people can be traced back centuries and has been widely popular in modern times, Chambers notices that its systematic utilization as a method for research and knowledge creation has really been developed in the last 20 years within the specialized areas of geography, social anthropology (see also Grasseni, Chapter 6, and Pink, Chapter 7, this volume), participatory action research, visual sociology, and education (Chambers, 2006: 2). This changed dramatically in the late 1990s, with the diffusion of modern spatial information technologies and the development of Geographic Information systems (GIS) that peaked in 2005 and 2007 with the creation and public distribution of projects such as Google Earth, Google Maps and Google My Maps. These and other mapping projects and tools (Wikimapia, OpenStreetMap, Photosynth, etc.) have deeply influenced GIS-based participatory mapping tools (PGIS, Participatory Geographic Information Systems) across the world. Today PGIS are widely used to create 'mashup' maps (a term used primarily to indicate new electronic practices of VGI sharing) that:

> combine a range of geo-spatial information management tools and methods such as sketch maps, participatory 3D models (P3DM), aerial photographs, satellite imagery, Global Positioning

> Systems (GPS) and Geographic Information Systems (GIS) to
> represent people's spatial knowledge in the forms of virtual or
> physical, 2 or 3 dimensional maps used as interactive vehicles
> for spatial learning, discussion, information exchange, analysis,
> decision making and advocacy. (Rambaldi et al., 2006: 2)

Liu and Palen make a case for the use of participatory mapping, or mashup maps, as a research method to conduct research in the sociology of disaster (and as a tool to respond to disasters) (Dynes, 1970; Neal, 1997; Powell, 1954; Stoddard, 1968 – all in Liu and Palen, 2010). The sociology of disaster uses 'spatial and temporal models to describe and anticipate macro social behavior' (Liu and Palen, 2010: 69). Typically, the real-time codification and classification of time-and-space models are important heuristic devices in the sociology of disaster: since disasters are generally characterized by different phases and zones. Liu and Palen describe the geography of disaster as based on a series of concentric zones: a centre affected by a very severe impact, surrounded by fringe areas characterized by a diversified level of damage and disruption. Four phases are used, traditionally, to describe the macro-behaviours in the event of a disaster: 'preparedness, response, recovery, and mitigation' (Powell, 1954, in Liu and Palen, 2010). Kraak (Kraak, 2001, in Liu and Palen, 2010) and Liu and Palen point out that maps are fundamental tools that help prompt decision-making in the actual event of a disaster. They are also key tools that aid us to rethink the dynamics of disasters. The rise of what is known as Geospatial Web has supported the growth of web-based map mashups that result from the increased use of social media and Web 2.0 practices that support participatory forms of 'neogeography' (Goodchild, 2009) in which many users share collaboratively – with applications such as Google My Maps – minute-by-minute updated information about the events of a disaster. Liu and Palen (2010) maintain that these practices increase the 'ability to tease apart actual behavior in disasters and pinpoint the multi-dimensionality of the experience and its effects on social life'. They go on to suggest that 'in particular, map-based "mashups," through the use of frequently updated data from multiple sources, allow us to "see" micro-behavior spatio-temporally' while providing up-to-date information that helps the 'practical work of reporting on, assisting in, and managing emergencies' (Liu and Palen 2010: 69–70).

Conclusions

This example demonstrates the evolving social functions, and the possible methodological potential, of new direct information visualization techniques that use volunteered geolocational data to study, and contextualize, complex and evolving social occurrences and phenomena. The full potential of direct visualization-based methods is still emerging, as is its theoretical and methodological definition. In this article I have suggested that existing geolocational software and applications (such as Google My Maps and Photosynth) can be interpreted and used as new research tools for direct visualization-based methods and investigations. Very much like the photographs and videos of the visual sociologists of the analogue age (who observed these media through the lens of established sociological theories, methods and aims), new augmented reality (AR) and geomedia can be used by the skilled researcher of the digital age to tap into the vast research potential of volunteered geographic information and participatory geographic information systems.

It is in this context that virtual maps, and the algorithmic software that support them, can become methodological tools that skilled, media literate scholars might use to compare, merge and interpret the increasing amount of geolocationally tagged multimedia data and information (shared by contemporary Web 2.0 media users) to explore meanings and/or causes behind the patterns that may be observed in geolocationally synthesized visualizations. Such patterns and meanings might indeed not have been visible in the unorganized chaos of forms and contents of the unarranged data. These new technologies thus become meaningful elements to project, organize, make visible and study the social performances, personal identities, mediated interactions and the 'imagined' communities of the media users that created them.

Bibliography

Anderson, B.R. (1991) *Imagined Communities: Reflections on the Origin and Spread of Nationalism.* London: Verso.

boyd, d.m. (2007) 'The significance of social software', in T.N. Burg and J. Schmidt (eds), *BlogTalks Reloaded: Social Software Research & Cases.* Norderstedt: Books on Demand. pp. 15–30.

boyd, d.m. (2008) 'None of this is real', in J. Karaganis (ed.), *Structures of Participation in Digital Culture.* New York: Social Science Research Council. pp. 132–57.

boyd, d.m. and Ellison, N.B. (2007) 'Social network sites: definition, history, and scholarship', *Journal of Computer-Mediated Communication*, 13 (1): article 11. Available at http://jcmc.indiana.edu/vol13/issue1/boyd.ellison.html

Brennan-Horley, C., Luckman, S., Gibson, C. and Willoughby-Smith, J. (2010) 'GIS, ethnography, and cultural research: putting maps back into ethnographic mapping', *The Information Society: An International Journal*, 26 (2): 92–103.

Cairncross, L. (1997) *The Death of Distance: How the Communications Revolution Will Change Our Lives.* Boston, MA: Harvard Business School Press.

Card, S.K., Mackinlay, J.D. and Shneiderman, B. (1999) *Readings in Information Visualization: Using Vision to Think*. San Francisco, CA: Morgan Kaufmann Publishers.

Chambers, R. (2006) 'Participatory mapping and geographic information systems: Whose map? Who is empowered and who disempowered? Who gains and who loses?', *The Electronic Journal on Information Systems in Developing Countries (EJISDC)*, 25 (2): 1–11.

Chambers, R. (2008) 'PRA, PLA and pluralism: practice and theory', in P. Reason and H. Bradbury (eds), *The Sage Handbook of Action Research: Participative Inquiry and Practice*. London: Sage.

Culler, J. (1990) *Framing the Sign: Criticism and its Institutions*. Norman, OK: University of Oklahoma Press.

Debord, G. (1983 [1967]) *Society of the Spectacle*. London: Rebel Press.

Donath, J. and boyd, d.m. (2004) 'Public displays of connection', *BT Technology Journal*, 22 (4): 71–82.

Dueker, K. and Kjerne, D. (1989) *Multipurpose Cadastre: Terms and Definitions*. Falls Church, VA: American Society for Photogrammetry and Remote Sensing and American Congress on Surveying and Mapping (ASPRS-ACSM).

Fuchs, C. (2008) *Internet and Society: Social Theory in the Information Age*. London: Routledge.

Giddens, A. (1990) *The Consequences of Modernity*. Stanford, CA: Stanford University Press.

Goodchild, M.F. (2007) 'Citizens as sensors: the world of volunteered geography', *GeoJournal*, 69 (4): 211–21.

Goodchild, M.F. (2009) 'Neogeography and the nature of geographic expertise', *Journal of Location Based Services*, 3 (2): 82–96.

Goodchild, M.F. and Donald, G.F. (2003) *Spatially Integrated Social Science*. New York: Oxford University Press.

Goodchild, M.F., Anselin, L., Appelbaum, R. and Harthorn, B. (2000) 'Toward spatially integrated social science', *International Regional Science Review*, 23 (2): 139–59.

Hine, C. (2000) *Virtual Ethnography*. Thousand Oaks, CA: Sage.

Jameson, F. (1991) *Postmodernism, or, the Cultural Logic of Late Capitalism*. London: Verso.

Kerren, A., Stasko, J.T., Fekete, J.D. and North, C. (eds) (2008) *Information Visualization – Human-Centered Issues and Perspectives. Volume 4950 of LNCS State-of-the-Art Survey*. London: Springer.

Kozinets, R.V. (1997) 'Want to believe: a netnography of the "X-Philes" subculture of consumption', in. R.V. Kozinets (ed.), *Advances in Consumer Research*. Provo, UT: Association for Consumer Research.

Kozinets, R.V. (1998) 'On netnography: initial reflections on consumer research investigations of cyberculture', in J. Alba and W. Hutchinson (eds), *Advances in Consumer Research* (Volume 25). Provo, UT: Association for Consumer Research. pp. 366–71.

Lapenta, F. (2008) *Define Geomedia*. Online publication available at www.francescolapenta.wordpress.com/2008/06/26/define-geomedia-and-web-30.

Lapenta, F. (2011) 'Geomedia: on location-based media, the changing status of collective image production and the emergence of social navigation systems', *Visual Studies*, 26 (1): 14–22.

Levy, P. (1997) *Collective Intelligence: Mankind's Emerging World in Cyberspace*. Cambridge: Perseus.

Liu, S.B. and Palen, L. (2010) 'The new cartographers: crisis map mashups and the emergence of neogeographic practice', available from www.thefreelibrary.com/The new cartographers: crisis map mashups and the emergence of...-a0219655235 (retrieved 25 October 2011).

Manovich, L. (2010) 'What is visualization?' Draft available at http://manovich.net/articles/ (accessed March 2011).

Manovich, L. (2011) 'What is visualisation?', *Visual Studies*, 26 (1): 36–49.

Masten, D. and Plowman, T. (2003) 'Digital ethnography: the next wave in understanding the consumer experience', *Design Management Journal*, 14 (2): 75–81.

Matthews, S.A., Detwiler, J.E. and Burton, L.M. (2005) 'Geo-ethnography: coupling geographic information analysis techniques with ethnographic methods in urban research', *Cartographica*, 40 (4): 75–90.

Mirzoeff, N. (ed.) (2002) *The Visual Culture Reader*. London: Routledge.

Mitchell, W.J. (1996) *City of Bits, Space Place and the Infobahn*. Cambridge, MA: MIT Press.

Palfrey, J. and Gasser, U. (2008) *Born Digital: Understanding the First Generation of Digital Natives*. New York: Basic Books.

Pink, S. (2011) 'Sensory digital photography: re-thinking "moving" and the image', in *Visual Studies*, 26 (1): 4–13.

Poster, M. (ed.) (1988) *Jean Baudrillard: Selected Writings*. Stanford, CA: Stanford University Press.

Rambaldi, G., Kwaku Kyem, A.P., Mbile, P., McCall, M. and Weiner, D. (2004) 'Participatory GIS' (retrieved 15 January 2011 from: www.iapad.org/participatory_gis.htm).

Rambaldi, G., Kwaku Kyem, A.P., Mbile, P., McCall, M. and Weiner, D. (2006) 'Participatory spatial information management and communication in developing countries', *EJISDC*, 25 (1): 1–9 (retrieved 30 September 2010 from: ejisdc.org).

Steinberg, S.J. and Steinberg, S.L. (2005) *Geographic Information Systems for the Social Sciences.* Thousand Oaks, CA: Sage.

Sundén, J. (2003) *Material Virtualities, Approaching Online Textual Embodiment.* New York: Peter Lang.

Thomas, J. and Cook, K.A. (eds) (2005) *Illuminating the Path: The R&D Agenda for Visual Analytics.* National Visualization and Analytics Center: IEEE Press.

Toffler, A. (1984) *The Third Wave.* New York: Bantam Books.

Uricchio, W. (2011) 'The algorithmic turn: Photosynth, augmented reality and the changing implications of the image', *Visual Studies,* 26 (1): 25–35.

Vincent, J. (2006) 'Emotional attachment and mobile phones', *Knowledge, Technology, and Policy,* 19 (1): 29–44.

West, R. and Turner, L. (2008) *Understanding Interpersonal Communication: Making Choices in Changing Times.* Belmont, CA: Wadsworth.

PART 4
PUBLIC SCHOLARSHIP, ARTS AND VISUAL INTERVENTION

With an increasing demand for the social sciences to have 'impact' outside academia and the enthusiasm of visual scholars to do research that reaches a wider public, new methodological questions and approaches are being generated. The three chapters in Part 4 reflect on how visual methodologies can produce creative connections between scholarship, arts and public/applied interventions. They continue themes established in earlier sections, to examine the senses, interdisciplinarity, applied research and how digital technologies reshape visual practices. Each author engages with arts practice and its relationship to scholarship from a different perspective. Yet collectively they demonstrate that theory, arts practice and the production of public texts are co-implicated in the ways visual methodologies are advancing. In Chapter 9, Maggie O'Neill draws on 20 years of research to discuss a methodological process that connects ethnographic practice, participatory arts and public scholarship through her work in the field of cultural criminology. In Chapter 10, Christina Lammer reflects on a set of collaborative research practices she has developed over the last 10 years, working across social sciences, medicine and arts practice. Originally trained in sociology, Lammer works in collaborative relationships with surgeons and established artists (across a range of different media), as well as with the participants in her research. In Chapter 11, Rod Coover, a documentary artist, develops an innovative conversational essay. Coover collaborates with scholars and artists in his very text as he talks with Pat Badani, Flavia Caviezel, Mark Marino, Nitin Sawhney and William Uricchio, sounding the reader with their discussion of how digital technologies are transforming visual practices. Each chapter creates a truly interdisciplinary blend of approaches that involves arts and documentary practice, the social sciences and humanities in creating routes to public and applied scholarship.

9

ETHNO-MIMESIS AND PARTICIPATORY ARTS

Maggie O'Neill

This chapter draws upon two decades of interdisciplinary ethno-mimetic[1] research conducted with marginalised groups to both illustrate and think through the relationship between ethnography (especially biographical research), participatory arts and public scholarship. It argues that interdisciplinary analysis is required to deal with the complexity of the issues involved and offers understanding as praxis (purposeful knowledge) drawing upon innovative, participatory, performative and policy oriented research. Visual interventions with sex workers, refugees, asylum seekers and community arts organisations are discussed with reference to the developing field of cultural criminology and the transformative role of art.

In the early 1990s, whilst researching Adorno's aesthetics of modernism (that was rooted in previous research on the transformative role of art and creativity), I began to reflect upon the methodological advances of bringing together sociologists and artists to work together on specific issues. At that time, my scholarly work was rooted in critical theory, western Marxism and feminism. I defined my research as being committed to challenging and changing sexual and social inequalities with individuals/groups/communities using participatory approaches. This involved exploring the inter-textuality across the arts and social sciences when examining lived cultures, as well the transformative role of connecting arts-based work and social research in research projects. I aimed to explore the sensuousness of ethnography and our immersion in the life worlds of participants as well as valuing their knowledge, experience and expertise, so I looked for ways of exploring and representing the complexity of psychic and social lived relations by combining art and ethnography. One of the central themes of this early work was the development of renewed methodologies for socio-cultural research as ways of working and writing in societies that are post-traditional but are marked also by the traditional; and, if we agree with Stjepan Mestrovic (1997), in societies that are post-emotional but also contain possibilities of and for authenticity.

Mestrovic argued that contemporary western societies are entering a new phase of development where 'synthetic, quasi-emotions become the basis for widespread manipulation by self, others, and the culture industry as a whole' (1997: xi). What he calls 'Postemotional types' are able to 'feel' a vast array of emotions without necessarily being motivated to action. In the post-emotional society, emotions have not disappeared but rather – a 'new hybrid of intellectualized, mechanical, mass produced emotions has appeared on the world scene' (1997: 26). Moreover, in the West we are suffering in part from compassion fatigue (1997: 33). Post-emotionalism, for Mestrovic, is a 'new theoretical construct to capture the Balkanization, ethnic violence, and other highly *emotional* phenomena of the late 1990s that are being treated mechanically – and not just in the Balkans but throughout the industrialized West' (1997: 40). Mestrovic draws upon Adorno's thesis regarding the growth and power of the culture industry in helping to create and sustain an almost totally administered society, where spaces to think and feel critically are constantly diminishing.[2] Our cultural life is being turned into a perpetual round of entertainment; we absorb media images in a state of relative inattention. Post-emotionalism is indicative of a contemporary 'me dominated' and media-saturated society that induces a degree of pessimism and paralysis in our responses to the crisis and plight of others. This paralysis is a marker of post-emotionalism. We turn the page, switch off – unmoved. Keeping open spaces to think and feel is central to the developing field of cultural criminology. Rooted in the Birmingham school of Cultural Studies, in critical criminology, as well as symbolic interactionist and ethnographic approaches to crime and deviance, there is a focus on the everyday meanings of crime and transgression, phenomenological analysis, as well as methodologies that are predominantly ethnographic, textual, and visual: 'Cultural criminology explores the many ways in which cultural dynamics intertwine with the practices of crime and crime control in contemporary society' (Ferrell, 2007).

Working in participatory ways (at that time with sex workers and communities affected by sex working) involved resisting such paralysis, blurring boundaries, questioning the notion of universal knowledge and the division between knowledge, reason and power and 'whose knowledge counts'. I felt that my research was in many ways indicative of what Bauman (1992) described as characteristic of 'interpretive sociology' but that we might also call 'public sociology' or 'public scholarship': 'a clarifier of interpretive rules and facilitator of communication: this will amount to the replacement of the dream of the legislator with the practice of the interpreter' (Bauman, 1992: 204). This interpretive sociological work is rooted in Marx's dictum that as philosophers we should not only aim to understand and explain the social world but should also seek to change it, to transform it. In order to understand the world we need to engage with lived experience as well as to explore structures and processes which serve to enable and/or constrain our actions and meanings and practices (Giddens, 1984);

but we also need to engage with intra-subjectivity and the more sensory ways that people engage in, describe and explore their social worlds.

For example, 'Not all the time ... but mostly ...', a partnership between myself and Sara Giddens, a performing arts lecturer, that began in 1996, involved working with a dancer (undergraduate student), a sound recordist, a film maker, and a photographer to create ethno-mimetic retelling of the life stories of sex workers through a live art performance and a short video of the performance piece. We were interested in the process of working at the borders of social research and arts practice and in reflecting upon the transformative, change-causing gesture involved in participatory action research and, in this case, performance art. We worked with some of my interview transcripts, which were anonymised. The process also involved discussion about the transcripts, which included interpreting the data based on key themes, images, rhythms and moments – parts of the many stories contained within the transcripts that were meaningful and resonant to us. The text, images and sounds used in the video were finalised and agreed through discussions between the collaborators (copyright for the dance and video/DVD are with Sara, as the artist). The material was shared with my interviewees to get their feedback before we went public with the work. Their responses were very positive indeed. The sensory nature of the performance and sharing this work with a broader audience beyond the usual academic one was important to us. The work challenged myths and stereotypes around 'the prostitute' and enabled the audience to engage with the flesh-and-blood woman behind the label and understand something of her life and lived experiences.

Hence, the work described here takes a primarily phenomenological approach to understand the processes and practices of our socio-cultural worlds, and the everyday lived experiences and meaning-making practices we engage in. There is also a focus upon collaborative and participatory ways of working with groups and communities that might include praxis (purposeful knowledge) to reach a broader audience beyond academic communities, challenge identitarian thinking and support interventions in policy and practice. In other words, there is a focus upon public scholarship.

Public scholarship

Public sociology is defined by Michael Burawoy and Jonathan Vanantwerpen as:

> a sociology that is oriented toward major problems of the day, one that attempts to address them with the tools of social science, and in a manner often informed by historical and comparative perspectives ... designed to promote public reflection on significant social issues. (Burawoy and VanAntwerpen, 2001: 1)

Burawoy and VanAntwerpen (2001) see sociology as organised around four types that can overlap and even be conducted by the same individual. These types are: professional (claiming an Archimedean point outside of the world it studies); policy (marked by instrumentally serving the needs of various clients); critical (marked by reflexivity and critical analysis of professional sociology that 'denies the very possibility of detachment and insulation, and denounces the pretence of professional sociology as an act of interested self-deception') (Burawoy and VanAntwerpen, 2001: 2–3); and public (designed to promote public reflection on significant social issues). What underpins these debates and other contributors to the debate, such as Loader and Sparks' (2010) *Public Criminology*, is the analysis of the role of the state and governance in the commissioning, production and dissemination of social science research.

Haggerty (2004) discusses the impact of the rise of neo-liberal forms of governance on the increasingly superfluousness and interventionary potential of criminological research. Alongside the growth of administrative criminology the neo-liberal focus on the individual as responsible for her own fate, welfare and security has impacted upon a shift away from criminology rooted in sociological analysis to a focus upon the 'monitoring and control of risky individuals and dangerous places' (Haggerty, 2004: 218) through increasingly technocratic and administrative criminology. For Haggarty, the bottom line is that 'the state is interested in a fairly narrow set of questions: They want help in running the state. They want research based on the problems as defined by the state ... Research evidence is rapidly becoming subservient to political expediency' rather than 'being the soil from which sound governmental policy emerges' (Haggarty, 2004: 219).

For Bauman (1992) there is little choice to be made between an engaged or neutral way of doing sociology. For a 'noncommittal sociology is an impossibility ... The job of sociology is to see to it that the choices are genuinely free and that they remain so, increasingly so, for the duration of humanity' (Bauman, 1992: 369). With this in mind I propose that critical and cultural analysis using participatory methods could move us beyond the binaries of legislative research that serves the purposes of the state and interpretive research that is easily ignored by government. Such research could also help us: access a richer understanding of the complexities and experiences of marginalised groups; develop knowledge and analysis that might foster a more radically democratic imaginary that challenges the exclusionary discourses which feed the paralysis Mestrovic talks about; and connect to more relational ways of promoting social justice and social change.

Participatory action research is one way of doing this, and combining arts and ethnographic/participatory research through what I termed 'ethno-mimesis' is another. In recent work (O'Neill, 2010), within the framework of cultural and critical criminology, I argue that ethno-mimesis can lead to the production of knowledge and a radical democratisation of images and texts that can move us, pierce us, challenge identity thinking and bring us in touch with our feeling worlds in subjective, reflexive ways that might intervene in public scholarship.

Participatory action research (PAR)[3]

Participatory action research (PAR) involves a commitment to research that: develops partnership responses to facilitate learning and social change; and includes all those involved where possible, thus facilitating shared ownership of the development and outcomes of the research (stakeholders). 'Inclusion' involves working with participants as co-researchers – community members as experts through democratic processes and decision-making. This involves mutual recognition, what Paulo Fréire calls dialogic techniques. PAR uses innovative ways of consulting and working with local people, for example, through arts workshops, forum theatre methods and stakeholder events. PAR is transformative and it is also rigorous and ethical. PAR is a process and a practice directed towards social change *with* the participants. It is interventionist, action-orientated and interpretive. At every phase of the PAR model there is the possibility for change: when conducting life-story interviews this process can validate the experience of the interviewee; and in the process of involving and including interviewees into the research as co-researchers this validation is transformed into constructive and creative responses for themselves and their communities. Outcomes of participatory research can inform, educate, remind, challenge and empower both those involved and the audiences of the research outcomes. Outcomes can be print based, performance based or art/exhibition based.

Conducting participatory action research (PAR) with individuals and groups promotes purposeful knowledge that may be transformative, and certainly counters the paralysis and pessimism that Mestrovic writes about. The relationship between thinking, feeling and doing (Arendt, 1970; Fals Borda, 1983; Tester, 1992); commitment and collective responsibility; the subject–object relationship; as well as the relationship between knowledge, power and reason are central to PAR, as is illustrated later in this chapter through the participatory action research with women and young people working as prostitutes, and communities/neighbourhoods affected by sex work.

Hence, my ongoing research involves working with the 'stereotypical subjects' of research through PAR, often with co-researchers as well as with community artists, photographers and performance artists in the doing, representation and analyses of social research. This approach to doing research is one that I have worked with consistently over time. It not only operationalises my feminist and socialist consciousness but also creates space for the possibility that things may be otherwise, that deconstructing and reconstructing are part of an interpretive approach to research whether one is a social researcher or an artist.

Ethno-mimesis

Ethno-mimesis is a term that captures the combination of ethnographic participatory work and the visual/artistic or poetic representation of research. Exploring the micrology of lived cultures and lived experiences through the frame of reference of sex workers, asylum seekers, the homeless and the marginalised, through sensuous knowing using biographical materials, I argue that both the narrative and visual can be defined as critical theory in practice and an example of public scholarship.

For example, in earlier work I argued that in representing ethnographic work in visual/artistic form we can reach a wider audience, beyond academic communities, to facilitate understanding, interpretation and maybe even action/praxis in relation to social issues such as prostitution and forced migration. Certainly, in representing ethnographic data in an artistic form we can access a richer understanding of the complexities of lived experience that can throw light on broader social structures and processes. Hillis Miller (1992) draws upon Walter Benjamin's work to illustrate how works of art bring something new into the world rather than reflecting something already there. This something new is constitutive rather than being merely representational, or reveals something already there but hidden. Works of art make culture. Each work makes different the culture it enters (Hillis Miller, 1992: 151). Indeed, through art works – performing arts/live arts, painting, poetry, literature, photography – we are able to get in touch with our 'realities', our social worlds and the lived experiences of others, in ways which demand critical reflection, similar to Barthes' use of 'punctum'. Thus the transformative nature of art and creativity are fostered in the space between art and ethnography. I have described this as a third space – the hyphen between art and ethnography (O'Neill, 2008).

Thinking about the performative dimension of ethno-mimesis was instrumental for me in articulating the relationship between knowledge, representation and praxis. Ethno-mimesis as performative praxis is reflexive and phenomenological but it is also critical and looks to praxis, as in the theatre work of Boal (1979) and Mienczakowski (1995), the socio-cultural research of Fals Borda (1983) or the filmic work of Trinh (1989, 1991). For Trinh, writing and filmmaking produce alternative representations of women's multiple realities and experiences. In undoing the realist ethnography project, she seeks to show that there is no single overriding vision of the world but rather multiple realities, multiple standpoints, multiple meanings for 'woman'. Trinh deconstructs the classic documentary film and her work provides a counter-documentary text which is reflexive, a site for multiple experiences and for seeking the truths in life's fiction. It makes a case for the development of interpretative and representational forms that transgress the traditional boundaries of ethnographic writing and representation via the hybrid, inter-textual relationship between ethnographic, biographical narratives and art forms, including performance art, photography and sculpture. In the next section I present three case studies that go some way to illustrate the points I make above.

Case 1: working together to create change

In 2000 I was commissioned with Rosie Campbell by Walsall South Health Action Zone (South HAZ) to undertake participatory research into the problems caused by prostitution in South Walsall. The project involved consulting all those involved and producing a baseline of information from which integrated programmes of action could be developed to more effectively address street prostitution. South HAZ at that time was a body made up of representatives from a range of community and voluntary sector organisations from across South Walsall who came together to try and solve some of the intractable health problems facing the area. We combined PAR and participatory arts (PA) and involved local people and organisations in the entire research trajectory from design to dissemination so that the ideas that came out of the work would be understood by those involved and create policy which would be in line with what people think locally.

At the beginning of the research we talked to a range of agencies and groups and recruited and trained local community researchers from the residents and steering group of South HAZ. We also argued that by using the arts as part of the PAR approach it might be possible to break down some of the perceived barriers between the community and the sex workers. We felt that an arts-based approach to consulting sex workers and young people at risk of involvement in sex work might be less confrontational and intimidating to groups who are not used to taking part in research. Such an approach would also provide visual representations that could be shared with and accessed by a wider population than a typical research report. The research was subsequently documented online by the research participants, the community researchers we worked with and the community artists and arts organisations that supported our work (see www.safetysoapbox.co.uk).

Working in partnership with local arts agencies, we discovered that safety was a common theme in interviews with sex workers, residents, local businesses and young people living in the area. Using safety as a theme, participants were able to think more broadly and creatively about some of the issues facing them in their community and focus less on the idea of prostitution as a cause of all the problems. Kate Green, the arts worker, worked with three groups of residents: sex workers, residents affected by street sex work, and young people living in the red light area. The website created by the resident participants describes the project as follows:

> During open discussion, participants reflected on their feelings and transformed thoughts into expressive artworks using a digital camera and a computer.
>
> Such an emotive issue as prostitution evokes an enormous array of opinions and attitudes, most of which are unheard and invisible. The social silence surrounding this issue has been confronted through this project and the spectrum of experiences, thoughts and feelings expressed through these striking digital artworks.

The leaflet created by the participants can be found at Safety Soapbox: sharing our true colours (see www.safetysoapbox.co.uk/leaflet.htm).

In an article discussing the benefits for creative consultation using research and community arts or participatory arts, O'Neill and Webster (2005) suggest that the most telling part of the research became apparent in the images on show at the art gallery. Although the different groups of people had come up with very different and sometimes painful or challenging images of what safety meant to them, the most obvious and uniting feature evident from viewing the images was what was similar about what the participants wanted to express, not what was different. Moreover, Safety Soapbox shows very clearly that working creatively across communities can transgress barriers; by engaging the imagination, people may see the issue from different perspectives.

O'Neill and Webster (2005) discuss how when the final report appeared – *Working Together to Create Change* (O'Neill and Campbell, 2002) – the recommendations were presented to the community and the key agencies involved but inevitably the recommendations were not universally accepted by either the local authority or the health authority. Additionally, the key recommendation, supported by a broad range of communities and agencies, that Walsall should move toward the idea of creating a safety zone (away from residential accommodation, where sex workers could work with the support of health and other agencies), was officially rejected by the police. However, neither South HAZ nor the local communities stood by and in their support of the findings an action group was formed to take the recommendations forward. This group has worked consistently to raise the issues wherever it could. The Safety Soapbox website was created and money was raised to develop and print the leaflet (found on the website) which summarised the outcomes of

Figure 9.1   Safety Soapbox. Photo: Kate Green

the research to local residents. The leaflet was posted to every single household in three wards of the Borough of Walsall: Caldmore, Pleck and Palfrey. The group ensured they had a representative on the Walsall Prostitution Action Forum, which contributed to the government review of prostitution, that in turn led to the Home Office strategy on prostitution in 2006. This research project, combining community arts and social research, evidences quite clearly the power of participation when local communities get involved in genuinely participatory research.

Case 2: arts, migration and diaspora – making the connections

The second example draws upon a decade of research funded by the AHRB and then the AHRC across four inter-linked projects. 'Global refugees: exile, displacement and belonging' was conducted in 1999–2001 with the artist Bea Tobolewska and a Bosnian community living in the East Midlands (fleeing war and ethnic cleansing) using participatory action research, arts and biographical methods. 'Towards a cultural strategy for the inclusion of refugees and asylum seekers' (2001–2) was followed by two inter-connected projects: 'Making connections: arts, migration and diaspora' (2006–8), and a knowledge transfer project, 'Beyond borders' (conducted with Phil Hubbard, 2008–9).

'Making connections: arts, migration and diaspora', was a two-year programme of workshops and seminars and was funded by the AHRC. In our work together we aimed to better understand the experiences of exile and displacement as well as to facilitate processes and practices of inclusion and belonging with new arrivals by encouraging collaboration and exchange of ideas and partnerships among artists, practitioners, academics, policy makers and new arrivals in the East Midlands. Themes of belonging, home, place-making and identity were central to the work, along with ideas and art-making expressed by participants. Exploring the social role of the arts in processes of social change and the space between ethnographic, participatory research and arts-based work, the partners engaged in three strands of activity taking forward the key aims of the regional network:

- to enhance the lives of recent arrivals in the East Midlands;
- to stimulate high-quality inter-disciplinary research and the production of art works;
- to facilitate connection, communication and feed into public policy; and
- to contribute to public awareness of the issues facing new arrivals.

The fourth project, 'Beyond borders', was a partnership between the University and four community arts organisations. Our collaborations in the knowledge-transfer project examined how the arts – defined in their broadest sense – might help mediate and represent the experience of arriving in a new country and what it means to feel a sense of belonging. The project also looked at how the arts might deliver cultural, social and economic benefits to new arrivals in the East Midlands region.

The project aimed to deliver social and cultural benefits to refugee/asylum seekers/migrants in the East Midlands region, as well as to wider communities, by developing three strands of participatory research and arts activity that: contributed to public awareness; examined the role of arts and cultural activity in social policy agendas; and facilitated knowledge, communication and understanding *with* new arrivals. The three strands of activity were as follows.

First, there was a diversity pool event (bringing together artists and programmers/schools and community organisations that employ artists for various projects). At this event, artists showcased their work, met other artists as well as programmers, schools, arts development officers and local authority representatives, and thus aided not only connection and communication but also the employment of artists. The event sought to build capacity and aid the professional development of artists as well as connect people through dialogue and the sharing of art forms. An economic impact was the employment of artists and funding to build upon this work in two of the community arts organisations.

Second, an electronic web resource was developed as an outcome of the participatory action research activities of the AHRC-funded regional network and partner organisations in order to house the database of artists (see www.beyondbordersuk.org).[4] The aim of the website resource is to build and maintain a database of artists who have arrived in this country from around the world, alongside regional artists, in order to: promote their work; explore the issues they face; and to support work with new and established 'arrival' communities.

Finally, an arts/research project, 'A sense of belonging', took place simultaneously in four geographical areas of the region – Derby, Nottingham, Loughborough and Leicester. Launched by a series of guided walks,[5] following the arts practice of Misha Myers (artist, educator and consultant to the walks), the project explored relationships between cartography (mapping), home, emplacement, and belonging in the lives of new arrivals. Participatory arts/research workshops explored and documented visually and poetically the various senses of belonging and the themes and issues raised during the walks and launch event. Narrative and visual outcomes were exhibited at the Bonington Gallery, Nottingham, in January 2009[6] and subsequently at one international and three regional and local conferences. They are also documented on the 'Making connections' gallery pages (see www.makingtheconnections.info) and online at the *Guardian* Society pages (www.guardian.co.uk/society/gallery/2009/jan/13/sense-of-belonging-exhibition).

The arts/research workshops were designed to put art at the heart of social research and to explore the issues raised on the walks. The arts/research workshops were led by the community arts organisations and supported by Phil and myself.

The arts practice communicated what *belonging* meant to those participating in the research, exploring their experiences and feelings about home, dislocation, place-making, belonging and friendship. The arts practice showed what it is like for new arrivals to live in Nottingham, Derby, Leicester and Loughborough, as well as highlighting the perilous journeys people had made to seek freedom and safety from nations including Zimbabwe, Congo, Iraq, Iran, Eritrea, Albania, Turkey and Afghanistan. The emotional and physical impact of these journeys, and the experiences of 'double consciousness' and being 'home away from home' were represented alongside the rich cultural contributions and skills migrants bring to the region's cities, towns, cultures and communities.

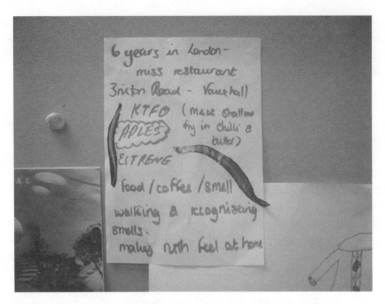

Figure 9.2   'A sense of belonging' workshops. Photo: Maggie O'Neill

Walking as ethnography and arts practice

Inspired by the walking arts practice of Misha Myers (2010), the guided walks involved a participatory, performative process of reflection, conversation and embodied movement/mapping following maps created by the new arrivals. We make places through an embodied process of finding our way. The walks were led and directed by 'new arrivals' (important given that the voices of new arrivals are often mediated by others), so they held situational authority. Following Misha's guidance, people drew a map from a place they call home to a special place and they then walked the map in Derby, Nottingham, Leicester or Loughborough with a co-walker. Co-walkers were policy makers, practitioners, residents and network members. What emerged through the process of walking and talking and subsequent reflection at a post-walk lunch event was a relational, sensuous, kinaesthetic, democratic and participatory process of collaborative co-production. This highlights the impact of arts and cultural activity for social policy agendas in participation with new arrivals.

PAR/ethno-mimesis, as a methodology and artistic practice, offers the opportunity for such groups to represent themselves, without a cultural or political intermediary talking 'on their behalf'. PAR/ethno-mimesis transgresses the power relations inherent in traditional ethnography and social research as well as the binaries of subject/object inherent in the research process. The participants involved in PAR are both objects and subjects (authors) of their own narratives and cultures. PAR/ethno-mimesis can facilitate and envision a more holistic model of social justice (O'Neill and Hubbard, 2010).

Crucially, PAR/ethno-mimesis is reflexive and phenomenological but also looks to praxis. Thus, it is vitally important to develop innovative methodologies in order to: (1) interpret the issues of migration both forced and free; (2) share the experiences of new arrivals; and (3) facilitate the production of new knowledge and counter hegemonic texts to offset, borrowing Roger Bromley's words, 'the circulation in politics and the media of a set of negative images and vocabularies relating to refugees and asylum seekers [that] has become part of a new exclusionary process' (2001: 20). Such corporeal and participatory ways of researching and knowledge production are included in my final example.

Case 3: community, politics and resistance in DTES, Vancouver

The third example is in progress. In Canada, Vancouver's Downtown East Side (DTES) is consistently described as: a problem community marked by 'human degradation' (Wente, 2008); 'Canada's poorest postal code' (Matas and Peritz, 2008); and presented as offering significant resistance to 'regeneration' (Huey, 2007: 133). The research currently underway conducts critical recovery of the history of DTES through the work of four organisations[7] and arts-based research that presents many stories, narratives and images that offer multiple, rich experiences and presentations of communities of interest, well-being and connection – based upon the lived experiences of residents and workers in DTES.

In partnership with local agencies, the research explores ways of seeing the spaces and places of community through the eyes of DTES residents and workers by using participatory and arts-based methods, including photography, video and walking (Pink, 2007). The project builds upon O'Neill and Stenning's (2011) collaborative work and Stenning's photographs of DTES in 2002 and 2008. The research involves:

a) a critical recovery of the history of the agencies involved and the DTES 'community';
b) using walking, storytelling and visual methods to capture what community means to residents working with local agencies; and
c) exhibiting the work in the community, producing a collaborative research report and articles in local media outlets.

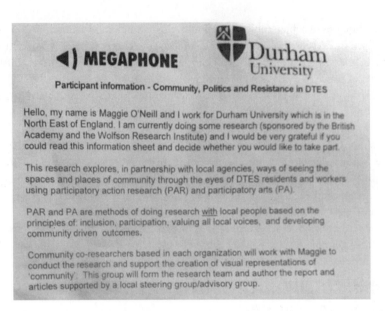

Figure 9.3   Participant information. Photo: April Smith

Four or five community co-researchers based in each organization are conducting the research and the creation of visual representations of 'community'. This group forms the research team and will author the report and articles supported by a local steering group/advisory group.

Partnership and collaboration are at the heart of the research. The aim is to produce knowledge that is useful both locally and internationally, that better articulates the communities that make up DTES and the sense of 'community' experienced by the denizens of the Downtown Eastside area. Using photography, digital storytelling and mapping and walking as community arts practice, the outcomes presented here powerfully inform, educate, remind and challenge us to think differently about the DTES. A complex, multi-layered and incredibly rich account of community/ies emerges that can tell us much about the workings of 'community' and which we can learn from and which will be meaningful to policy makers, organisations and developers not only in Vancouver, Canada, but internationally in the UK and Europe. The photographic exhibits and digital stories powerfully represent 'community' and in the stories that unfold there are important messages for us all about community building, community well-being, community sustainability and the greening of communities.

Taking a phenomenological approach, the arts-based research both documents and analyses the politics of community and resistance in DTES. Difference is visualised and we are given other ways of seeing the spaces and places of 'community' through the eyes of some of the most marginalised

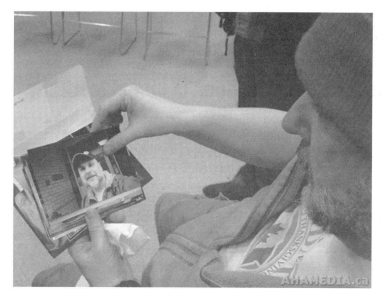

Figure 9.4   Representing community. Photo: April Smith

inhabitants. Just as the trials, tribulations, joys and successes experienced by an individual become inscribed in his or her face, the same could be said of a community; the well-being (or otherwise) of a community can be read from visual

Figure 9.5   Community dialogue. Photo: April Smith

images of it. The picture that emerges contrasts with the hegemonic image and instead uncovers rich, multi-layered stories that speak of community, politics and resistance in ways that I had not expected.

Ways forward: advances in visual methods

In a recent talk, Bauman delineated a genealogy of sociology and especially sociology's relation to society. He spoke about the shift from the first managerialist approach to society, the development of de-traditionalisation and individualisation (see Ulrich Beck, 1992, on individualisation and Giddens, 1992, on life politics), to the rise of the latest version of managerialism – lamenting the focus upon the growth of individual solutions to social problems that are created socially. Hence he described our current situation as one where we are individual by decree but not de facto – because we do not have access to the resources for de facto.

One clear point concerned Bauman in his talk. How do we reconnect our work with the public and with the public arena? He made a plea for work to be undertaken where people needed help. Moreover, Bauman offered a recipe, or heuristic advice, that we might take up in our mission as social scientists to avoid ossifying and codifying society and allowing for the fact that we are bound to act under conditions of continuing uncertainty. Bauman offered an invitation to develop an agenda for sociology in the 21st century (that we can interpret in inter-disciplinary ways) that includes the following.

First, de-familiarise the familiar and familiarise the unfamiliar. Here Bauman made reference to Milan Kundera using the tear in the curtain to see through to reality, avoiding cheap convictions and stereotypes (or in Adorno's terms, 'identity thinking'). Kundera, like Adorno, calls for artists and humanities to join forces. Second, he called for what E.M. Forster describes as 'only connect': take-up interaction with other spheres of human life, showing the interconnections. Thus inter-disciplinarity is a positive way forward in this respect. Third, 'unravelling doxa' – 'knowledge with which you think but of which you don't know': here he means the art of thinking consciously. For me, this is synonymous with critical thinking, reflexivity and the writings of Benjamin, Adorno and Bauman. As methodologists we need to concern ourselves not only with the art of thinking, but the art of listening and seeing too. Fourth, he urges us to open, and keep open, dialogue, and spread the art of sociology around through dialogue and participation.

Advances in visual research methods are, for me, captured eloquently by Bauman's invitation and encapsulated in the approach to participatory and visual methods I have undertaken for the last couple of decades, documented and discussed here.

Participatory approaches involve de-familiarising and refamiliarising; they can be a 'refreshing antidote to the somewhat alien intrusion of impersonal analytic methodologies' (Ryan, 2011: 5). Partnership and collaboration are at the centre of the research documented above. Dialogue is a crucial aspect, indeed a driving force: dialogue that is unfinished, that opens and keeps open the spaces for critical thinking, resistance and reflection; dialogue that is inter-disciplinary in scope, and fosters mutual trust and subject–subject relationships as far as possible – valuing communities sharing knowledge and expertise and setting the horizon for further development. Unravelling doxa involves the importance of the process of reflexivity of relationship building and sustaining, hence 'art can be a mediator and a way of creating relationships'. Art is also a way of overcoming barriers, challenging stereotypes, producing more complex knowledge, and creating safe spaces for dialogue to listen and communicate experience across linguistic and cultural divides. Research findings offer social and cultural impact, and, as in the second case discussed above, participatory methods can also elicit economic impact too.

On the other hand, the tensions and problems of participatory approaches are numerous. PAR is difficult to put into action, is time consuming, and involves lots of time, energy, commitment and emotional labour. It is a relational and collective enterprise involving serious ethical consideration and constant reflexivity on issues of accountability, trust, risk, respect, recognition – who is invited to the table and whose voice is heard in research and publications? The tension between academic researcher and community researcher involves a deep awareness of power relations and cannot be entered into lightly or naively. The risk of harm to communities, groups and individuals is obvious, as is the risk of collaborative research that raises expectations, and may even set groups up to fail.

Other challenges relate to the risk of instrumentality in research and include: appropriation, use value, navigating uncertainty, and managing disciplinary territories. Finally, a common accusation from discipline-bound and purist colleagues might be to what extent is the combination of social research and arts practice research?

In conclusion my answer is to agree absolutely with Bauman: avoid cheap convictions and stereotypes, take risks, and undertake creative critical research rooted in deepening knowledge and analysis with the very communities and groups we usually study. Show the interconnections, the intersections, the inter-disciplinarity in our work as sociologists, criminologists and visual psychologists. Concern ourselves with thinking critically, reflexively, as interpreters, not legislators. This is the legacy of critical theory, feminist theory and cultural criminology, and it involves the role of public intellectuals in uncovering identitarian thinking through critical analysis. It involves: acting as interpreters not legislators (Bauman, 1992); fostering democracy through ongoing critical analysis; ensuring the critical recovery of history (hidden histories); recognising the objective mediation of subjects and subjectivity and the vital importance of examining societal conditions; and reading these against appearance, against the grain (Adorno, 1884, 1997, 2005: 281), using creative and participatory methodologies (ethno-mimesis).

Notes

1   In my work, ethno-mimesis is a combination of ethnography and arts-based practice; it is a theoretical construct, a process and a methodological practice. See also Cantwell for whom the term means the representation of culture (1993).
2   See Adorno and Horkheimer (1979), especially the essay, 'The culture industry: enlightenment as mass deception'.
3   PAR originated in the countries of the south. The methodology emerged from developmental politics and interpretations of the works of Marx (we need to understand the world *and* to change it) and Gramsci (the combination of 'common sense' and 'critical knowledge' through mutual recognition and collaboration is more likely to develop greater knowledge and understanding but also solutions).
4   This strand of activity is looked after by Charnwood Arts in Loughborough.
5   For example, see John Perivolaris Walking with Thaer (www.flickr.com/photos/dr_john2005/sets/72157605115882016).
6   Over 300 people attended the private view and 1005 people visited the exhibition between 9 January and 29 January, averaging 60 visitors per day (not including the numbers attending the private view).
7   Megaphone, a street-level newspaper, similar to the *Big Issue* in the UK; PACE society, a project that supports sex workers; Enterprising Women Making Art, a strand of the Atira Resource society, part of Atira women's resource social enterprise that provides social housing and responses to sexual violence and abuse; and United We Can, a recycling social enterprise dealing in bottles and cans, and Aha Media.

References

Adorno, T.W. (1984) *Aesthetic Theory* (edited by G. Adorno and R. Tiedemann, translated by C. Lendhart). London: Routledge.

Adorno, T.W. (1997) *Aesthetic Theory* (translated by R. Hullot-Kentor). Minneapolis, MN: University of Minnesota Press.

Adorno, T.W. (2005) *Critical Models: Interventions and Catchwords*. New York: Columbia University Press.

Adorno, T.W. and Horkheimer, M. (1979) *The Dialectic of Enlightenment*. London: Verso.

Arendt, H. (1970) *On Violence*. New York: Harcourt Brace.

Bauman, Z. (1992) *Intimations of Post Modernity*. London: Routledge.

Beck, U. (1992) *Risk Society: Towards a New Modernity*. London: Sage.

Benjamin, W. (1985) *One-Way Street and Other Writings* (translated by E. Jephcott and K. Shorter). London: Verso.

Boal, A. (1979) *Theatre of the Oppressed*. London: Pluto.

Bromley, R. (2001) 'Between a world of need and a world of excess: globalized people, migration and cinematic narrative', unpublished paper, from personal communication with the author.

Burawoy, M. and VanAntwerpen, J. (2001) *Berkeley Sociology: Past, Present and Future*. Berkeley, CA: University of California.

Cantwell, R. (1993) *Ethnomimesis: Folklife and the Representation of Culture*. Chapel Hill, NC: University of North Carolina Press.

Fals Borda, O. (1983) *Knowledge and People's Power: Lessons with Peasants in Nicaragua, Mexico and Colombia*. New York: New Horizons Press.

Ferrell, J. (2007) 'Cultural criminology', in *Blackwell Encyclopedia of Sociology* [on-line]. Available from: www.culturalcriminology.org/papers/cult-crim-blackwell-ency-soc.pdf.

Ferrell, J., Hayward, K., Morrison, W. and Presdee, M. (eds) (2004) *Cultural Criminology Unleashed*. London: Glasshouse Press.

Giddens, A. (1984) *The Constitution of Society: Outline of the Theory of Structuration*. Cambridge: Polity.

Giddens, A. (1992) *The Transformation of Intimacy: Sexuality, Love and Eroticism in Modern Societies*. Cambridge: Polity.

Haggerty (2004) 'Displaced expertise: three constraints on the policy relevance of criminological thought', *Theoretical Criminology*, 8 (2): 211–311.

Hillis Miller, J. (1992) *Illustration*. London: Reaktion Books.

Huey, L. (2007) *Negotiating Demands: The Politics of Skid Row Policing in Edinburgh, San Francisco and Vancouver*. Toronto: University of Toronto Press.

Loader, I. and Sparks, R. (2010) *Public Criminology?* London: Routlede.

Matas, R. and Peritz, I. (2008) 'Canada's poorest postal code in for an Olympic clean-up?', in Toronto's *Globe and Mail*, Friday 15 August 2008 11:14 (retrieved 5 May 2011 from: www.theglobeandmail.com/news/national/article704374.ece).

Mestrovic, S.G. (1997) *Postemotional Society*. London: Sage.

Mienczakowski, J. (1995) 'The theater of ethnography: the reconstruction of ethnography into theater with emancipatory potential', *Qualitative Enquiry*, 1 (3): 360–75.

Myers, M. (2010) 'Walk with me, talk with me: the art of conversive wayfinding', *Visual Studies*, 26 (1): 50–68.

O'Neill, M. (2008) 'Transnational refugees: the transformative role of art?' *FQS*, 9 (2) (retrieved from: www.qualitativeresearch.net/index.php/fqs/article/view/403).

O'Neill, M. (2010) *Asylum, Migration and Community*. Bristol: Policy Press.

O'Neill, M. and Campbell, R. (2002) *Working Together to Create Change*. Staffordshire University and Liverpool Hope University College. Available from www.safetysoapbox.co.uk (retrieved September 2011).

O'Neill, M. and Hubbard, P. (2010) 'Walking, sensing, belonging: ethno-mimesis as performative praxis', *Visual Studies*, 25 (1): 46–58.

O'Neill, M. and Stenning, P. (2011) 'Politics, community and resistance in skid row: a photo essay', unpublished paper.

O'Neill, M. and Webster, M. (2005) *Creativity, Community and Change: Creative Approaches to Community Consultation*. Internal report published by Staffordshire and Loughborough Universities.

Pink, S. (2007) 'Walking with video', *Visual Studies*, 22 (3): 240–52.

Ryan, K. (2011) 'Foreword', in M. O'Neill, K. Ryan et al. *Beyond Borders: A Sense of Belonging*. Loughborough: Charnwood Arts.

Tester, K. (1992) *The Inhuman Condition*. London: Routledge.

Trinh, T. M.-H. (1989) *Woman, Native, Other: Writing Postcoloniality and Feminism*. Bloomington and Indianapolis, IN: Indiana University Press.

Trinh, T. M.-H. (1991) *When the Moon Waxes Red*. London: Routledge.

Wente, M. (2008) 'Meet Vancouver's next mayor', Toronto *Globe and Mail*, 19 June, p. A15.

10

HEALING MIRRORS
Body Arts and Ethnographic Methodologies

Christina Lammer

Prologue

In this chapter I discuss the development and application of audiovisual ethnographic methodologies in the context of body-oriented projects with patients
who are being treated through plastic and reconstructive surgery. Inspired by
the medieval *Speculum Humanae Salvationis* (*Mirror of Human Salvation*), an
illustrated assemblage of popular theology in the Late Middle Ages, I suggest
how photographic and video cameras function as a contemporary *Heilsspiegel*
(*Healing Mirror*). In doing so I evoke the *doing* of methodology through ethnographic research at the Medical University Vienna (MUV) over a period of
10 years (2000–2010). The processes I describe are part of a methodological
framework influenced by approaches from body art and physical theatre. This
includes video interviews, action research in a broad and experimental sense,
audiovisual participatory observation, work with movement and voice, as well
as portraiture and self-experiments. Theoretically, my discussion is informed
by *The Image and Appearance of the Human Body* (Schilder, 1978 [1950]), *Art
and Agency* (Gell, 1998) and *The Corporeal Image* (MacDougall, 2006) – works
that bring to the fore pivotal points around which human modes of experience, emotionality and expressiveness unfold. The 'healing mirror', an apparatus
invented for a study with facially paralysed patients, is used here as a metaphor
to capture the expressive capacities of the *inner face* – an emotional smile, for
instance, or a promising twinkling – as sensory categories of oneself.

It is this very bringing together of methods, practices and approaches that
constitutes the methodological advance that is the focus of the chapter, through
a discussion of the *FEATURES* project. In *FEATURES* – Vienna Face Project
(2010–2014), my research project on facial expressiveness, people suffering
from partial facial paralysis are invited to talk about their disability and how

they perceive themselves in everyday life. Since the human face is studied in plastic surgery and in the visual and performance arts, the *FEATURES* project has been developed together with plastic surgeons and contemporary artists. One important issue that is explored is body image and how we perceive, experience and express ourselves on a daily basis. The methodological framework is interwoven with the Russian literary critic and theorist Mikhail Bakhtin's approach to speech and expressiveness, and with the Polish theatre director Jerzy Grotowski's studies on the 'organicity' of the 'actor's act' (Bakhtin, 2000 [1975]; Grotowski, 1991 [1968]). However, I depart from the psychoanalytical methods and theories that may be expected of a researcher living in Vienna and brought up in its intellectual atmosphere. My attention instead passes through the living and moving flesh of personal and subjective impressions and expressions of disability and otherness in the mirror of a self that is in constant flux. In particular, I search for ways to analyse physical actions and their socio-cultural and symbolic meanings. This is comparable to the theatre work of the Russian director Constantin Stanislavski (1863–1938) who claimed, before Grotowski, that the nature of a figure is *organic* (Stanislavski, 1984 [1948]: 21). According to the anthropologist Richard Schechner, the major goal of acting 'and the basis of Stanislavski's great work is to enable actors to "really live" their characters. Nature ought to be so skilfully imitated that it seems to be represented on stage' (2003: 46). Stanislavski aspired to a life-like style on stage. As he wrote:

> FACE
>
> Facial expressions are brought about of their own accord, naturally, as a result of intuition, inner feelings. Nevertheless their effectiveness can improve through the exercise and development of flexibility of the facial muscles. Yet … to accomplish this one must be familiar with the muscular anatomy of the face. (Stanislavski, 1963: 62)

Imagine yourself as an actor or dancer doing physical exercises in front of the mirror. The self is always possessed by the *other* and perceived as mediated. Thus subjectivities are shared. In the words of David MacDougall: 'Although there is pain and danger, there is also humour and an acceptance of the shared subjectivity of bodily experience' (2006: 15). In my research I compare patients who exercise their facial and bodily expressiveness with the training of actors. My approach takes into consideration their personal impressions of themselves.

Sharing subjectivity

The mirror apparatus that was developed for *FEATURES* has to fulfil various functions: it has to allow me to video record patients while they do their exercises; it has to be as simple as possible and easily transportable since the glass sheet is used in various locations; and it has to let me create individual portraits of patients, both videos and stills, with the aim of illuminating one of the most vulnerable parts of their bodies. My considerations led to the construction of a square mirror with a small circular hole in its centre. The device is placed on a tripod. The *sitter* is on the reflective side of the sheet while I, as *portraitist*, stay with the photo or video camera on the opposite side, which is painted black.

The hole in the 'healing mirror' functions like a mediating channel, creating a lively encounter between *sitter* and *portraitist*. The Viennese psychiatrist and neurologist Paul Schilder (1886–1940) was particularly interested in the phenomenon of *autoscopy* (seeing one's own self). He noted, 'we create a mental point of observation opposite ourselves and outside ourselves and observe ourselves as if we were observing another person' (1978 [1950]: 84). Schilder asked (healthy) persons to close their eyes and imagine what they would look like if they were standing or sitting in front of themselves. They all imagined themselves as pictures rather than in a three-dimensional way.

This finding corresponds with the photographic self-portraitures developed at the very beginning of the 20th century by the Vienna-based artist and anatomist Hermann Heller (1866–1949) in order to create 55 mimic masks.

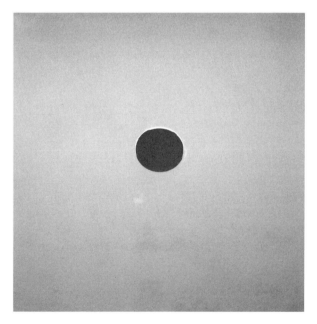

Figure 10.1   Christina Lammer, *Healing Mirror*, 2010

Heller was a professor of artistic anatomy at the Academy of Fine Arts between 1906 and 1936. He was familiar with the Austrian painter Egon Schiele (1890–1918), who is recognized as a major figure in the history of modern art and in the development of the Expressionist movement. For some time they even had their ateliers in the same building at Wattmanngasse 6, in the 13th district.

> The portraitist does not co-opt, does not eat up, does not ana-
> lyze – in the Freudian sense – the sitter and leaves him [or her]
> in his [or her] personal consistence. It is incredibly beautiful that
> one can see faces in this way. (Hermine Heller, 2006)[1]

The visual and sensory ethnographic methodologies I outline in the following pages are inspired by a historical context that is specific to Vienna, including the diverse and intersecting relationships between some of its inhabitants.

I introduce the process of working with the healing mirror with persons who have partly 'lost their face' as an example to illuminate a methodological and theoretical grounding. Patients who suffer facial palsy and are treated in plastic surgery need to do physiotherapy in front of the mirror in order to adequately smile or close their eyes. This form of therapeutic movement is an integral part of their healing process. Thus healing is deeply connected with re/learning bodily as well as emotional skills through exercise. In developing the healing mirror methodology I borrowed ideas from Jerzy Grotowski, suspending the differentiation between acting in theatre and everyday acts for the development of a test arrangement with patients who suffer facial paralysis (Goffman, 1959). According to Grotowski, the:

> actor's act – discarding half measures, revealing, opening up,
> emerging from himself as opposed to closing up – is an invitation
> to the spectator. This act could be compared to an act of the most
> deeply rooted, genuine love between two human beings – this is
> just a comparison since we can only refer to this 'emergence from
> oneself' through analogy. (1991 [1968]: 212)

In advancing this methodology I produce a variety of different portraits – of disabled persons, clinicians, artists, and of myself. According to Maggie O'Neill, 'through art works – performing arts/live arts, painting, poetry, literature, photography – we are able to get in touch with our "realities", our social worlds and the lived experiences of others, in ways which demand critical reflection' (O'Neill, this volume, Chapter 9). Using my body as a sensory research instrument, the practice of portraiture builds relationships of trust between the sitters and myself. In his anthropological theory of art (1998), anthropologist Alfred Gell studied agent/patient relationships. This notion of agent/patient enabled me to understand the power dynamics I encountered, both when I accompanied patients to their treatments or appointments with physicians and during my own encounters with clinicians and artists. Connecting methodologies and power relations related to body art – such as physical theatre and contemporary video art – with biomedical issues is an integral constituent of the audiovisual tools developed within my ethnographic and artistic work. I collaborate with four artistic colleagues, amongst them the Polish artist, Artur Zmijewski. His video installations are impressive examples of how video analyses of the social realities of sick and disabled persons – whether visually or hearing-impaired – can at once be painful and ironic, even grotesque. Artur creates situations in front of the camera, showing sick persons in the nakedness, vulnerability and loneliness of their everyday lives. Mirroring the agent/patient relationship of medical practices, he applies the camera like a surgeon uses the knife to lay bare the qualities of life beyond the skin.

Creating embodied dialogue

My research is based on the idea of taking an organic approach to advancing dialogues. Some dialogues are already established in clinical contexts. For example, during their treatments, patients learn to recognize themselves as objects of a medical scientific theory of signs. The dialogue between the sick and their healers is interpenetrated with visual media, such as endoscopic imaging and video-based diagnostic testing. In this dialogue, the body is discussed on two levels, which in phenomenological terms we would call *Körper* and *Leib*:

> the term *Leib* refers to the living body, to my body with feelings, sensations, perceptions, and emotions. … *Körper* takes its root in the Latin corpus and refers to the structural aspects of the body. It is the objectified body (somebody else's *Körper*), and also the dead body or corpse. (Ots, 2003 [1994]: 116)

I consider the concept of *Leiblichkeit*, or living embodiment, to be an important ingredient in any dialogue. In *Doing Sensory Ethnography* (2009), Sarah Pink emphasizes 'that the talk of an interview is not simply performative and embodied, but that it is more fully situated in that it is an emplaced activity that engages not only the performative body but the sensing body in relation to its total environment' (2009: 83–4). To a certain degree, this argument corresponds with what Mikhail Bakhtin refers to as: 'dialogic communication, [where] the object is transformed into the subject (the other's *I*)' (2002: 145). In Bakhtin's approach, meanings accompany one another and build a context.

Healing Mirrors has the character of a self-critical review – illuminating the modes of ethnographic sound and video production in a clinical environment, including the creation of installations presented in the context of art exhibitions (Lammer, 2007a: 208–15, Lammer, 2007b: 91–116, Lammer, 2009: 264–75). However, as a concrete project, *Healing Mirrors* is at its very beginnings. In *Picturing the Self* (2005), Gen Doy discusses what:

> writers on photography and autobiography say about the self as single self, or multiple selves. The main point of contention is whether there exists a self with agency and consciousness, which changes through time but is essentially an individual self, or whether the self as multiple, decentred and fragmented, results not from human agency, but is constructed by social discourses including, most importantly, language. (Doy, 2005: 144)

According to the art historian Janet Kraynak, Mikhail Bakhtin 'develops an idiosyncratic approach to the problem of language, focusing upon its aspects as speech. ... The utterance, Bakhtin emphasizes, is not an autonomous unit but always arises, either directly or indirectly, in response to another utterance' (Kraynak, 2005: 4). Bakhtin's broader concept of *dialogue* includes *utterance* as an integral part of any linguistic exchange:

> The domain of speech-act philosophy brings attention to precisely those aspects that structuralist and formalist linguistics cast aside – material context, human action, and subjectivity – and as such, to what the art historical reception has suppressed in its assessment of language-based artistic practices. (Kraynak, 2005: 5–6)

In light of this, I stress the importance of *speech* – for personal contact and in its mutual expressive intonations and incantations – as a methodological category within the framing events of sensory ethnographic and art-based research activities. I do not present an already executed and finished piece of work, but rather invite you, the reader, to follow me along the way through a labyrinth of approaches.

Dialogue plays an important role in the development of my approach (O'Neill, this volume, Chapter 9). For example, I recognized chains of meaning in a public discussion between Manfred Frey, head of the plastic and reconstructive surgery unit at the MUV, and the Austrian artist, Günter Brus, known for his active role in the Viennese Actionist art movement, with whom I collaborated to produce *Günter Brus Kleine Narbenlehre* (*Günter Brus' Small Theory of Scars*) (Lammer, 2007c). The conversation between the plastic surgeon and the artist took place at the book's presentation at the Museum of Modern Art in Vienna, in February 2008. The volume confronts surgical practices with the artist's violent and self-injuring performances of the 1960s and 1970s. In the late 1990s, Brus had a cancerous growth in his stomach and underwent two operations. By creating the *Bilddichtung* (works that combine poems with drawings, paintings and photographs) *Theory of Scars* (1999), Brus ironically self-documented his hospital stays. He 'put himself in the picture' as a patient (Radley, 2009; Spence, 1988 [1986]; Tembeck, 2009). The confrontation of visual arts and surgery in the frame of the book presentation was particularly fruitful for the development of *FEATURES*. Their exchange is interwoven in the methodological and theoretical fabric of the project's ongoing hospital-based audiovisual and sensory ethnographies:

> Günter Brus: Initially, I was at the hospital and it was not a stomach operation, which had taken place earlier, but rather a ruptured scar. That's why the book is known as 'Kleine Narbenlehre'. I felt relaxed, as I sometimes am, and bored, so I decided to capture a few situations in photographs, then I wrote verses to accompany them. My wife photographed me in a hospital bed. I then went out into the corridor. The nurses were very surprised to see me standing there in my nightshirt and funny slippers and white socks. I asked one of them to take a picture of me. I pressed the camera into her hand. She burst out laughing and went back to her room saying, 'Mr. Brus, Mr. Brus, nobody has ever done that before!' I said, 'Please do it for me as an experiment.' So she took eight photos. I photocopied them, without intending to do anything special with them, and stapled them together to make eight or nine copies, to which I added verses and sent to friends. There was no speculation about me being a suffering invalid – you can't really say a funny invalid either.

In Brus's conceptualization of his art piece, dialogue – between the nurses and the artist – played a crucial role. Without the help of his caregivers who took the photographs, the work would not have come into existence.

Fairytale surgery

Referring to a range of arguments in *Günter Brus Kleine Narbenlehre*, Frey raised a question of *aesthetics*: 'What is aesthetic? ... I am a plastic surgeon who also performs cosmetic surgery, but that's something entirely different. Even then, I do not have any freedom of design.' Brus, the artist, on the other hand, regarded the issue from a different perspective, focussing on the technical aspects of dissection in order to get a better understanding of how the human body is perceived in surgery: 'You [surgeons] are trained in dissecting bodies. Simply put, you use the same techniques for living people when they are anaesthetised. What is the difference between a corpse and a living person who has been anaesthetised?' This was a controversial remark for the surgeon. He responded that the symbolic meaning of the human body is unmistakable, as is the respectful treatment that must equally be given to each individual. The difference between operating on a living or dead body is self-evident in his field of practice. 'I would never and should never be able to pick up a knife and cut open a living, feeling body with circulation without undertaking many years of study.' According to the historian Ivan Illich in his study *Medical Nemesis – The Expropriation of Health* (2002 [1975]: 150), Descartes 'constructed an image of the body in terms of geometry, mechanics, or watch making, a machine that could be repaired by an engineer. The body became an apparatus owned and managed by the soul, but from an almost infinite distance.' In a socio-cultural order of functionalities, the suffering *Leib*, as living bodily experience, and the articulation of pain in the form of speech, are increasingly neglected. In contemporary medicine, aesthetic experience is merged with functionality. A diagnosable body is the necessary precondition for surgical treatment. Within our exceptional research collaboration, Manfred Frey and I aim at deepening our understanding of practices of self-presentation and portraiture today. Gen Doy refers to the 'photo-autobiographical' work of Jo Spence, who 'examines conflicts between the fragments of the self/selves, but believes that, through photo-therapy, a process she devised together with Rosy Martin, the agency of the self can develop and become more conscious' (Doy, 2005: 144–5; Hogan and Pink, Chapter 13, this volume). According to this approach, the self as *agent* acknowledges the alienating processes of fragmentation (in the clinical context), but brings the broken pieces into a novel dialogue.

'Sono operatore' (I am an operator), wrote the Italian author Luigi Pirandello (1867–1936) in his novel *Quaderni di Serafino Gubbio operatore* (2010 [1926]: 4), in order to bring the main figure of the story, the cameraman Serafino Gubbio, into being. As opposed to an *agent*, the *operator*, in Pirandello's sense, operates nothing:

> But, as a matter of fact, being an operator, in the world in which I live and upon which I live, does not in the least mean operat-ing. … This is what I do. I set up my machine on its knock-kneed tripod. One or more stagehands, following my directions, mark out on the carpet or on the stage with a long wand and a blue pencil the limits within which the actors have to move to keep the picture in focus. (Pirandello, 2010 [1926]: 2–3)

Inspired by Pirandello, Walter Benjamin compares the *cameraman* with the *surgeon*, and the *painter* with the *magician* or general practitioner in *The Work of Art in the Age of Mechanical Reproduction* (1977 [1936]).[2] These comparisons strongly inspired my fieldwork activities in the *operating theatre* of plastic and reconstructive surgery. According to Benjamin, the *magician* keeps a 'natural distance' from the sick person while the *surgeon* has no interpersonal encounter in the 'decisive moment' (1977 [1936]: 31). The central topic raised by Pirandello and Benjamin is the dehumanization of mankind in modern industrial societies (Lammer, 2009: 272). In the aforementioned dialogue between Frey and Brus, a variety of theoretical and methodological implications of the figure of the *operator* were addressed. They are still of importance in my project.

Malfunctions and pathologies inside the body are rendered visible with the help of imaging technologies and media, enabling surgeons to navigate through inner bodily structures, detecting and removing lesions, limiting invasiveness and scars. Minimally invasive surgical techniques increase with the multimedia creation of a virtual body proper, projected on screens in real time. The gastroenterologist Michael Häfner, head of the Department of Internal Medicine at the St Elisabeth Hospital in Vienna, used the term 'functional aesthetic' to explain the meaning of beauty or aesthetics in his profession: 'A cut is beautiful for me when I remove a malignant tumour'. Phenomenological approaches in medical anthropology and sociology make distinctions between notions of *illness* and *disease*. According to the physician and philosopher Drew Leder, in 'disease, one is actively disabled. Abilities that were previously in one's command and rightfully belong to the habitual body have now been lost. ... When sick, I no longer can engage the world as once I could' (1990: 81). Leder refers to this phenomenon as an aspect of disappearance, which goes hand in hand with a withdrawal from personal experience of the self and sensibility. Frey, the plastic surgeon, neatly sums up the relationship between the *operator* and the body as object: 'Subjectivity is not reliable in surgery. I cannot operate because I enjoy it, but rather I do it because it needs to be done. Objectivity is required with the object, being the patient, who is at the centre of all actions, thoughts, feelings and design.'

During my work at the hospital I developed a fascination for mucosal and connective tissues. This led to a voracious lust to explore the organic unfolding of the human being. With respect to my ongoing explorations of these fabrics, however, my interest is strongly related to degrees of 'personality-ness', and much less to its 'thing-ness'. Bakhtin's studies on dialogue and language are nurturing: 'Any object of knowledge (including man) can be perceived and cognized as a thing. But a subject as such cannot be perceived and studied as a thing, for as a subject it cannot, while remaining a subject, become voiceless, and, consequently, cognition of it can only be *dialogic*' (Bakhtin, 2002: 161). My conversations with Brus about his self-injuring artistic operations in the late 1960s and the surgeries he later underwent helped me to see the clinical encounters I observe on a daily basis in a different light. He sharpened my senses and enabled me to perceive, for instance, the material components used in the surgical operating theatre under the phenomenological aspect of *Leiblichkeit*, or living bodily experience. During our collaboration I was frequently reminded of a form of personal knowledge that does not exist in isolation but only in communion.

Connecting tissue

In his speech at the presentation of our book, Frey referred to Günter Brus's *Bilddichtung* and to its section '*Einblick in ein Innenleben*' ('*Insight into an Inner Life*') as follows:

> Manfred Frey: There is a relatively bloodthirsty image of the middle of an operating room with a stomach cut open and the bloody gloves of the surgeon. Beneath the image are the words, 'Fairytale surgery penetrates the belly and paunch. Hollow probes furrow in the orchestra pit. Snow White anaesthesia snoozes in the glasshouse. And seven bloody ravens flap from his mouth.' I won't bother to interpret this, but this connection between fairytales and fairytale surgery often features the term 'dream' throughout its correspondence and interpretation. I don't know whether this relates to the fear of reality or the possibility of experiencing and processing reality through this, or indeed, allocating it to a person, a place. (2008)

The depictions of the artist's opened torso during surgery indicate a radical breach of taboos. According to the cultural historian Jonathan Sawday, in *The Body Emblazoned*: 'Modern surgeons or physicians are careful to shield, wherever possible, any possible sight of our own interiors when we become "patients". Indeed, the very word "patient" hints at the taboo connected with the body interior' (1996 [1995]: 12). In the context of studying Brus's *Narbenlehre* I began to investigate modes of becoming a *patient* with my own body.

Photographs of my stomach taken during an endoscopic examination were integrated into the book *Kleine Narbenlehre* as research materials. In the course of working with these pictures I quickly realized that I would always connect this colourful and glossy appearance of my interior with childhood memories – seeing myself sitting alone at the dining table, a full plate in front of me, and not being able to eat (Hogan and Pink, this volume, Chapter 13). My mother would not let me go to play until I had finished my lunch, which could take hours. Eating and digesting are problematic for me and often merge with unhappy feelings, not only in relation to food but also towards the cook (my mother), and recalling a nightmare-like image of myself as a skinny little

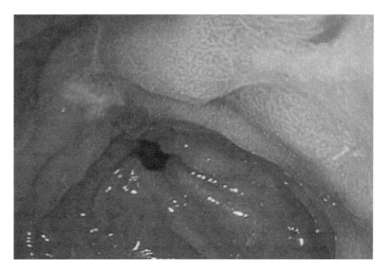

Figure 10.2   Michael Häfner, 2009

girl that is written deeply into my persona. A common saying in English is: 'The way to a person's heart is through the stomach'. This part of my body is highly sensitive. I raise this childhood anecdote because I consider my psychological and emotional conditions to be uncannily mirrored in the shiny walls of my intestines. This consideration has an important impact on the epistemological grounding with which I build my personal and subjective methodologies.

Inspired by the feminist artists Mona Hatoum and VALIE EXPORT, who produced medical images of their fleshy interiors with the help of endoscopy and presented them as video installations in art galleries, I use my own body as material for ethnography. Both artists experiment with the perception of the body's viscera. In *Corps étranger* (1994), Hatoum evokes issues of identification with her inner flesh, turning it into a terrain through which viewers can travel, while EXPORT's '*glottis* pieces emphasise that language and speech, commonly understood as channels for sharing thoughts, ideas, and emotions, can also be seen in terms of power and domination' (Sichel, 2010: 212). In both video works, healthy-looking bodies become subjects of inquiry and self-examination. Showing movement beneath the skin with the help of medical camera technology furthermore reveals different aspects of performativity and utterance – plunged into a delicately personal but synchronously reifying and distanced interpenetration, as in normal medicine. They mimic the characteristic features of a biomedical setting, for instance, with the use of a typical circular form to mark out the image of internal cavities. Endlessly caressing the boundaries of taboo, they put visitors in a rare and peculiar position, allowing their eyes to zoom into secret spaces.

In what was probably the last text he wrote before his death, *Toward a Methodology for the Human Sciences* (2000 [1975]), Bakhtin argued that the 'natural sciences have an object system (subjectless)' and, in comparison, 'our *thought* and our *practice*, not technical but *moral* (that is, our responsible deeds), are accomplished between two limits: attitudes toward the *thing* and attitudes toward the *personality. Reification* and *personification*' (Bakhtin, 2002: 168). In the course of developing the *Healing Mirrors* project with facially paralysed patients, I borrowed methodologies that are used in physical theatre and for the training of actors (Grotowski, 1991 [1968]; Leabhart, 2007; Richards, 2008; Stebbins, 2009 [1886]; Toporkov, 2001). The integration of daily yoga exercises and physical therapy in my work incidentally went along with one of my own stories of recovery. Movement increasingly became a part of my everyday life.

Mucosa speeches

While I was still in a weak condition, I continued to collaborate with Elke Krystufek, a renowned Austrian visual and performance artist. Elke has made hundreds of self-portraits. In her feminist art performances, she used her own body as a canvas and surface for ideological projections, often employing masquerade as a powerful element within her work. But this was in her former life. Last year she decided to stop producing art and to convert to Islam, wearing veils as working clothes. 'I always covered my head', she remarked recently in a discussion with the writer and filmmaker Chris Kraus at the Academy of Fine Arts Vienna. In her study, *The Art of Reflection* (1996), Marsha Meskimmon links the 'concept of masquerade … to the idea of excess and the carnivalesque body as described in the work of Mikhail Bakhtin'. According to the Russian literary theorist, she writes, 'carnival represented the space in which sharp boundaries between bodies could be less fixed or even removed' (Meskimmon, 1996: 122). The exchange with Elke Krystufek is *healing* for me in an unconventional way. She introduced me to her critical attitude towards allopathic medicine during our encounters and invited me to take belly-dance classes and to travel to Egypt together. Our collaboration helps me discover a form of self-healing through movement that is carried over into my work in *FEATURES*.

Elke and I both witness ongoing processes of transformation in each other – her conversion to Islam and my change of lifestyle with a strong curative aim, which includes dancing and other liberatory forms of movement. 'Intimacy does not arise when we gaze into Annie Sprinkle's uterine orifice. It is formed within relationships', she declared in a video interview at my studio in 2006. I included images of our adventurous desert tour in Egypt in a short movie about love, referring to a theatre piece Elke is currently working on. Her shift away from art production corresponds with her desire to engage with people in a way that allows for a more lively and energetic quality of being together.

In his essay, 'Hunger of an Ox', Italian philosopher Giorgio Agamben poses the question, 'What is dance other than the liberation of the body from its utilitarian movements, the exhibition of gestures in their pure inoperativity?' (2011: 111). Drawing on the relational qualities outlined above, Elke encouraged me to elaborate the endoscopy video recordings of my stomach as a material basis for the development of my illness story as *autopathography* (Tembeck, 2009). In January 2010, she was appointed curator of the exhibition *Hidden Passengers in Contemporary Art*, 2000–2009, at *Montehermoso* in Vitoria-Gasteiz (Spain) and asked me to contribute as one of eight video artists selected for a show entitled *STOWAWAYS*. My gastroenterologist, Michael Häfner, collaborated with me. Using the footage of an endoscopy examination of my intestines that revealed various benign ulcers, we prepared the art piece *Brot + Rosen* (*Bread + Roses*), about which Elke wrote:

> stomach ulcers turned her [Christina Lammer's] attention towards her own body and frailty, putting her in a different position from that of a researcher, with her gaze fixed on others. The minor or major illnesses of the participants in the artistic field are still not a widely discussed topic in the public arena; nevertheless they define the way we act professionally and politically – as we know very well that weak or injured people do not fight in the same way, and that their activism takes on a different form. (Krystufek, 2010)

As I frequently watched the medical images of my own '*organicity*' during the preparation of *Brot + Rosen* (2010), I tried to locate the injured spots within myself that could be identified in these video sequences. I naively thought that there must be a connection between what I perceived as painful internal sensations and what I saw on the gastroscopic movie. Instead, I learned that I was left alone with my living, bodily experience. My personal perception had hardly anything to do with the depicted signs of disease I saw on my computer screen. So I searched for ways to align my subjective impressions with the uncanny but beautiful *reifications* of myself in the image. By synchronizing this internal hollow *thing* with the sound of my breathing, the work took on a fleshy *personalization* and a vibrant rhythm. My gastroenterologist, however, found it to be slightly too vivid. Michael accompanied me to the opening of *STOWAWAYS*, and as we observed visitors' reactions towards the videos, he mentioned that he found our piece's soundtrack to be quite disturbing. His point of view immediately converged with the situation of image-making at the hospital and with his daily encounters with patients. 'Your breathing is totally relaxed during the procedures', he declared. I could not know because I was unconscious during the examination. I had recorded my breath that very morning, while feeling at ease.

Epilogue

This chapter has addressed the interrelations of epistemic cultures that are usually carefully set apart: for example, the intersections of plastic surgery and *Vienna Actionism*, or video arts and internal medicine. It explored advances in visual methodology that are strongly informed by *organic* and *personalized* expressive modes of knowledge production, including body-oriented approaches nurtured by theatre, sculpture, painting and filmmaking. Artur Zmijewski, for instance, a contemporary Rabelais in the world of visual arts and performance, actively transcends the boundaries between art and science. How far can the limits between the visual methodologies applied in sociology or anthropology and in artistic practices be stretched? I argue that social scientists can learn from the phenomenological and experiential knowledge that artists like Brus, Krystufek and Zmijewski continually produce.

Purse lips – doing physical therapeutic exercises to improve one's facial expressiveness is crucial in the frame of the *Healing Mirrors* video project. *Purse lips with lips open* – these orders are executed in front of the mirror by facially paralysed patients after they undergo plastic surgery. *Push mouth forward* – to date I have accompanied four people who are being treated by Frey and his team. *Suck in cheeks* – a seven-year-old girl from Switzerland.

Figure 10.3   Christina Lammer, Video still, Léonie 2011

I asked her to document scenes and experiences of her everyday life with a video camera. *Stretch mouth wide* – with the aim of teaching her caregivers about what it means to live with her condition (Chalfen and Rich, 2007: 53–70). *Stretch mouth wide with eyes closed* – a Norwegian man in his 20s who studies engineering, a Viennese woman who just turned 30 and works at her parents' company distributing medical apparatuses. *Show teeth* – she did her exercises at my studio and allowed me to videotape her while she was moving her face. *Pull top lip over bottom lip* – filming her through the orifice in the mirror apparatus. *Pull bottom lip over top lip* – the circular hole in the glass sheet hints at an analogy with medical imaging technologies like endoscopy. *Raise chin and pull down top lip* – similar to the Italian *tondo*, a circular picture or sculpture, which has a long tradition in art history. *Puff out cheeks with eyes closed* – the little one is comically grimacing at me. *Push air in and out* – an Italian mathematician living in Sweden is the fourth amongst patients suffering from this peculiar disability who are working with me. *Whistle* – when he tries to smile he has the impression that his face looks sad. *Make a big 'O' shape (open mouth wide)* – understandably, he does not like to appear sad. *Bring lips together to make a small 'o' shape* – so he still avoids smiling. *Wrinkle nose and move nose up and down* – in the style of Arnulf Rainer's art experiments *Face Farces* (1969–1971) and his series of *over-paintings* (1975–1978), and of Franz Xaver Messerschmidt's *Character Heads* (after 1770). *Wrinkle nose with eyes closed* – practising the expressive capacities with Tamar Tembeck who is trained in *Corporeal Mime*, another physical theatre method. *Open and close eyes and flutter eyelashes* – Artur Zmijewski gives me video lessons. *Raise forehead (surprised look) and move quickly up and down and back to centre* – I love his video installation, *An Eye for an Eye* (1998). *Raise forehead (surprised look) and stretch mouth wide* – healthy persons embracing amputees. 'They have been taken into the greatest confidence, allowed the most shameful touch, the greatest ignominy – they touch the scars' (Zmijewski, 2005: 176). *Raise forehead (surprised look), stretch mouth wide and close eyes*[3] – shame is an important issue in the dialogue among able-bodied and disabled human beings.

The 'healing mirrors' discussed in this chapter include heterogeneous aspects of *doing* methodology – experimentation, movement and the use of material components in order to develop a plastic vocabulary, comparable with the creation of a sculpture. Human expressiveness involves the body as a whole and is not confined to the features of the face or to particular gestures. In contrast to the artistic act of creation, the illumination of the body's exterior and interior for diagnostic and therapeutic reasons through allopathic medicine goes hand in hand with a loss of expressive personification. 'Healing mirrors' are not restricted to visual methodologies but rather emerge through internal and external sounds and forms of touch – for example, the peristaltic movements within the digestive pipes or the pulse rhythm. I argued that human agency is infused with an organic quality that is difficult to capture with scientific methods. In front of my video camera, Léonie, the Swiss girl, massaged her face as she did with her speech therapist. At some point I asked her to do it gently, avoiding anything that does not feel good. The movement of her features changed through this soft quality of touching. She was tenderly sculpting herself.

Acknowledgements

First I would like to thank Gerhard Lang and Tamar Tembeck for correcting my English. They made this chapter readable and understandable. Further thanks go to all the people who worked together with me during fieldwork at the hospital and beyond (without my collaboration partners this project would not be possible): Manfred Frey, head of the Department of Plastic and Reconstructive Surgery, Medical University, Vienna, and his team and patients; Michael Häfner, head of the Department of Internal Medicine, St Elisabeth Hospital, Vienna; Günter Brus, visual artist; Elke Krystufek, visual artist; Tamar Tembeck, physical theatre practitioner, art historian and curator; Artur Zmijewski, video artist and filmmaker.

Notes

1   The art historian Hermine Heller (†) was the daughter of Hermann Heller. She invited me to her house to study original historical materials of her father's bequest. In a video interview conducted in the frame of CORPO*realities* (2004–2009, www.corporealities.org), my research on body images in the medical context, Hermine Heller (2006) refers to her father's 55 mimic masks.

2   Luigi Pirandello died in the year of publication of Walter Benjamin's *The Work of Art in the Age of Mechanical Reproduction* (1936).

3   Source: Fialka-Moser, Veronika, 2007, University Clinic for Physical Medicine and Rehabilitation, MUV. List of exercises and drawings for facially paralysed patients.

References

Agamben, G. (2011) *Nudities*. Stanford, CA: Stanford University Press.

Bakhtin, M.M. (2000 [1975]) *The Dialogic Imagination*. Austin, TX: University of Texas Press.

Bakhtin, M.M. (2002 [1986]) *Speech Genres and Other Late Essays*. Austin, TX: University of Texas Press.

Benjamin, W. (1977 [1936]) *Das Kunstwerk im Zeitalter seiner technischen Reproduzierbarkeit*. Frankfurt am Main: Suhrkamp.

Chalfen, R. and Rich, M. (2007) 'Combining the applied, the visual and the medical: patients teaching physicians with visual narratives', in S. Pink (ed.),

Visual Interventions: Applied Visual Anthropology. New York and Oxford: Berghahn Books. pp. 53–70.

Doy, G. (2005) *Picturing the Self*. London and New York: I.B. Tauris.

Gell, A. (1998) *Art and Agency: An Anthropological Theory*. Oxford: Clarendon Press.

Goffman, E. (1959) *The Presentation of Self in Everyday Life*. New York: Anchor Books.

Grotowski, J. (1991 [1968]) *Towards a Poor Theatre*. London: Methuen Drama.

Illich, I. (2002 [1975]) *Limits to Medicine – Medical Nemesis: The Expropriation of Health*. London and New York: Marion Boyars.

Kraus, C. (2011) *Where Art Belongs*. Cambridge, MA: MIT Press.

Kraynak, J. (ed.) (2005) *Please Pay Attention Please: Bruce Nauman's Words*. Cambridge, MA and London: MIT Press.

Krystufek, E. (2010) *Stowaways: Hidden Passengers in Contemporary Art, 2000–2009*. Vitoria-Gasteiz: Montehermoso.

Lammer, C. (2007a) 'Sociology of breast tissue', *European Surgery*, 39 (4): 208–15.

Lammer, C. (2007b) 'Bodywork: social somatic interventions in the operating theatres of invasive radiology', in S. Pink (ed.), *Visual Interventions: Applied Visual Anthropology*. New York and Oxford: Berghahn Books. pp. 91–116.

Lammer, C. (2007c) *Günter Brus: Kleine Narbenlehre*. Vienna: Löcker Verlag.

Lammer, C. (2009) 'Empathographies: using body art related video approaches in the environment of an Austrian teaching hospital', *International Journal of Multiple Research Approaches*, 3 (3): 264–75.

Lammer, C. (ed.) (2010) *CORPOrealities*. Vienna: Löcker Verlag.

Leabhart, T. (2007) *Etienne Decroux*. London and New York: Routledge.

Leder, D. (1990) *The Absent Body*. Chicago, IL and London: University of Chicago Press.

MacDougall, D. (2006) *The Corporeal Image: Film, Ethnography, and the Senses*. Princeton, NJ and Oxford: Princeton University Press.

Meskimmon, M. (1996) *The Art of Reflection*. New York: Columbia University Press.

Ots, T. (2003 [1994]) 'The silenced body – the expressive Leib: on the dialectic of mind and life in Chinese cathartic healing', in T.J. Csordas (ed.), *Embodiment and Experience*. Cambridge: Cambridge University Press. pp. 116–36.

Pink, S. (2009) *Doing Sensory Ethnography*. London: Sage.

Pirandello, L. (2010 [1926]) *Shoot! The Notebooks of Serafino Gubbio, Cinematograph Operator*. Milton Keynes: Dodo Press.

Radley, A. (2009) *Works of Illness – Narrative, Picturing and the Social Response to Serious Disease*. London: InkerMen Press.

Richards, T. (2008) *Heart of Practice: Within the Workcenter of Jerzy Grotowski and Thomas Richards*. London and New York: Routledge.

Sawday, J. (1996 [1995]) *The Body Emblazoned*. London and New York: Routledge.

Schechner, R. (2003) *Performance Theory*. London and New York: Routledge.

Schilder, P. (1978 [1950]) *The Image and Appearance of the Human Body*. New York: International Universities Press.

Sichel, B. (2010) 'To us all. VALIE EXPORT'S Film and Video Works', in A. Husslein-Arco, A. Nollert and S. Rollig (eds), *VALIE EXPORT Time and Countertime*. Köln: Verlag der Buchhandlung Walther König. pp. 207–13.

Spence, J. (1988 [1986]) *Putting Myself in the Picture*. Seattle: The Real Comet Press.

Stanislavski, C. (1963) *An Actor's Handbook*. Berkshire: Methuen Drama.

Stanislavski, K.S. (1984 [1948]) *Die Arbeit des Schauspielers an der Rolle*. Berlin: deb.

Stebbins, G. (2009 [1886]) *Delsarte System of Dramatic Expression*. Charleston: Bibliolife.

Tembeck, T. (2009) 'Performative autopathographies – self representations of physical illness in contemporary art', doctoral thesis, Montreal, McGill University.

Toporkov, V. (2001) *Stanislavski in Rehearsal*. London: Methuen.

Zmijewski, A. (2005) *If It Happened Only Once It's As If It Never Happened*. Warsaw: Zacheta National Gallery of Art.

11

DIGITAL TECHNOLOGIES, VISUAL RESEARCH AND THE NON-FICTION IMAGE

Roderick Coover with Pat Badani, Flavia Caviezel, Mark Marino, Nitin Sawhney and William Uricchio

Midway through a conversation which is the centerpiece of this chapter, Flavia Caviezel, whose multimedia project *Check on Arrival – Borderland Airport* takes users into the in-between spaces of airport security checkpoints, describes the use of interactive tools such as hyperlinks and keywords as *a superior form of editing*. Take it more broadly – both literally and metaphorically. Practices and logics of ordering and sequencing that have long been central to work done by film editors infuse digital projects in research, production/post-production and reception, and they do so across programmes and disciplines.

That the film editor's job has always been metaphorically hypertextual is a good place to begin a chapter about the impact of digital technologies on visual research and documentary production. Once upon a time, the film editor who cut film at a Moviola or flatbed searched among hanging strands and labelled cores of clips and sequences, mixing, taping, gluing, and marking-up films with her white pencils and sharpies. She might have imagined countless possible versions, voices, and angles before arriving at a final, linear (single-channel) print. Similarly, the videotape editor would speed and jig through tapes, more often than not stacked in piles on shelves around the edit station, with its decks, mixers, controllers, text generators, scripts, logs, and log notes. Maurice Halbwachs (1992) famously describes unshared memories as being as illusive as dreams – that memories gain meaning, value and endurance by sharing them. Much the same is true for the experience had by the film editor, whose countless imagined alternative versions vanish with the release of the answer print because they had no shared expression.

There are many practical ways that digital technologies offer *a superior form of editing*. Programs make materials simultaneously accessible so that editors can collate clips into many differing bins, build multiple sequences and compare versions. The editor moves easily between visual, audio and effects work, and between poetic and rhetorical modes or logics. She can readily undo, redo and juxtapose differing versions of a project. Materials can be input from many sources and output in many formats such as those for tape, disc, web, etc.

More significantly, layering and compositing found in editing and effects programs have altered cinematic premises about the frame, continuity and montage; they have expanded cinematic rhetoric and poetics, perhaps defining an increasingly hybrid language that fuses writing and images (Coover, 2011a, 2011b; Manovich, 2002, 2006). The attention to mise-en-scene given by framing and the qualities of time provided by continuity are not dialectically opposed to montage as they were considered to be in traditional filmmaking. Layering and compositing allows for, among other things, co-existence: the uncut image can share screen-space with the edited one; the motion image may share space with the still; the framed detail may be juxtaposed with a panoramic long shot. However, most significant for those participating in this chapter's conversation may be the ways that digital technologies have altered fundamental theories about how documentary images work and how to work with them.

The first important way that digital technologies have transformed visual research projects is organizational. In single-channel, time-based work, a shot plays in time and when it ends, the next shot plays; time is the primary structuring force. Interactive and non-linear works use diverse structures, such as spatial ones. A time-based object (a clip, sequence, etc.) may have links (paths, routes, threads) to other time-based objects; these may even be mapped through a program's interface, as is the case with hypertext writing packages such as Eastgate Storyspace® and interactive DVD programs like DVD Studio Pro®. Similarly, such objects and their icons may be spatially arranged together on a webpage. Alternatively, organizational models may be designed with data sets in which materials are accessed by keywords or by other connections, such as randomized ones.

Furthermore, practices of editing occur across once-distinct practices. Video-editing tools are writing tools alongside word processing programs. Not only are researchers and makers combining ways of editing images, text, photographs, sounds, and so forth, they are also increasingly producing works in many differing formats; a single project may result in a combination of films, websites, essays, books, performances, etc. While digital technologies may invite an integration of diverse kinds of writing and audio-visual media, they also allow for varied and multiple dissemination. This allows for the inclusion of diverse perspectives and expressive modes; while some things are better said directly in an essay, others may be better said, for example, through first-person accounts, motion images, music, or even dance or poetry. Further, positions offered using one approach can sit next to different or even contradictory positions arrived at via another approach *without needing to be reconciled or mediated in the same fashion.*

This integration of practices is facilitated by the fact that editing tools are increasingly common and easy to use; many programs are even designed to look alike or work alike, particularly those produced by a single company (for example, Microsoft Office or Adobe Suite software). Sharing tools among differing practices is challenging disciplinary concepts and methods (Bartscherer and Coover, 2011) and provoking exciting discussions about where disciplinary approaches may merge and where borders between disciplinary practices are becoming redefined.

Figure 11.1 *The LA Flood Project*, Mark Marino

Los Angeles seems to be a basin of crises, whether being destroyed in film or undergoing a fire, earthquake, or mudslide on the nightly news. Its history is also marked by social unrest: the Watts Riots and Chicano Moratorium in the 1960s and 1970s and the LA Rebellion in the 1990s. Covering almost 500 square miles of land, the city brings together 70-some smaller cities and many ethnic and social enclaves. Anna Deveare Smith may have discovered the perfect narrative structure for depicting such a city in her one-woman-performing-many-voices show, *Twilight: Los Angeles*.

The LA Flood Project builds on her model by presenting a collection of oral histories and fictional testimonies through the one medium that connects more in the city than cars or personal computers: mobile phones. By connecting these histories to GIS data, the project seeks to add a layer of metadata to the city through which travellers can encounter voices of the city in crisis while living in the city in between the exclamation points of most recent and forthcoming traumatic events. Together with an emergency simulation of a flood, the oral histories and fictional narrative triangulate to help visitors discover their own place in this landscape of crises. (See http://laflood.citychaos.com/.)

The participants in this conversation also address how computer technologies are facilitating collaboration. In their projects, collaboration occurs by working with teams or inviting subject contributions in project development and production, and by working with others to exhibit, screen, stream or perform works. In a couple of works cited, collaboration also includes inviting user feedback or user-generated versions. Interactive documentary and visual research projects can readily incorporate differing voices, perspectives and arguments. As with conversations, linear arguments and narratives may co-exist with alternative and diverse forms of expression. Collaboration propels theoretical and practical considerations. While the researcher may still advance focused arguments, she may not be in control of all the elements that make up a work or of all the ways it is used. Of course, collaborations were frequently necessary in managing the apparatus of cinema production and, in ethnographic projects, in creating the conditions that might allow for filmmaking. Due to the cross-disciplinary and multimedia conditions of contemporary documentary arts, the range of perspectives that may be incorporated has been growing wider. For example, Nitin Sawhney draws together videos recorded with youths on the Gaza–Israel border, provoking expressions on the ground and producing responses across international borders, while Pat Badani records cafe-goers speaking in several languages.

The collaborative nature of these contemporary working methods is fostering learning and exchange across fields and, in the process, creating individuals like those in this conversation who move fluidly between research, art and critical discourse. Pat Badani uses video interviews recorded in cafes in different countries to study what it means to have a home in the age of global travel; these are embedded in an interactive installation project inviting user responses. Flavia Caviezel takes her camera on both sides of X-ray machines at airport security checkpoints to examine human aspects of the security ritual. Roderick Coover's interactive cinema project examines production(s) of place in the American desert West using a navigational environment that stimulates choice-making. Mark Marino's lexia-structured *LA Flood Project* takes a quasi-documentary approach to imagining the experiences that might surround a flooded city. Nitin Sawhney works with youths on the Gaza–Israel border to stimulate discourse on how physical barriers shape narratives and their attending metaphors. William Uricchio writes about multimedia technologies and works with creative teams at MIT to develop interactive cinema projects which invite user participation in documentary editing processes.

All are redefining the concept of what constitutes the non-fiction image. The approaches discussed in this chapter do not deny the value of single-channel documentary work. The approaches described in this chapter present alternative approaches to working with documentary images that may be particularly

Figure 11.2 *'Where are you from?'* stories, Pat Badani

In 2001, wanting to explore the Internet as a means of bridging cultures and geographies around ideas of foreignness and migration, Pat Badani conceived a project called *'Where are you from?'*, a hybrid project that exists both in the web as a large interactive archive of video on demand, and in physical space as participatory installation/events in six world cities. The project explores where people come from and where they go to in search of a better life, raising questions of migration, globalization and cultural identity along with probing the fundamental question of how to define notions of 'home'. The work crosses media formats as well as borders and uses interactivity and keyword selections. It also explicitly draws attention to its own production, locations in which interviews were gathered and the recording conditions (see www.patbadani.net/where_from2.html).

exciting in the context of the kinds of research projects that take place in the humanities and social sciences. The projects discussed in this chapter demonstrate ways to integrate video with text, sound, movement, maps, and infinite other kinds of materials and activities in the research process.

It may be particularly apt, under such conditions, that this chapter takes the form of a conversation. In a departure from expository formats that dominate critical writing, the work is open-ended and shaped by the diverse perspectives of the participants. Where conventional exposition frequently edits away divergent issues to maintain focused attention upon a primary argument, conversations may suggest multiple directions when participants propose threads not followed as well as the ones picked-up and continued. Thus, this conversation engages a set of issues in form as well as content.

It begins with the fundamental question: What is new and different about making documentaries and other non-fiction works with digital tools?

William Uricchio: One difference from the analogue tradition is *what* we have access to in terms of where our cameras can go and whose voices we can reach. New digital technologies are enabling us to reach places, people and conditions that have long been inaccessible. The ubiquity of recording and transmitting technologies – the camera equipped cell phone for example – is a game changer. It has changed not only what we can access, but who does the accessing. The great mass of the public is now potentially engaged in recording life as it unfolds, and better, crafting it into coherent form, into documentary. The digital turn has also offered more than tools: it has also led to the development of new environments such as the network. The Internet has effectively done away with the institutional filters that long stood between organizers of sounds and images and the public. The world's largest stock footage library is at our fingertips; and anyone's documentary is guaranteed distribution. This unfettered access to the public is terrific; but it also has a price that we can see when we turn the formula around: the public also has unfettered access to individuals' footage and documentaries. They can remix it, repurpose it, see it in contexts and ways that its creator never imagined – and perhaps never intended. The long reign of the author or artist as a controlling presence is under siege. The challenge can be as simple as that also afforded by DVDs and DVRs, allowing viewers to fast-forward, freeze or repeat; or as extreme as allowing deconstruction, reassembly, and radical new uses. Ideally, of course, sympathetic collaborations between author and audience will lead to productive interactions, constructive dialogue, and perhaps even new kinds of texts and audio-visual terrains.

Mark Marino: There are also different forms of navigational systems for traversing collected narratives. For example, the Literatronica engine on which *A Show of Hands* is built uses a spatial metaphor of lexias. Remember how Eastgate *Storyspace®* gave you that visual map? Literatronica does that with lexias, although distances are signified by numbers, and the numbers make a difference. *The LA Flood Project* uses a more literal space-navigation system. The user travels through the map or the space to encounter the text pieces, much as they might travel through a museum. So, space is important in both, though in different ways. One is tied to the historical city; the other is tied to narrative logic.

Nitin Sawhney: For me, the mapping work is a part of the workshops we conduct with youth. It's a way to begin to perceive their neighbourhoods, using photography, maps and interviews that lead to richer narratives they develop further in their films in the project, *Voices Beyond Walls*. Our documentary, *Tarya Warakiya* (*Flying Paper*), is a parallel project, which also engages these youth in extended work with us. The mapping for us is an intermediate part of the process, but one that is revealed in the presentation of the work in exhibits. Last summer in Jerusalem, we had two groups of kids in parallel workshops use mapping to understand each other's neighbourhoods across the dividing wall and then go on to make films that built on those narratives. The city was their canvas and mapping surely helped them develop the storyboards and scripts for their projects.

There tended to be three main zones – the city, the refugee camp and the buffer zone. One of the things we did with kids who lived there was to work with them to design a kite camera that takes aerial photography/ video of their buffer space from above. The 'Kite Cam' was used as part of the documentary to provide aerial views during the kite festival, though we only managed to get some footage before it crashed. So, in a sense we tried to get participants to think about their space and buffer zone through the filmmaking process.

Coover: I get the sense that *making* the film is as important and valuable in creating connections as *showing* it. This emphasis on process and participation seems to emerge in many differing ways among documentary makers of our time. Thinking back to the kinds of exchanges offered by Jean Rouch and Edgar Morin in *Chronique d'un été* (*Chronicle of a Summer*, 1960), are collaborations of our time different?

Pat Badani: Well, there probably isn't a radical shift per se, but rather one that is part of the media continuum.

In terms of 'making' documentary film, Rouch and Morin's project already pioneered a new aesthetic by changing the connections made between author and subject. Their strategy was simple yet groundbreaking: they would ask non-actors to speak about their personal experiences while being filmed, an approach that turned the process of documentary making into a collaborative and participatory one. Interestingly, this was facilitated by what was then a 'new technology', namely 16mm film, sync sound, and light hand-held cameras that allowed them to take the project to the streets and to document 'true life' in a spontaneous way. However, when I think back at some of the conversations Rouch and Morin had about their project, I remember Rouch expressing serious doubts about the possibility of recording a conversation naturally with the camera present. A similar intervention would seem less awkward today because of the way that media technology is part of our everyday lives. If Rouch and Morin had to overcome people's uneasiness in front of the camera due to the lack of familiarity with media broadcasting in 1960, today the problem is a diametrically opposite one. For me, the question is still how to document conversations naturally, but – due to expanded media being here, due to the technology – for me the question has become: What is natural?

Figure 11.3   *Voices Beyond Walls*, Nitin Sawhney

Voices Beyond Walls is a participatory media initiative that supports creative expression and human rights advocacy among marginalized children and youth (aged 10–25) through digital storytelling workshops, new media production, and global dissemination of their work. It was founded in 2006 to serve young Palestinians living in refugee camps in the West Bank, Gaza and East Jerusalem. The project consists of a programme of digital media training and capacity building with local community centres, collaborative digital storytelling and neighbourhood mapping workshops conducted with youth, as well as ongoing evaluation and follow-up opportunities for learning and creative media engagement. Like many of the works discussed in this chapter, *Voices Beyond Walls* has taken on many forms, including the 'Re-imagining Gaza' programme in the Gaza Strip and a parallel workshop in Al Aroub camp in the West Bank (see www.voicesbeyondwalls.org).

The shift in process and participation that you ask about is perhaps more evident in terms of today's connections created in 'showing' the documentary material. While Rouch and Morin relied on traditional methods of distribution for showing the film *Chronicles of a Summer*, *'Where are you from?'* is part of a generation of works making use of an interactive Internet-based archive of video on demand, a new type of broadcasting having as a precedent the community-based video projects of the 1970s and similar to these in terms of their intentionality, but with a major feature that separates them from their media precedents (and ultimately making them more effective, in my view). Instead of a 'one to many' form of communication as with film or video, Internet broadcasting is a platform for showing documentary material that offers communication from 'many to many' and is furthermore openly accessible worldwide, any time, to anyone with Internet access. The question of access is huge because this feature creates unprecedented connections and new collaborations with viewers who also become to a certain degree participants and co-editors.

Flavia Caviezel: When you put your video recordings or other materials online after the recordings there is an immediacy. The exchange process with the participants is suddenly, virtually represented. I anticipated that this might be very sensitive. During our research project at Zurich Airport (2004–2006) on control procedures, we had to negotiate with the officials of the airport police and customs about the final presentation form of research results (videos, photos, statistics, texts). Our aim was to develop an interactive and collaborative online platform, but they didn't give us the permission to put the material online because it was still considered subversive and uncontrollable. Concerning the collaboration with the controllers at the airport, we had to create an atmosphere of trust to get the permission for interviewing and observing control procedures. This took quite a long time. Our topics included not only visible unveiling but also invisible phenomena like the so-called 'profiling' and 'routing' and how these become manifest in the heads of the control agents. Furthermore, the guards' perceptions of the border area and working places were points of analysis. To approach these different phenomena it was crucial to create intimacy with the airport employees during approximately one hour of interviewing, and this was best achieved in filming only by one person. You might say that we, as researchers, performed as 'accomplices' for one hour with persons who could have completely different points of view, and after finishing we changed our roles back again to be critical outside-observers – a classical situation of research in social sciences described in the concept of 'becoming and othering'.

Badani: I think that both Flavia's project and mine are good examples of the kinds of different collaborations that are shaped by context. You have had to develop an extraordinary process to enter into the world of the security checkpoints that requires all sorts of collaborations that also reflect the institutional contexts, and meanwhile they had to be carried out in places where maybe you had less control over the environments; and I had to enter different communities and contexts as well for my project.

There are different levels and notions of collaboration that emerge in a variety of ways in the making of my work, for example: collaborations between researchers and institutions; collaborations with funding sources; collaborations with coffee shop owners and staff; collaborations with city park officials; with city government officials; with community centres and their staff; collaborations with about 130 individuals (total strangers in six cities and in three languages) who came to tell me their stories in front of my camera; and lastly there is a collaborative process established with online visitors who navigate, make choices and, in a way, co-edit the work.

Caviezel: I would say the degree of intimacy might be different, but we wouldn't have got anything specific about unseen phenomena and mind concepts without trust and intimacy.

Another point you mentioned before is the possibility of interactive online media to allow for collaboration, for example, in getting feedback from the user. Because we couldn't put the project online and let users comment or add materials, we tried to find an appropriate interactive computer alternative. Along with representing the heterogeneous, often-changing controlling processes of the airport is reflection upon knowledge representation and processes of cognition where an interrelation of authors and users become manifest.[1] So, the idea of our *interactive form* of reception is to offer a user in the exhibition situation the possibility to surf with his or her own 'dramaturgy' through the research material and, therefore, to create an individualized 'narrative'.

Figure 11.4   *Unknown Territories*, Roderick Coover

In *Unknown Territories*, users navigate vast, scrolling, symbol-rich landscapes evocative of the canyon lands of the Colorado River in the American Southwest. The project asks: How do we learn to picture a place, and what impact does that have on how the land is used? The symbols and icons reveal fragments of visual information, archival recordings, historical narratives, and imaginaries. These are based on the writings of John Wesley Powell and the crew of his Colorado River Exploring Expeditions of 1869 and 1871 in one gallery, and of writer Edward Abbey and his compatriots in another. The environments offer something that a linear documentary cannot: choices. Viewers become users. The spatial structure allows users to navigate among primary texts. It allows users both to follow the researcher's narrative choices and to create their own connections through the paths they weave (see www.unknownterritories.org).

Coover: In a way, then, such projects give agency to both the subject and the reader – connecting them not in time but in a virtual space that spans time, and a narrative structure gives way to some other kind of activity . . .

Marino: Story gives way to space the way Victor Hugo and those miserables give way to Paris. One can narrate a trip through a city, but their experience is not necessarily narrated: that is what I learned from reading the transcripts and trails of users in *A Show of Hands*. Contemporary digital productions might be best thinking not in lines of flight but in land and cityscapes. While we used to talk of a reader making their own stories, maybe we need to think about encounters between visitors and spaces.

William Uricchio: I think we've touched on an important aspect of computing in the capacity of digital tools to open up participation – not just in allowing an audience to see things, but also to produce things. In MIT's HyperStudio project, *Berliner sehen* (developed by Kurt Fendt and Ellen Crocker), we incorporated 18 hours of documentary footage centred around eight people. The footage was broken into about two-minute clips. Each of those clips was coded according to things the individuals talk about, neighbourhood, history, politics. Users call up the characters and themes that they are interested in learning about, and the program might provide 24 or so randomly organized but appropriately coded thumbnails. Each thumbnail represents a two-minute clip. Click! Users can then play and explore that material – repeating the process through all 18 hours of footage if they want! – in a coherent way, based on human characters and themes. They can then drop and drag those thumbnails into a linear framework and build their own narrative or argument. Kurt Fendt and Ellen Crocker did that about 15 years ago with initial filming starting in 1995 and the release of the first online version in 1997. But, in fact, it's a documentary project. It was shot in a traditional way (a film crew), and its main innovation lies in the recombinatory nature of the shot assembly process and the viewer's role in exploring the material and putting the pieces together. In the decade since *Berliner sehen* first appeared, lots has changed ... including the fact that most cell phones have video cameras. Most people are now potential filmmakers – not just potential editors – and with online live streaming repositories such as Qik, there are many new possibilities to help support a new approach to documentary. We're now developing a project in the area of collaborative documentary production (the repurposing of *Berliner sehen* is a first step), taking advantage of the camera-equipped public. We are also trying to generate an online editing tool, so that any of the people who put their footage up there can use any of this footage, and re-edit it afterwards into some sort of coherence. In order to keep the process social, to keep the emphasis on a creative community, if someone uses your footage, you're notified, and you can access the page where it is used and re-edit it if you wish. So it becomes an intricate process where ordinary people generate the footage and then mix and remix it in a collaborative way.

Coover: How do we understand some of the limits or problems of revealing the process? Many of the projects we have been discussing partially reveal a process but not entirely, and it would seem one major cause for this is the sheer quantity of research that goes into a project that in the end is only distantly related to a work's thesis.

Badani: This is a very valid point. There is so much material related to the making of projects of this magnitude that never is shared or viewed, material that is nonetheless an intrinsic part of the work's meaning. Because so much of my work is process-oriented, I have often tried to think of solutions to this question, and I've found that there exist certain conventions for doing this that can be adapted to new media works. For example, an exhibition catalogue with an introduction and visual documentation can serve this revelatory function, and in my piece, *'Where are you from?'*, it was practical to create a separate page with this information, enabling me to catalogue, describe and contextualize the work. I located some of my process descriptions in the 'credits', including my interview permission papers. In this way, the credits page also becomes an information space that provides the visitor with archival material with which to contextualize the work and gain greater depth and understanding. For example, I include details of a specific recording instance in Chicago that is pretty much like how the projects were done in other world cities. However, the question remains: How much does the public need to know when you show a work, when you exhibit a work? If one is a researcher working in culturally sensitive issues or making a work for other researchers, perhaps one has a stronger reason for revealing each small step of the process. But the visual artist exhibiting in visual art forums like galleries, museums and new media festivals may not be likely to reveal the process unless the curator is doing a process-based exhibition because, in many cases, too much information can be more distracting than helpful at the level of viewer experience. Having said that, there are new curatorial approaches that pay attention to the challenges in question due to the emergence of art projects informed by interdisciplinary practices (such as scientific research) that are an intrinsic part of the work's coherence.

Caviezel: It's probably a difference between art and social science projects, especially those in anthropology, which has a very strong tradition of examining individual research processes. To get over (self)reflecting forms which we found either lengthy, redundant or euphemizing the power relationship between authors and protagonists, we tried to include more subtle forms; the library-like organization of the research material with linking keywords allows the user to unveil relations or interdependencies between the different topics. If, for example, you take the keyword 'forbidden', you are provided with

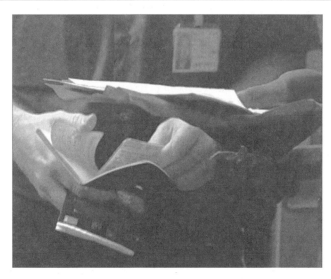

Figure 11.5   *Check on Arrival – Borderland Airport*, Flavia Caviezel

Zurich Airport demarcates borders in the middle of Switzerland. It is a hub for more than 17 million passengers and a terminal for about 400,000 tons of freight per year. In this constructed space, borders are crossed every day to our closest neighbouring countries or via flight destinations such as Lagos, Tel Aviv or Beijing. In 2005, a research team spent time at the airport to look at recent tendencies in the checking of people, baggage and goods, focusing on the issues of control systems and the role and interpretation of technologically produced visualizations. Using a platform that was developed by Flavia Caviezel and Susanna Kumschick at the University of the Arts Zurich and realized in collaboration with Videocompany Zofingen and V2_Lab Rotterdam, the interactive work organizes 90 minutes of edited videos, photos and other documentation to focus on the airport as a border space, becoming a controversial stage for current changes: What is the significance of country borders in a globalized world? What are they supposed to protect, and against what? (See www.ith-z.ch/forschung/check+it.)

a spectrum of what doesn't pass the controlling devices at the border – from dangerous goods to micro-organisms to migrants. All are perceived in a similar way by the controlling personnel. To put those materials under the same key-word and show them side by side may be seen as our reflection on the political impact of control. I would describe these linkages as *a superior form of editing*. Another example is the keyword 'stop', which triggers reflections about the limits of research in a border area.

Coover: Yes, that's a huge part of what happens in anthropology which is concerned both with the process of gathering information and the canons and discourse to which it speaks. On the other hand, practitioners of interpretive anthropology, and visual anthropology in particular, frequently note the dilemma of what to do with all those field notes and other data that may be tangentially related to the primary question or final work. This is one place where the impact of other arts and methods, including many made newly accessible through new media such as Panorama and visual kinds of indexing, are shifting the discussion. With these tools materials can be organized in more than one way and disseminated in differing formats, as was the case of *Unknown Territories*, which was presented as a multi-monitor exhibition, a web-work, a film, a set of photographs and a series of essays. But then, even with all those options, only a small portion of the research is likely to be used or even relevant.

Marino: When I was writing *A Show Of Hands*, I became very conscious of the number of lexias since the system relayed the percentage read – answering an age-old (maybe a tiny age) complaint about hypertexts that you never know where the bottom is, and so often, you feel like you are free-falling. If I went over 100 lexias, each page read would make less than 1 per cent of impact. Talk about a bottomless pit for contemporary reading on the net. Both the oral history and narrative components of *LA Flood* take on a different philosophy; the content can be nearly infinite. The number of histories are unlimited, or relatively unlimited, because the pine tree is in the pinecone, or pine nut, if you are in Providence, and the mountain is in the pine tree.

Coover: That sounds like a moment in Italo Calvino's *Invisible Cities* (1974) when Marco Polo is talking to Khan about the emperor's chessboard and in the knot on one square begins to read a history of the empire …

Marino: Yes, and the chessboard is, of course, so fitting there too, because Calvino was so mathematical about his constraints. Have you ever seen the constraints for *If On A Winter's Night A Traveler*? (1981). It's like lambda calculus. It would send Lacan into the asylum. I think that's true of many of us, when we stop tracing plot lines, we turn to other rules to create the thingness – the properties that will hold it all together … the accent or shape of jaw that distinguishes a Hatfield from a McCoy. For my work, it is a characteristic of the prose that emerges in each work like an identifier that indicates the piece belongs to the whole …

Uricchio: One of the big challenges comes in the area of coherence. When we have linear narrative or an argument in an academic journal, coherence is guaranteed, or, at least, promised. Coherence is not necessarily lost when we give the user more freedom; however, with that freedom comes a greater chance of incoherence or something else, a meta-coherence. One of the interesting things to emerge here is that this is driving scholars and artists to find other strategies for coherence. We used to rely upon narrative as a primary structuring form. Now we have cartography, which enables a kind of coherence without necessarily linking the whole video to the story. That's really quite interesting to me.

Figure 11.6   *Berliner sehen*, Kurt Fendt and Ellen Crocker, MIT

Documenting the many facets of how the Fall of the Wall has impacted eight personal life stories in Berlin is the focus of *Berliner sehen*, an interactive documentary expressively created for a multi-linear viewing experience. Eighteen hours of video-taped conversations between residents of two neighbourhoods in the former eastern and western part of the city were segmented into short clips of about 90 seconds in length and tagged with thematic and geolocation data, combined with six hours of historical documentary footage and hundreds of public documents from public and personal archives to form a network of dynamically connected video clips, photos, and texts. Users access *Berliner sehen* through an interface that presents them with a randomized selection of materials based on the selected person and/or theme/s. Documents can be viewed by pulling them into the centre of the user interface, simultaneously also highlighting related themes, and thus allowing further exploration in different yet connected thematic or character-based directions. The resulting remixes represent the users' views on issues of change, hopes, and memory, a specific look at a personal life story, or a combination of several life stories. In the future, spatial and time-based representations of the materials and the user-created mini-documentaries allow for yet more perspectives on the multi-faceted issues in the aftermath of the fall of the Berlin Wall (see www.mit.edu/~fll/projects/BerlinerSehen.shtml).

Argument, though, is trickier. Argument is often about sequence, and meaningful sequence is less tolerant of manipulation. So with argument, we have more of a limited case. However, on the experience side of things, we are seeing greater affordances. Compelling experiences are key for many artists, offering them a way to keep viewers engaged and to encourage viewers to explore and reflect upon the work. The less artists can use narrative as a crutch to lean on, and the more navigational choice they give to their audience, the more important experience will be in binding the work into something coherent and satisfying.

Sawhney: In conflict and contested spaces like the ones we work in, the 'sense of coherence' that William mentioned plays a crucial role for youth living there to function and support resilience. It is informed both by a coherent narrative of the conflict and also by their ability to retain freedom to navigate the urban spaces they inhabit. I know this is a meta response to what William was saying, but what I like to think is that in the process of the neighbourhood mapping and photo work they do, they actually link this sense of narrative and space quite well. This helps to make their films so compelling. For the viewer/audience it's a different thing. When I show the Gaza sensory footage from our documentary work – it all seems a bit ephemeral until I locate those narratives on a map of the Gaza Strip. This helps audiences recognize the spatial context of the places we investigate visually and the contested realities of the place, whether it's the war-torn city, the congested camp or the tense buffer zones. The film footage often contradicts many of the perceptions of those places, and this is quite interesting for us as filmmakers. So we have to find ways to locate the film spaces for the viewers and I think that's where an online dimension that complements the linear film may indeed be crucial.

Badani: I remember all of 10 years ago, when the first Internet-based art works emerged, it was fairly standard to find lengthy texts not only explaining to the user what to do – how to navigate through the site and what plug-ins to download – one also had to go through a lengthy description of the project written by the artist before finding gratification in experiencing the work itself (provided all the technology worked). We don't see that anymore now that web tools and web-interface are more efficient and intuitive, and now that the public-at-large is used to navigating the web. Instead there are new pressures to employ fancier tools, and to see how artists use these tools as a kind of game play. This is also very important in the structuring of online works. It has to be said that rewarding the viewer in some way is at the core of a lot of Internet-based art works, both those that explicitly utilize game strategies and those that discretely integrate a sense of play. In some cases, part of the pleasure is simply experiencing the 'cause/effect' phenomenon; seeing how one action might be rewarded by an interesting result. So, the user may be engrossed with the play involved in navigating and might seem to forget about content, and that's interesting as well. As an artist creating in and for this environment, I need to acknowledge this phenomenon and work with it.

Marino: However, if the narrative becomes the space, it is foolish to create long cues through that space or to require that your guest see every room. You can no longer count on people reading to the end. It seems like vanity to expect readers to find all your Easter Eggs, to want to follow the tree to the ends of all your branches. Your work is part of their multichannel, many-tabbed, multi-tasking narrative encounters. For example, there's no reason to expect that they have closed their email, chat, or Facebook windows while they are encountering your work, any more than that they stop answering their phone when they are walking through your city (or locative media narrative). So, our job is not to be their tour guide but instead their cruise director or perhaps merely the host who invites all the guests to the party.

Caviezel: Yes, though it's not so easy because you have to accept that users might miss the 'raisins' of the material you offer. In developing the interactive platform and reflecting on processes of cognition we had to let things go and didn't implement an author controlled and guided tour for users through our favourite research material.

Marino: As authors, we are used to being the ringmaster, but in this environment, we are at best selling the peanuts or raisins. We are creating our works in an overloaded ecology where they will no longer enjoy the codex luxury of monopolizing the reader's attention, which has been so well trained to watch many more than three-rings at once.

Note

1   See *Science Studies* and authors like Hans-Jörg Rheinberger or Karin Knorr-Cetina. They have described an interest of the sciences on alternative forms of knowledge presentation because of the circumstances that knowledge is constituted through experimental systems itself as well through the formats in which it is presented. This means that media-based presentations of research results and processes of cognition are interdependent. The formats are diverse; knowledge is not only inscribed in language and text but also in non-textual forms.

References

Bartscherer, T. and Coover, R. (eds) (2011) *Switching Codes: Thinking Through Digital Technology in the Humanities and Arts.* Chicago, IL: University of Chicago Press.

Calvino, I. (1974) *Invisible Cities* (Translated by W. Weaver). New York: Harcourt Brace Jovanovich.

Calvino, I. (1981) *If On A Winter's Night A Traveler* (Translated by W. Weaver). New York: Harcourt Brace Jovanovich.

Coover, R. (2011a) 'The digital panorama and cinemascapes', in T. Bartscherer and R. Coover (eds), *Switching Codes: Thinking Through Digital Technology in the Humanities and Arts.* Chicago, IL: University of Chicago Press. pp. 119–217.

Coover, R. (2011b) 'Interactive media representation', in Eric Margolis and Luc Pauwels (eds), *The Sage Handbook of Visual Research Methods*. London: Sage. pp. 619–38.

Halbwachs, M. (1992) *On Collective Memory* (Translated and edited by L.A. Coser). Chicago, IL: University of Chicago Press.

Manovich, L. (2002) *The Language of New Media*. Cambridge, MA: MIT Press.

Manovich, L. (2006) 'After effects, or the velvet revolution', *Millennium Journal*, 45/46: 5–20.

PART 5

TOWARDS AN INTERDISCIPLINARY VISUAL METHODOLOGY?

Visual scholars have long since crossed disciplinary boundaries, yet in a contemporary context interdisciplinarity is becoming an increasingly prevalent theme. This final part of *Advances in Visual Methodology* reflects on the contemporary context of interdisciplinary practice – exploring when it is and is not appropriate, and new routes to knowing that it can create.

Yet we should note that, as I highlighted in Chapter 1, the question of interdisciplinarity has already been addressed, if in a less direct way across most of the chapters of this volume. The questions raised by visual ethics discussed in Chapter 2 extend across disciplines and in some cases emerge between the conflicting epistemologies of different disciplinary traditions. Part 2 sees further crossovers. In Chapter 3, references across disciplines continue, as the sociologist Lydia Martens engages with anthropological theories of vision alongside philosophical and sociological theories of practice. In Chapter 4 Jon Hindmarsh and Dylan Tutt note how the type of video-based studies of work practices they discuss are engaged across disciplines, going beyond sociology. Chapter 5, by the anthropologist Elisenda Ardévol, brings together anthropology and media studies in the form of an exploration of the methodological implications of the growing relationship between visual anthropology and Internet studies. In Part 3, with a focus on spatial concepts, new interconnections come to the fore. In Chapter 6, Cristina Grasseni, also an anthropologist, finds herself working in a museum context, using a 'community mapping' method originating in urban studies. Sarah Pink, in Chapter 7, brings together anthropological and geographical theories of place and movement to inform a methodology for doing visual ethnography in ways that incorporate the Internet, and thus also, like Ardévol, engages with media/Internet studies. Similarly, in Chapter 8, Francesco Lapenta draws on sociological and media theory to explore what he calls 'geomedia'. Part 4 is explicitly interdisciplinary, bringing interrelationships between arts practice, sociology and anthropology into focus, through connections with cultural criminology (O'Neill in Chapter 9) and medicine (Lammer in Chapter 10), and by connecting the analysis of practitioners and scholars (Coover in Chapter 11).

Here in Part 5, we encounter two contrasting stories relating to the engagement of approaches between disciplines, reminding us that there is no single way of understanding the potential of interdisciplinary methodological potentials. Rather, the methods that we engage should always be the best ones to answer the research question. In some cases these will be best situated in one discipline, in others they will reach out to others. In Chapter 12, the anthropologist Marcus Banks considers his own research task, working with archival film in India. He discusses a series of existing methods that are already available for analysing film, originating from outside anthropology. Yet, as his chapter unfolds, he explains how these were not suitable for his work. Indeed the approach he took developed along its own path, in a way that reminds of ethnography as he navigated the possibilities and opportunities that arose during the process of his encounters with archives, texts and the persons responsible for them. In Chapter 13, Susan Hogan and Sarah Pink again make connections with the field of art, taken up in Part 4, but this time to develop an approach that interweaves visual ethnography practice as developed by Pink and feminist art therapy practice as developed by Hogan. Taking up the question of visual practices from Part 1, here each discipline engages different visual practices, but they share ways of looking, with rather similar understandings of notions of truth. The authors suggest that by bringing together these approaches, researchers and participants may establish collaborative routes through which to arrive at closer understandings of personal interior dialogues and conflicts – an area of experience social science methods rarely encounter.

In Chapter 14, Luc Pauwels reflects on the contemporary opportunities and challenges for the advancement of visual methods in a way that is applicable across the 'visual' disciplines. Pauwels is critical of the current state of visual research, suggesting that in a contemporary context it needs to move forward in new ways that are relevant to scholars from different disciplines. Indeed, he argues against the polarisations that have tended to develop between visual researchers interested in different elements of images of their production and representation, thus pointing out that visual scholars ought to attend to the implications of each of these domains in the pursuit of visual research, scholarship and communication of their work. Such an endeavour as Pauwels suggests, would benefit from our attending to the expertise of scholars from other disciplines, increased collaboration and a departure from claims that one 'visual' discipline should stand at the centre of visual research. As he notes, the visual has something of an 'invisible' presence in many disciplines. Pauwels' call for a renewed approach is significant to this volume as a whole in several ways. On the one hand, it invites us to turn back to the previous chapters, to interrogate how the ways of working with the visual, across disciplines, through new theoretically informed methodologies and with the new technologies that they describe, might begin to meet the changes he is calling for. On the other, it outlines the scale of the task ahead, for the *further advancement* of visual methodologies.

12

AN ANTHROPOLOGIST IN THE FILM ARCHIVES
Interdisciplinary Approaches

Marcus Banks

Introduction

In line with trends in anthropology more generally, visual anthropology has increasingly taken on a historical dimension. Concerned almost exclusively in the 1960s and 1970s with the production of ethnographic film (for example, Hockings, 1975), the field has widened to encompass the study of historical materials produced by others, most notably archival ethnographic photography. While this is to be welcomed, there still remains a media imbalance: visual anthropology as a field practice is still almost exclusively concerned with film (or today, video) produced by the anthropologist him- or herself, while visual anthropology as an analytical enquiry is almost entirely concerned with the study of historical photography produced by others.[1] How and why this should be so is not entirely clear – nor is this the place to examine the reasons for the imbalance – but the fact remains that the anthropologist seeking to work with archival film (or contemporary photography) must of necessity look beyond the discipline for methodological assistance.

There are, for example, numerous 'how-to' discussions related to the production of ethnographic film and video (for example, Chapter 4 of Pink, 2007; the whole of Barbash and Taylor, 1997) and many methodological insights to be gained from reading about contemporary ethnographic film (for example, MacDougall, 2005). There is far less written from a methodological perspective about photography, certainly on taking photographs, and as with MacDougall's work, insight into analytical methodology is largely to be gained by reading examples, such as Elizabeth Edwards' work (for example, 2001). Edwards in fact refers to her methodology as 'forensic' (by which she means a close and detailed examination of informational content, rather than pertaining to the law or to public debate – e.g. 2001: 106). In my own work, I have referred to the 'internal' and 'external' narratives of an image, which can be read by the social analyst (Banks, 2001: 11), though I provide no detailed instructions as to how this reading should proceed.

In general, there is very little produced by visual anthropologists on the techniques of visual analysis,[2] and to the best of my knowledge there is nothing at all on working with archival film (as opposed to archival photography).[3] In this chapter I therefore lay out some of the possible ways in which we could advance the anthropological study of archival film by assessing some of the ways in which film (and video) has been analysed by researchers in the social sciences and humanities.

Why archival film?

I use the term 'archival film' very loosely in this chapter, simply to mean any length of film, edited or otherwise, that was shot more than 80 or so years ago – that is to say, material for which there is almost certainly no-one living who could be interviewed about the production, or whose only memories of it would be very thin childhood ones. This is simply to by-pass the most obvious research technique of all, which would be to speak to the film's producer, or someone else intimately involved in the production, about the profilmic context, the intention behind shooting the footage, and so forth. With archival film one enters the methodological space where anthropology and history normally differ most sharply: with exceptions, an anthropologist interested in some matter can go and talk to those involved, observe them and even participate in the activity, and a historian cannot. With archival film, as with historical photography,[4] one is faced with the image itself and sometimes nothing more, if there is no associated archival material such as letters, official records, and so on.

However, before discussing strategies by which one might approach the study of archival film, it is worth asking why a social scientist of the contemporary world would want to do so. The most obvious reason is that no one today lives in ignorance of their past. While one cannot assume that research subjects' relationship to the past is necessarily positive, even stated objections to knowledge of the past must be treated as a form of relationship. Thus to investigate visual representations of that past must provide a starting point for insights into how others see their past. Such approaches can be linked to visual repatriation projects, common with archival still photography (for example, Peers and Brown, 2006), but much less so with archival film footage. Through viewing footage with research subjects, and seeing the use they subsequently make of it, one can gain a sense of how they understand their past, and how they wish to call upon it in the present. Taking the many well-documented cases of photographic repatriation, it should not be assumed that responses are always positive. Peers and Brown, for example, found a strong acceptance among First Nations Kainai people of the Beatrice Blackwood photographs from the 1930s that they took from Oxford to Canada, largely because they had prepared the ground extremely thoroughly and ensured that they were returning the photographic copies into a social and cultural space that had been defined by Kainai people (for example, an educational programme was set up with local schools). Bell, however, reports that the younger men in the Purari Delta, New Guinea, found the images of their semi-naked forefathers to be rather embarrassing (Bell, 2010: 360), while Niessen provoked disquiet and even anger among the Sumatran villagers to whom she showed images of old textiles now in Dutch and German museums: by what right did she have access to these textiles, and therefore images of them, when they did not (Niessen, 1991: 421)?

Niessen's project highlights another, more prosaic, use to which archival images – film and photographs – can be put, by creating a proxy for a longitudinal study. Archival images of objects, but much more so footage of action, such as ritual action, or dancing, allows past and present comparisons to be made. Changes in material culture can be studied through comparison between contemporary objects and those held in museum collections, but past forms of more intangible aspects of cultural heritage such as song, or dance, may only be recovered from film records.

With such potentially compelling reasons to study archival film, why is it such an under-utilized resource? Part of the answer is simply practical: it is difficult to obtain information about what material is available, and even when located it can be difficult, time-consuming and expensive to view it. Part of the answer, however, is methodological: anthropology, and the other human sciences, have few if any tools by which to address the study of film. Of course, it could be argued that there is nothing distinctive to address: there are (or are not) data to be extracted from a filmic source for those who address the film material carefully, and the simple act of observation alone will reveal such data. Take, for example, a famous (for the day) scandal from colonial India.

Visual evidence in the archive

In 1911, King George V and Queen Mary visited India for a Durbar – a ceremonial bringing-together of all the Indian Native Rulers. These occasions allowed the encompassing authority of the British Empire to be asserted, while recognizing the right to rule of – and minutely observed status distinctions between – the Rajas, Maharajas and other traditional rulers of the Native or Princely States, that is, those parts of British India which were not under direct rule. The correct observance of etiquette when the Native Rulers were presented to the King was of paramount importance, and although film cameras had been present for an earlier Durbar in 1902–3, in 1911 a great deal of importance was attached to filming the event and ensuring that the footage was seen as widely as possible and as quickly as possible.[5] It was immediately noted that one of the Native Rulers, the Gaekwar of Baroda (a state in western India), had 'bobbed' when presented, rather than bowing formally, and had turned and walked away with his back to the King-Emperor rather than walking backwards until he was out of the royal presence. This was seen as a sign of great disrespect and much commented on in the British and other press at the time (Bottomore, 1997: 331–3). However, conducting the kind of 'forensic' analysis advocated by Edwards some eight decades later, film historian Stephen Bottomore has come to the conclusion that while the Gaekwar probably did behave in the manner described, still images taken from the footage at the time and published in the British press were probably of another Native Ruler, as the footage shows that other Native Rulers behaved in a similar fashion. Close examination of the 1911 Durbar footage does allow a re-evaluation of factual data: the Gaekwar of Baroda almost certainly did 'bob', but so did several others, and there are other reasons, part of the external narrative, that determined why his actions were singled out at the time (the Gaekwar was a reformist, and suspected of encouraging anti-British feeling). Bottomore is able to do this, in part, because he examines all the 10 or so surviving short films of the Durbar, rather than relying on a single source. He also demonstrates quite nicely that sometimes film viewers see what they want to see, and that all readings of film are heavy with meaning brought to, rather than within, the film text – both points I return to below.

A similarly evidential approach is taken by the independent scholar Barry Salt in his sweeping approach to fiction film history (1992). Salt, who has a background in theoretical physics, adopts a materialist and at times statistical approach to the study of film, in order to see 'film style' as an outcome of certain historically specific technical conditions. On a decade (or half-decade) by decade basis, he considers what kinds of shots were used (and possible), the kind of lighting available, the differences between different kinds of lenses, and so on. Salt is particularly interested in editing and in the actual and average length of shots in a film, seeking to establish some kind of correlation between average shot length and the psychological effect a film has on the viewer.

Two kinds of content analysis

Such 'forensic' examinations of content (Bottomore) and of technique (Salt) are not in themselves especially anthropological, nor indeed would either scholar claim them to be so, although both could provide a helpful model if an anthropological research question were framed in a certain way. For example, Salt's average shot length analysis approach could have been (and presumably still could be) applied to the filmic outputs of Worth and Adair's now classic Navajo film project (Worth and Adair, 1973). Considered from a more socio-logical standpoint, however, the modes of analysis most commonly seen are variations on the idea of content analysis.

There are, broadly, two approaches to content analysis. On the one hand, that of scholars such as Bell (2001) relies on an enumeration of features identified in the content of film or a corpus of photographs created by others, which can serve to reveal latent features which may not have been intentionally placed or given prominence by the film's maker or photographer, but which can be uncovered through coding and analysis. While Bell's approach employs quantitative tech-niques, not all content analysis approaches do so. For example, Iedema demon-strates how his analysis of a documentary film about failings in the Australian hospital system contains a number of 'patterns' (typically, repeated sequences of shots with similar content) that serve to semiotically promote one particular interpretation of the failings and their resolution (Iedema, 2001: 184).[6] In order to identify these 'patterns' (for example, hospital administrators 'usually' appear alone in shots and sequences) Iedema needs to compile a descriptive shot list for the entire 30-minute film, something he notes is 'laborious' (Iedema, 2001: 200). Iedema does not apply any form of statistical analysis (unlike Salt or Bell) although he could have done so. There is, however, a rough and ready sense of a building weight of evidence: he notes, for example, that shots of the hospital administrators are 'often' filmed from a low angle, which he suggests denotes their power (Iedema, 2001: 185). This is in marked contrast to a completely different kind of content analysis, championed primary by Christian Heath and other colleagues working within an ethnomethodological paradigm (for example, Heath et al., 2010; see also Hindmarsh and Tutt, this volume). Yet not only is their form of analysis not quantitative (*contra* Bell but apparently in keeping with Iedema), in their recent book on video and video analysis (Heath et al., 2010) they explicitly reject it, something they note is markedly at odds with many other approaches in the social sciences (2010: 84). They do this for two reasons. The first is simply that they generate the video data themselves; therefore while they could analyse it for latent meaning, deducible via content ana-lysis of the former kind, this would on the face of it be a pointless task as they have already been quite self-conscious in how they set the camera up, framed the shot, and so forth. They are explicit about the fact that they pre-select 'perspicu-ous' settings; that is, they choose to film arenas of social action most likely to generate the data they are seeking to capture.[7] Therefore, as they have selected these arenas, and gained the advance permission of the actors to be videotaped in those arenas – such as doctor–patient interactions in the consulting room

(Heath et al., 2010: 30, 45) – there is little point in scrutinizing the ensuing video tapes for latent meaning, at least at the level of authorial intention. The authorial intention is manifest to the researchers precisely because they knowingly created it.

Their second reason for rejecting quantitative content analysis is, however, the more significant, and a direct outcome of their conversation analysis approach. Put simply, at the micro-sociological level social life demonstrably works, most of the time: through whatever means, human social actors effect meaningful linguistic and extra-linguistic communication, and get on with life. There is therefore no need to collect a large enough sample of communications in order to demonstrate efficacy by statistical means. Heath et al. (2010) quote Schegloff (1993) who points out that if, in any instance, the parties to a conversational exchange treat the linkages between conversational items as relevant, then that single instance, in its context, is robust and need not to be supported by a statistically significant body of other such instances.

For Heath et al. (2010), content analysis (not a term they use themselves) is about the meticulous transcription and analysis of micro-components of social action. There is still, however, an unspoken concern with latency, this time with the latency of subject comprehension and motivation as captured by the researchers' video, rather than the latency of authorial intention.[8] But before going on to consider how the approaches above might be of benefit to the study of archival film, there is a further set of cross-disciplinary perspectives to consider.

Studying media

In contrast to the research strategies discussed above are the methodologies developed by the discipline of media studies (which of course has a developed tradition of content anlysis as well, going back to the early work of the Glasgow Media Group). Unlike conventionally framed film studies, media studies has paid particular 'ethnographic' attention to audiences. Film studies of course considered audiences, but as Stephen Hughes has recently pointed out, the classic paradigm was to consider the audience to have been constructed by the film (Hughes, 2011). That is, film studies in the 1970s and 1980s (but resting on an older 'classic' foundation in the work of Kracauer, Bazin, and so on) created a theory of spectatorship (rather than a theory of audience), viewing film as a series of encodings that stitched ('sutured') the spectators into the narrative. From this perspective, the sociology of audiences ('those who actually attend the cinema' as Hughes puts it – 2011: 300) is an irrelevance. Although he is deeply antithetical to this kind of film studies scholarship (Salt, 1992: Chapter 2), Salt actually shares this stance with scholars such as Metz and Wollen in that he seems to regard the textual analysis of the film as sufficient to understand how it works (Salt, 1992: Chapter 6).

However, media studies, of the kind developed by the British tradition of cultural studies,[9] began from the 1980s, to consider 'real' audiences. Through their work they showed that audiences formed their own contexts for their viewing practice, that they brought to their viewing their age, gender, ethnicity and so forth. From this perspective, audiences were not considered to be especially interested in questions of evidentiality (except perhaps in special instances, such as slow-motion action replays of disputed referee decisions in televised sports), and – by definition – could not be consciously aware of latent meaning. However, while media studies approaches such as those above drew more directly on, and were therefore in dialogue with, anthropology, because of the reliance on ethnography (however understood), they prove little direct help in the study of archival film. This is for the very reason stated at the start of this chapter, that the audiences – if ever known – are no longer present to be the subjects of ethnography. For the rest of this chapter, therefore, I will present what I have been able to learn and the methodologies I have had to adopt, in order to study archival film anthropologically. I will do this with reference to a form of cinema I have already briefly discussed – film from and of colonial India.

Into the archive

Most histories of cinema in India point out that it arrived early – a programme of Lumière brothers short films was screened in Bombay in 1896, only a few short months after they had been screened for the first time in Paris (e.g. Chabria, 1994: 3–4). By 1901, if not earlier, the first Indian-made footage had been shot – a now-lost sequence showing a reception that was held to celebrate the success of an Indian student who had been awarded a prize in mathematics at Cambridge (Mohan, 1990: 3).

A century later I entered the archive to conduct research on these early films.[10] I took with me a hypothesis: that a comparison of colonial-period documentary film made by Indian and British filmmakers respectively will manifest the culturally mediated contrast between two differently positioned ways of 'seeing India' (or *Imagining India* in Inden's (1990) sense). These differences would be partly revealed through internal narrative readings (a rough and ready formulation of Edwards' 'forensic' scrutiny), partly through external narrative readings (an examination, where possible, of contemporary documents relating to the film material: a kind of historical ethnography).

The starting point for this hypothesis was previous scholarship on early photography in India (for example, Gutman, 1982), which argued that there were strong continuities with pre-photographic painting techniques. These were characterized as a 'lack' of vanishing-point perspective and a general flatness, and in particular a sense that 'everything happens at once'. There is no narrative, no story that the viewer constructs as his or her eye is led through the picture by various icons and tokens; instead the viewer is plunged into the heart of direct experience. While this kind of approach has been challenged by Pinney as essentialist (1997: 93–5), it is certainly echoed in the work of scholars of early Indian cinema. Ashish Rajadhyaksha, an Indian film historian, sees early Indian cinema as a form of direct address to an audience, rather than a world populated by psychologically rich characters into which the audience is invited (1994: 28). Visually, the image is deliberately flattened, as with still photography: the audience encounters surface and then looks elsewhere (1994: 26).

Unfortunately for my hypothesis, the material required for a comparison did not appear to exist. Although I found a relatively large amount of British-produced documentary film footage (both professional and amateur) in the archives, I found almost no Indian-produced material, though some now lost material can be identified from other sources (such as the papers submitted to the 1927 Indian Cinematograph Committee of enquiry into the Indian film industry). These include a number of short documentaries: the 1901 film, mentioned above, of a reception for an Indian scholar who had been awarded a prize in mathematics at Cambridge (Mohan, 1990: 3); a 1902 film about a wrestler; a film from 1920 showing the funeral procession of Lokamanya Bal Gangadhar Tilak, which Gandhi attended (Mohan, 1990: 3) and so forth. One writer, however, dismisses this entire corpus of lost film (an estimated 1500 short films produced between 1920 and 1940) as 'just camera reportages without any attempt at interpreting or analysing the political and social events portrayed' (Ray, 1991: 1).

The relative absence of material does not in itself preclude analysis (as Cherchi Usai notes in his study of silent cinema, it is estimated that 80 per cent of the subject of his study has been lost (2000 [1994]: 18), but places great reliance on the analysis of the external narrative. Such a study would therefore rely heavily on contemporary documents, in particular those in official archives and those in newspaper archives. This is the approach adopted, for example, by the historian Kaushik Bhaumik in his study of early Bombay fiction cinema (2001): he draws upon newspaper and popular magazine reviews of films to gain some sense of the overall content, as well as which actors and directors were involved, and he uses the archived records of the colonial-era Bombay Board of Film Censors to gain some insight into the audience response to the public screenings of many of the films. Such an approach was not possible in my case, however, as the documentary and perhaps amateur footage I had hoped to find would rarely have been screened for public exhibition and would therefore not have attracted newspaper write-ups, nor passed through the Bombay Board of Film Censors for approval.

It might have been possible to conduct other kinds of analysis with the material that is available. Statistically grounded analysis of the extant material, such as that conducted by Salt or Bell, is not impossible with the small amount of available material but for a social scientist is a fairly problematic approach: there is simply too much that is unknown about the missing footage. Even non-statistically based content analysis, such as that conducted by Iedema, is problematic, given the highly unequal ratio between the British-made material I had identified – well over 100 films – and the small amount of Indian material available.

I was therefore forced to consider another way of approaching the topic, one which still in some way addressed the hypothesis I was interested in, and yet which made sense of the material available. To do this, I was forced to broaden the frame of reference and – following Hughes and others – to consider the audience, not the original or intended audience(s) of the films (as so little is known about them), but the 'audience' of modern scholars and others charged with curating, exhibiting, and writing about the films.

Out of the archive

Put briefly, by taking an ethnographic approach to my own experiences in the archive, I came across two principal narratives about – or, more appropriately, modes of seeing – India's colonial film heritage. One voice was centred on the Indian National Film and Television Archive in Pune, the other on the offices of a government department called Films Division in Bombay.

A body of contemporary scholarship working in or alongside the Pune archive has advocated the view that any documentary production in India by Indians during the colonial period is of no relevance in telling the visual history of India's nationalist struggle and independence. Instead, the history is to be found in the apparently ephemeral fantasies of the mythological dramas and other feature films of the colonial period. For example, when I first arrived at the archive to conduct my own research, before I could commence I was required to watch a videotape of D.G. Phalke's work, a man commonly referred to as the 'father of Indian cinema'. In requiring this of me, the archive's staff were doing two things. First, they were suggesting that I give due recognition to the 'father' of Indian cinema, D.G. Phalke, despite this not being the subject of my research. Second, they were preparing me for a further task, working my way through a set of reading materials in the archive that had been prepared for me and – I suspect – any foreign researchers visiting the archive for the first time.

In the archive's library and elsewhere I was presented with a nationalist and, as it were, culturalist reading of these early films. A small consideration in this literature is given to early documentary and actuality films, but for the most part attention is focused on Phalke himself and his discovery of cinema. This has assumed the status of legend in film historical circles. From his own account he was watching a Christian propaganda film, *The Life of Christ*,[11] sometime around 1910 when the revelation came: 'While the *Life of Christ* was rolling fast before my eyes I was mentally visualizing the gods Shri Krishna, Shri Ramachandra … Could we, the sons of India, ever be able to see Indian images on the screen?' (cited in Rajadhyaksha, 1987: 48). This much-quoted statement (composed by Phalke many years after the event), combined with another equally well-known statement in which he declares that his films are '*swadeshi*' (literally, of one's own country, but used by Gandhi to indicate self-sufficiency) in that 'the capital, ownership, employees and stories are *swadeshi*' (Rajadhyaksha, 1994: 38), is what confirms Phalke not only as the father of Indian cinema but also as a nationalist, a figure allied with Gandhi in the freedom struggle.

For film historians such as Rajadhyaksha and Chabria, it is not merely the content of Phalke's and others' films – a dramatization of India's glorious if mythological past – but the style: the reading (from Judith Gutman) of a 'planar flatness emphasising frontality' (Chabria, 1994: 3). With little evidence in support, Chabria goes on to claim that:

> the 'Indian images' which Phalke had imagined three years before struck a deep chord in the psyche of the spectators. They recognized and welcomed his integration of India's centuries-old traditions and culture with the new medium of cinema, finding in it a new 'self' or identity in the modern context. (1994: 8)

A very similar reading is also made by Ashish Rajadhyaksha (e.g. 1994: 28ff). In addition, he notes that by the late colonial period, the British had very effectively colonized the material and public space of India: through architecture and town planning, and through the institutions of governance, education, and administration. By contrast, the realms of the domestic and the spiritual had been left largely untouched, or had been changed inadvertently (for example, the crystallization of a religion called 'Hinduism' in the late 19th century) but then avoided for fear of inciting further Hindu–Muslim tension. As a result, according to Rajadhyaksha, it was precisely these realms that were taken up by Phalke and his successors. By focusing on the spiritual through Hindu mythology, and domestic space – especially as the location of women – Phalke sought to throw onto the big screen the very areas of Indian (Hindu) experience that might foreshadow full political independence. As examples, Rajadhyaksha cites the Phalke mythological dramas, but also social dramas such as *Pitru Prem* ('A Father's Love') (Harilal Bhatt, 1929, in Rajadhyaksha, 1994), a morality tale about a perfect family surviving the loss of the father's fortune, of which only a fragment now survives (Rajadhyaksha, 1994: 31).

I could go on, but I hope the point is made. In particular, Chabria, Rajadhyaksha and others (such as Paul Willemen, with whom Rajadhyaksha edited the monumental *Encyclopaedia of Indian Film*, 1999) would seem to confirm my initial hypothesis: that of a distinctive Indian vision of the colonial period, albeit one that is recoverable from pre-Independence fiction films rather than non-fiction.

There is, however, another view, that put forward by producers, directors and others associated now or in the past with the Ministry of Information's Films Division in Bombay. If the Pune archive view largely eschews consideration of documentary, the Films Division eschews consideration of feature film, though this is more understandable given that the unit and its precursors were entirely devoted to documentary and newsreel production. This view is a social realist one and, from interviews I conducted with staff there, and from various published accounts, the Films Division also had a project of uncovering a nationalist cinematic vision during the colonial period. The account however was largely one of failure and thwarted opportunity: banned or destroyed newsreel footage of Congress Party meetings, battles with the Bombay Board of Censorship to have the Shree Krishna Film Company's two 1930 films 'Civil disobedience at Dandi, 5th April 1930' and 'Civil disobedience at Bombay, 7th April 1930' released uncut, and so forth (Dharamsey, n.d.: 8) (both named films show the famous occasions when Gandhi and others broke the Government of India's 'Salt Law' that prohibited the manufacture of salt, thereby requiring it to be imported as planned for in the colonial economy).

As noted above, for the colonial period so little of the footage invoked in the argument remains, that it is difficult to assess it. However, the Films Division's view is largely focused on the political significance of the profilmic event rather than the style, or even the content of the films, and – in line with the Division's subsequent output – the assumption seems to be that the missing films were transparent, realist narratives that were 'Indian' by virtue of the circumstances of their production, and not by virtue of their shooting style or diegesic mode.

The Films Division's view is, however, somewhat compromised, at least as seen from the perspective of the Pune archive. In 1939, the Information Department of the Government of India founded the Film Advisory Board as a medium of propaganda to boost the war effort (see Woods, 2001). It was split into two in 1943, creating the Information Films of India and the Indian News Parade, the first a documentary production unit, the second an official newsreel company (commercial newsreel companies had been operating in India for at least a decade).

However, at the start of the war, opinion was divided within the Indian National Congress about the extent, if any, to which the Congress should co-operate with the British war effort. Consequently, JHB Wadia – a noted British supporter and anti-fascist – was appointed as Chair of the Films Advisory Board, and the chief producer was initially an Englishman, Alexander Shaw (Mohan, 1990: 15; Woods, 2001). Between 1940 and 1946, FAB and IFI produced more than 170 films, but to say they were unpopular would be an understatement; the Government of India had to introduce Rule 44A under the Defence of India Rules, making it mandatory for every commercial cinema house to show Films Division films 'at each and every show' (Mohan, 1990: 16).

When the newly independent government's Ministry of Information's Films Division was established, its mission was to continue the propaganda efforts of its predecessors: 'to harness this form of visual education to dispel ignorance and to enlighten our people and the world outside about the possibilities of this new nation' (Mohan, n.d.: 5). Thus, although the pre-history of documentary production could quite clearly be represented – in the absence of the films themselves, such as Bhatvadekar's 1901 film about the Cambridge mathematics prize winner – as blows against the imperialist colonizer, the actual history of the Films Division's activities reveals, in the worst light at least, the documents of collaboration, if not with the British as imperialists, then with the centrist state. Mriganka Ray, a Bengali documentary filmmaker, notes that although in its early years the Films Division was one of the largest such bodies in the world, containing many talented filmmakers, the focus was not on 'the reality of the country'. She goes on:

> The real India for which the freedom fighters strove eluded the political rulers who sought to guide the destiny of the official media … [the Films Division] was geared to the hidebound government policy of projecting the gilded image of a welfare state which was hardly the reality. (Ray, 1991: 2)

Thus both the Pune archives view and the Films Division view present an indigenous cinematic vision – the one encoded in the very films themselves, the other an initially more politicized but ultimately compromised set of actions around the use of the camera itself. The views differ quite sharply, but both in some ways are stories of failure. The ever present spectre at the Pune archives feast of mythological dramas is Hindutva – aggressive Hindu nationalism. Although Rajadhyaksha and others are quick to absolve Phalke and the other pioneers of Hindutva sentiment (e.g. 1994: 25), the fact remains that the vast bulk of the commercial cinema in the years leading up to independence centred on Hindu epics, and the files of the Bombay Board of Film Classification contain numerous instances of actual or potential communalist (that is Hindu–Muslim) violence at cinemas in the period; indeed, the prevention of such violence was a frequent cause for denying a film a release certificate. Moreover, while the popular Bombay cinema of the post-independence period – the direct descendant of Phalke's mythological dramas – has wide-ranging social ramifications, it has remained a commercial enterprise and has not contributed significantly to the post-independent nation-building project.

This last point is acknowledged by Rajadhyaksha as a partial failure of the proto-nationalist twinning of film and politics (1994: 38). While Phalke and his successors had positioned film within the uncolonized space of the domestic and the spiritual, after independence the Government of India – or more generally, the State – increasingly sought to claim that space for itself. Gandhi and others proposed a view of 'tradition' in the realm of the material that influenced India's economy for decades, while recent years have seen the rise of government-sponsored Hindutva (see Banerjee, 2006, for example). But the Films Division didn't really win the historiographic argument either. Its films remained unpopular, perhaps because of their patronizing stance. One producer reminiscing about his career with the Films Division in the 1950s says:

> We found, for instance, that the techniques employed in the modern documentary were more suited to educated audiences, who could understand devices like 'wipes', 'flash backs', 'dissolves', and fast tempo. Modern techniques rather confuse village and illiterate audiences, the film being still new and rare to many of them. Therefore technical devices were avoided, the tempo slowed down, and sometimes shots were repeated to stress the main idea of theme. (Mohan, n.d.: 5)

Identical sentiments are to be found in anecdotes from the UK's Colonial Film Unit in Africa (see Burns, 2000). Although a period of greater state freedom in the mid-1960s led to *cinema verité* and observational techniques being adopted, the 1967 elections that brought Indira Gandhi to power soon brought the heavy-handed techniques of government propaganda back into the Films Division productions (Mitra, 1991). The loss therefore was to documentary cinema itself, which had to wait until the 1980s to gain freedom, independence and maturity.

Conclusions

My initial research hypothesis was in the end proved partly correct, but not in a way that I had expected. I had to revise my initial categories of 'British-made' and 'Indian-made'; I had to discard a distinction between fiction and non-fiction; and I had to select carefully from a variety of methodologies in order to gain purchase on an unstable and contested terrain. Indeed, it was through seeking to make sense of the contestation that brought home to me that methodologies that address a single media type (such as 'film' or 'photography') or that focus on the media text alone (as in some kinds of content analysis) can only provide partial insight into the sociological significance of visual media. This is in part because many of those methodologies are fit for highly specific purposes, such as the analysis of work practice (see Hindmarsh and Tutt, this volume) and need to be adapted to be functional in other contexts.

More particularly, while the methodologies of 'forensic' image analysis, content analysis, audience and reception studies, and so forth all have their part to play in the study of archival film, it is the combination of these techniques and – most crucially – an appreciation of the historicity of the context of analysis that are required to bring the images out of the archive and to appreciate their social embedding.

My own research into colonial-era film practice in India still has many more avenues to explore – for example, how the quite substantial quantities of amateur British 'home movies' shot by transient residents and visitors to India compare to amateur footage shot in the UK; or about fears expressed to the Bombay Board of Film Censors, by both British and Indian subjects, concerning how the supposedly corrupting effects of imported American 'B' movies in India might mask other, more commercial concerns about India as a marketplace for film distributors. But my initial assessment of the material has convinced me that there are cautious grounds for optimism concerning the value that an anthropological approach can have when combined with methodologies derived from neighbouring disciplines.

Notes

1   This is, of course, a gross oversimplification. A great deal of attention has been paid to at least certain archival films (most notably Flaherty's 1922 *Nanook of the North* – see, for example, Jay Ruby's edition of Rotha, 1983) though there is still to date no authoritative history of ethnographic film. Similarly, the anthropological historian Elizabeth Edwards, while devoting much of her research to historical photographs, has also written about contemporary photography of interest to, if not produced by, anthropologists (see, for example, Edwards, 1997).

2   There is of course plenty of writing on visual methodology within anthropology, including my own work, but this on the whole tends to proceed at the level of general discussion, illustrated with apt examples, rather than rigorously examining the parameters and conditions under which research enquiries might take place; Collier and Collier (1986) probably comes the closest.

3   Away from anthropology, the *Historical Journal of Film, Radio and Television* occasionally carries methodological articles (for example, Fielding, 1987), and Cherchi Usai's *Silent Cinema* (2000) remains a definitive work.

4 I prefer the term 'archival film' to 'historical film', simply to avoid the confusion that the latter sometimes refers to film and video footage about historical events, especially in the world of fiction film.

5 The 1911 Delhi Durbar is well-known and much written about; for this account however I rely entirely on Stephen Bottomore's analysis of the film material (1997).

6 Iedema does not, in fact, refer to his approach as an example of content analysis. I have argued elsewhere, however, that his 'social semiotic' approach to the latent meaning of the film rests upon an approximated quantitative approach to the content of the film's scenes (Banks, 2007: 47–8).

7 The term is Garfinkel's (cited in Heath et al., 2010: 88) and although in my opinion this is an instance of what I consider to be the circularity of some ethnomethodological analysis, it is a key tenet in the field.

8 It is another premise of ethnomethodology that while human subjects are understood to be – normally – competent social actors, they are also understood to be unconscious of their competence; social life would be unbearable and unsustainable if we had to consciously plan all the micro-detail of social interaction.

9 In particular, the Birmingham Centre for Contemporary Cultural Studies, and the work of scholars such as Stuart Hall and David Morley.

10 Over the course of the research, which was partly funded by the British Academy, I entered several actual archives, chief among which were the National Film and Television Archive (Pune) and the Maharashtra State Archives (Bombay) in India, and the National Film and Television Archive (London) and the Centre for South Asian Studies (University of Cambridge) in the UK. I am grateful to all the staff at these and other institutions for helping me with my search requests and viewings.

11 Possibly Alice Guy Blaché's *Vie du Christ*, 1906, though this would require further research.

References

Banerjee, M. (2006) 'Neo-nationalism in India: a comparative counter-point', in A. Gingrich and M. Banks (eds), *Neo-Nationalism in Europe and Beyond: Perspectives from Social Anthropology*. Oxford: Berghahn. pp. 237–47.

Banks, M. (2001) *Visual Methods in Social Research*. London: Sage.

Banks, M. (2007) *Using Visual Data in Qualitative Research*. London: Sage.

Barbash, I. and Taylor, L. (1997) *Cross-Cultural Filmmaking: A Handbook for Making Documentary and Ethnographic Films and Videos*. Berkeley, CA: University of California Press.

Bell, P. (2001) 'Content analysis of visual images', in T. van Leeuven and C. Jewitt (eds), *Handbook of Visual Analysis*. London: Sage. pp. 10–34.

Bell, J. (2010) 'Out of the mouths of crocodiles: eliciting histories in photographs and string figures', *History and Anthropology*, 21 (4): 351–73.

Bhaumik, K. (2001) 'The emergence of the Bombay film industry, 1913–1936', DPhil Dissertation, Oxford University.

Bottomore, S. (1997) '"Have you seen the Gaekwar bob?": filming the 1911 Delhi Durbar', *Historical Journal of Film, Radio and Television*, 17 (3): 309–45.

Burns, J. (2000) 'Watching Africans watch films: theories of spectatorship in British colonial Africa', *Historical Journal of Film, Radio and Television*, 20 (2): 197–211.

Chabria, S. (1994) 'Before our eyes: a short history of India's silent cinema', in S. Chabria and P. Cherchi Usai (eds), *Light of Asia: Indian Silent Cinema 1912–1934*. New Delhi: Wiley Eastern. pp. 3–24.

Cherchi Usai, P. (2000) *Silent Cinema: An Introduction*. London: British Film Institute.

Collier, J. and Collier, M. (1986) *Visual Anthropology: Photography as a Research Method*. Albuquerque: University of New Mexico Press.

Dharamsey, V.K. (n.d.) 'Brief notes: early Indian shorts and newsreels', in O. Chanana (ed.), *Docu-Scene in India*. Bombay: Indian Documentary Producers' Association. pp. 7–8.

Edwards, E. (1997) 'Beyond the boundary: a consideration of the expressive in photography and anthropology', in M. Banks and H. Morphy (eds), *Rethinking Visual Anthropology*. London and New Haven: Yale University Press. pp. 53–80.

Edwards, E. (2001) *Raw Histories: Photographs, Anthropology and Museums*. Oxford: Berg.

Fielding, R. (1987) 'Newsfilm as scholarly resource: opportunities and hazards', *Historical Journal of Film, Radio and Television*, 7 (1): 47–54.

Gutman, J. (1982) *Through Indian eyes: 19th and early 20th century photography from India*. New York: Oxford University Press.

Heath, C., Hindmarsh, J. and Luff, P. (2010) *Video in Qualitative Research: Analysing Social Interaction in Everyday Life*. London: Sage.

Hockings, P. (ed.) (1975) *Principles of Visual Anthropology*. The Hague: Mouton.

Hughes, S.P. (2011) 'Anthropology and the problem of audience reception', in M. Banks and J. Ruby (eds), *Made To Be Seen: Perspectives on the History of Visual Anthropology*. Chicago, IL: University of Chicago Press. pp. 288–312.

Iedema, R. (2001) 'Analysing film and television: a social semiotic account of *Hospital: An Unhealthy Business*', in T. van Leeuwen and C. Jewitt (eds), *Handbook of Visual Analysis*. London: Sage. pp. 183–204.

Inden, R.B. (1990) *Imagining India*. Oxford: Blackwell.

MacDougall, D. (2005) *The Corporeal Image: Film, Ethnography and the Senses*. Princeton, NJ: Princeton University Press.

Mitra, A. (1991) 'The Indian documentary film in 1967', in P. Maitra (ed.) *The Short Film Scene in India*. Calcutta: Nandan Publications, West Bengal Film Centre. pp. 10–15.

Mohan, J. (n.d.) 'Movement: contribution of the independents', in O. Chanana (ed.), *Docu-Scene in India*. Bombay: Indian Documentary Producers' Association. pp. 9–16.

Mohan, J. (1990) *Documentary Films and Indian Awakening*. New Delhi: Ministry of Information and Broadcasting, Publications Division.

Niessen, S. (1991) 'More to it than meets the eye: photo-elicitation among the Batak of Sumatra', *Visual Anthropology*, 4 (3–4): 415–30.

Peers, L. and Brown, A. and members of the Kainai Nation (2006) *Pictures Bring Us Messages/Sinaakssiiksi Aohtsimaahpihkookiyaawa: Photographs and Histories from the Kainai Nation*. Toronto: University of Toronto Press.

Pink, S. (2007) *Doing Visual Ethnography* (2nd edn). London: Sage.

Pinney, C. (1997) *Camera Indica: The Social Life of Indian Photographs*. London: Reaktion Books.

Rajadhyaksha, A. (1987) 'The Phalke era: conflict of traditional form and modern technology', *Journal of Arts & Ideas*, 14–15 (July–Dec): 47–78.

Rajadhyaksha, A. (1994) 'India's silent cinema: "a viewer's view"', in S. Chabria and P. Cherchi Usai (eds), *Light of Asia: Indian Silent Cinema 1912–1934*. New Delhi: Wiley Eastern. pp. 25–40.

Rajadhyaksha, A. and Willemen, P. (1999) *Encyclopedia of Indian Cinema* (revised edition). London: British Film Institute.

Ray, M.S. (1991) 'Social documentary in India – an overview', in P. Maitra (ed.), *The Short Film Scene in India*. Calcutta: Nandan Publications, West Bengal Film Centre. pp. 1–9.

Rotha, P. (1983) *Robert J. Flaherty: A Biography*. Philadelphia, PA: University of Pennsylvania Press.

Salt, B. (1992) *Film Style and Technology: History and Analysis*. London: Starword.

Schegloff, E.A. (1993) 'Reflections on quantification in the study of conversation', *Research on Language and Social Interaction*, 26 (1): 99–128.

Woods, P. (2001) 'From Shaw to Shantaram: the Film Advisory Board and the making of British propaganda films in India, 1940–1943', *Historical Journal of Film, Radio and Television*, 21 (3): 293–308.

Worth, S. and Adair, J. (1973) *Through Navajo Eyes*. Bloomington, IN: Indiana University Press.

13

VISUALISING INTERIOR WORLDS
Interdisciplinary Routes to Knowing

Susan Hogan and Sarah Pink

In this chapter we explore interdisciplinary visual methodologies through an exploration of intersections between two practices for which visual methodologies are fundamental: feminist art therapy and visual ethnography. In using therapeutic techniques in ethnographic research we push beyond the boundaries of existing approaches and challenge the construction of binary oppositions between social science and arts practice. We suggest there are a series of congruities between a feminist approach to art therapy and strands of contemporary anthropologically informed visual ethnography practice which are concerned with understanding other people's interior thoughts, the potential of art to make critical interventions, and routes to knowing in practice. While our reflections are based mainly on debates that have developed in anthropology, we argue that the relationship between feminist art therapy and visual ethnography practice established here is applicable for research across cognate disciplines.

Our exploration of feminist art therapy practice as a route to ethnographic knowing was inspired by a question posed by Andrew Irving and Nigel Rapport[1] concerning the importance of interior dialogue, mood, reverie and imagination in anthropology. What ontological status, they asked, should we afford to inner dialogue, imaginative worlds and emotional reverie 'without turning them into reified states or static properties'? Here we approach this question through a methodological exploration of how feminist art therapy might be understood as a route to ethnographic knowing, and to communicating, about shifting interior states.

In its most simple form, making a work of art, and reflecting upon it, can involve for the participant moments of inner dialogue, the experience of fleeting urges, and visceral embodied emotions stimulated sometimes by the tactile qualities of the materials. These are fluid states rather than reified ones. In art therapy, we are precisely concerned with issues surrounding knowing about, and bringing to a 'surface', interior feelings. As a taster, and to give readers with no knowledge of art therapy a stronger sense of the kinds of processes we are referring to, we begin with an example from Susan Hogan's own practice. Here Hogan is describing her experience as a facilitator of an art therapy group; as she demonstrates, it is sometimes the pictorial *struggle* which can be revealing, and can lead to reflections on and awareness of one's own interiority:

> At the group's invitation I did make one artwork. I painted a picture of myself breast-feeding. However, I struggled with the piece. I had wanted the quality of the paint to be very watery creating an image like a reflection on a pond. Whilst painting it I became aware of the fact that I wanted to depict my baby both inside and outside of my body simultaneously. I imagined her suckling one breast whilst stroking the other with her little hand. But I was not able to achieve a satisfactory result with the materials and I spent the session working and reworking the image – struggling with the boundaries. The finished artwork, unresolved though it was, embodied my experience of merger and separateness. The act of painting brought to awareness and illustrated my feelings of conflict and ambivalence about these processes – my emotional struggle. Indeed, my *inability to resolve the image pictorially* was highly revealing. I had not experienced through conversation the full force of these conflicting emotions. Participating in the group reminded me of the power and poignancy of the art therapy process which yields the possibility for the articulation of powerful embodied feelings and responses which cannot necessarily be experienced or evoked through a verbal exchange alone. (Hogan, 2003: 168)

Thus the way the art work is constructed, reworked – areas obliterated and reshaped – can be deeply revealing, giving immediate access to areas of inner conflict and ambivalence. How the work is subsequently handled or destroyed can also become relevant, as it is an object embodied with emotions. Art therapy is a powerful and immediate method; there is also the possibility of exhibition, and though much art therapy work remains confidential, for some women the revealing image being revealed can be both cathartic and empowering. As a woman said to Hogan the other day, 'I feel heard'. Before elaborating further on art therapy practice, however, we first situate our discussion in relation to existing anthropological interests in art and in therapy.

Our discussion is informed by two existing strands of research that have related anthropology to arts practice and to therapeutic practice. In the next sections we outline some key points from these existing literatures to expand the context through which the contribution of a feminist art therapy as a way of doing visual ethnography can be understood.

Art and anthropological ethnographic practice

The making of connections between contemporary arts practice and ethnography is becoming increasingly popular across anthropology, sociology, geography and in interdisciplinary areas of practice that draw on these disciplines (e.g. Grimshaw and Ravetz, 2005; Pink et al., 2004, 2010, 2011; Schneider, 2008; Schneider and Wright, 2006, 2010). In qualitative research practice more generally, the use of participant-produced photography (e.g. Irving, 2007; Radley and Taylor, 2003), and drawing and other arts practices (e.g. Hogan, 2011a, 2011b; O'Neill, 2008; Tolia-Kelly, 2007) is also becoming increasingly popular as a research method; this is particularly within social-science research that seeks to explore experiences relating to health, physical movement thorough different environments, and feelings of exclusion. Bird working with refugees helped to produce an exhibition exploring themes of migration; one particular piece sought to capture the claustrophobia of the inside of a lorry container, arguably hard to describe, especially in a second language O'Neill (2010). While we cannot fully review this broader literature here, it is pertinent to note that these approaches are part of a trend in social science and humanities research that focuses on the experiential, the sensory, and ways of knowing, being and remembering that cannot necessarily be articulated in words. Linked with a wider emphasis on the concept of 'knowing', across anthropology (e.g. Halstead et al., 2008; Harris, 2007) and other ethnographic disciplines, these developments are also congruent with the concern with the senses in ethnography and a move beyond written text (Pink, 2009).

Within this literature concerned with knowing and arts practice, Amanda Ravetz's comments on the relationship between anthropology and contemporary art are particularly pertinent for our discussion. Ravetz suggests that anthropology and contemporary art involve different ways of knowing (2007: 269). Focusing in particular on 'modes of contemporary art where ways of knowing are not about producing certainties' (2007: 271), Ravetz proposes that:

> There are certain situations when opening up a space for *interrupting the certainty of knowledge* is appropriate; and that contemporary art's expertise in 'modes of interruption' provides an important challenge to the search for certainties that underpin much anthropological knowledge. (2007: 271; original italics)

The dichotomy that Ravetz sets up between the 'certainties' of anthropological knowledge and the 'interruption' of art is perhaps overly stark given the moves towards understanding ethnographic knowing as sensory, unspoken or contingent and shifting noted above. As we argue below, in the social sciences and humanities, scholarship is not necessarily a science of certainties. Yet Ravetz's understanding of art as a mode of knowing characterised by uncertainty is important. The knowing that art therapy practice is concerned with is also uncertain, and as implied through the example from Hogan's practice with which we opened this chapter, shifting, perhaps contradictory and multiple.

Thus the act of art making can be a moment of ontological uncertainty and potentially liberating. Consequently art making can become a route through which interiority might be considered not simply as something that comes to the surface and is recorded as a static event, or crystallised and *made static*, but rather, and importantly, it offers ways of understanding interiority through an anthropological paradigm that views inner states as being in progress, rather than ever static. Such understandings are also congruent with the understanding of art therapy that we advance here. Art in art therapy is of significance not only as a representation of the feelings of the individual at a particular moment in time – an inner 'snap-shot', if you like. Indeed, the art therapy approach we outline does not regard her (the client) as 'paranoid' or 'neurotic', or as arrested at an early phase of development. The self of art therapy does not become crystallised anywhere. Rather, in feminist art therapy, images are understood as containing multiple and contradictory selves, at odds with essentialist notions of unitary selfhood. A feminist art therapy sees images as producing and being produced through a 'self in process'.

To qualify our own distinction between the knowing of anthropology and feminist art therapy practice, we suggest that anthropological knowing (as well as that which is produced ethnographically in other academic disciplines) is also rather precarious, subject to revision, and rarely holds the certainties that its convincing written narratives might imply. Anthropological ethnography is usefully understood as a process of seeking routes to reflexively and self-consciously comprehend other people's 'ways of knowing' and make these meaningful in scholarly ways. Indeed, it is more appropriate to see anthropology itself (and scholarly modes of knowing more generally) as a way of knowing that is equally subject to transformation and shifts. However, returning to Ravetz's (2007) point, the concepts of uncertainty or interruption coincide with our understanding of art therapy as a route to understanding interiorities. Indeed, our approach offers the possibility of understanding interiorities precisely as Irving and Rapport suggested – 'without turning them into reified states or static properties'. Such an approach offers a way to resolve the relationship between the uncertainty and the contingency of knowing and the use of narrative in ethnographic representation and scholarly argument. First, however, we situate the methodological advance we are suggesting in this chapter through a consideration of how image-related therapeutic approaches have already been developed in anthropology.

Anthropological and therapeutic methodologies

The use of visual methods drawing on therapeutic practices has some history in social research. In his book *Guide to Imagework* (2004a), the anthropologist Iain Edgar argues for the use of imaginative research methods based on transpersonal psychology and the work of psychotherapist C.G. Jung in particular. Edgar makes a case for our imaginative worlds to receive scholarly attention, pointing out that, '... the use of the imaginative senses could be more extensively used across the full range of social science research' (2004a: 1). Moreover, he suggests, 'the mind's inner imagery' can be manifested in a number of external visual forms (2004b: 95). Edgar's work has established key connections between visual therapeutic and social research methods. The approach developed here, based in feminist art therapy, both builds on and departs from his contribution.

Edgar's term 'imagework' describes a range of techniques, which encompass the technique of creative visualisation and involve 'imagination-based research methodologies' (2004b: 90). His method is based on a therapeutic model used in experiential group work (2004b: 90), which he describes as 'an active process in which the person "actively imagining" lets go of the mind's train of thoughts and images and goes with a sequence of imagery that arises spontaneously from the unconscious' (2004b: 91). The commonsense assumption that we can 'think about nothing' or 'let the mind go' works well for this model. Yet we begin from a different premise that assumes modern western research, and in therapy, subjects do not actually engage in practices of *doing* or *thinking* in ways that are completely uninformed by moralities, values, and existing categories. Rather than separating out thought, reason, or moralities from ways of knowing, we suggest a focus on phenomenological notions of knowing. There are nevertheless a series of commonalities between Edgar's 'imagework' and feminist art therapy rooted in the categories of 'memory', 'spontaneous' and 'dream' imagework, which again we both build on and depart from.

'Memory imagework' involves guiding respondents into their memory of earlier events. For example, to examine household change across two generations and, in particular, 'changing Western domestic symbolism', Edgar invites research subjects to remember a house from childhood in their imagination and then to 'fast forward' to their current house to 'imagine the symbolic value of their chosen activity' (Edgar, 2004a: 25). Then 'a brief felt-tip picture of their imaginings' can be produced and discussed in the group or in pairs. The group 'can then make a meta-analysis of the emerging themes'. This is very similar to the group-interactive approach to art therapy in which a 'meta-analysis' might also be produced in therapeutic group work, though as a way of reiterating and consolidating dominant themes (Hogan, 2009). For example, the theme of loss might come to the fore following a particularly moving disclosure from an individual. This might then lead other participants to reflect on their own sense of loss, to articulate feelings about their losses verbally and pictorially. The echoing of common themes through art works is referred to as 'group resonance' in art therapy literature, and can take obvious or subtle forms. The facilitator might attempt to articulate or summarise emerging themes and issues. Commonly, this is done at the beginning of the session (relating to what happened in the group the previous week).

What Edgar identifies as 'spontaneous imagework' involves using the Jungian active imagination technique 'which facilitates a spontaneous journey into the imagination' (2004a: 10). Edgar elaborates the technique as one in which participants undertake a journey that leads them to a 'wise person' to whom they can discuss the questions they 'carry' with them (which might be about a predetermined subject) (Edgar, 2004a: 31). In art therapy, where this technique is referred to as 'guided fantasy' the only difference is that the client is usually free to ask their own question.

Edgar's technique of 'dream imagework' is described as 'the use of dreams for diagnosis and healing'. Respondents recount a dream or believe themselves led by dreams. The analytical processing of the work is firstly descriptive, in that respondents are asked to 'tell their story', then follows 'analysis by the partici-pants of the personal meaning of their experience of the symbols used' (2004a: 10). Likewise, in art therapy dreams may be recounted and reflected upon. For example, a young woman who usually dreamt of herself as white reflected: 'Guess what? I had a dream and I was black in my dream. And the people in my dream were black and that was OK. I was so happy' (Campbell and Gaga, 1997: 216). In this case the dream was significant in pointing to the young woman's sense of increasing self-acceptance, and shedding of internalised racism.

Dream imagework can also be developed into spontaneous imagework in what Edgar promotes as a 'communicative' approach which is interested in 'the psychodynamics of the social setting and the interpretative framework of the participants' (2004a: 49–50). There is a strong similarity between this approach and group-interactive therapy, but with different aims, because Edgar is inter-ested in exploring research questions, whereas art therapy is focused on the experiential learning and personal self-reflection of participants.

Above we highlighted the question of narrative, indicating that a feminist art therapy approach brings into relief differences between the 'uncertain', shifting and contingent ways of knowing that emerge from therapeutic and ethnographic encounters and narrative forms of scholarly writing that seek to convince. Edgar argues that 'imagework' is compatible with any social science research paradigm that 'seeks to account for the outcome of human cognition, imagination, emotion and intuition ...' (2004a: 19). Although Edgar employs techniques similar to those used in 'arts-based' research, and will ask respondents to draw, paint or enact an imagined image, these other products are then *translated* into words: 'Arts-based inquiry typically results in some form of artistic performance while imagework does not' (2004a: 18) and its research strategies lead 'to normative scholarly and academic outcomes' (2004a: 17). This a crucial point at which feminist art therapy departs from imagework. In doing so, it invites a challenge both to the text-based normative scholarly outcomes and the narrative of academic discourse, more akin to the challenge posed by contemporary art practice suggested by Ravetz (2007). We will return to this question of narrative. First, however, we digress for a section to outline why these issues are pertinent for the phenomenological ethnographer.

Knowing and narrative in ethnographic practice

Ethnographers are always faced with a problem: while we might aim to empathise with, understand, interpret and represent other people's experiences, imaginations and memories, their sensory and affective qualities are only accessible to us in limited ways. As Irving expresses it, 'The problem facing anthropologists during fieldwork, especially given the centrality of memory, reverie, and imagination to ethnographic practice, is how to bring events from the past into life when there is no independent access to people's consciousness, memories, or the past' (2007: 186). In his own collaborative research practice, Irving has invited participants in his work to walk around urban contexts while narrating and photographing their memories of pivotal moments in their lives. This has created a powerful medium for learning about other people's experiences. It also provides a route to communicating about them in printed text through visual and written narratives that do not reduce the experience of others to what Irving refers to as 'the static types and social categories that are often required in conventional social scientific and anthropological analyses' (2007: 204–5).

Concepts of 'knowing' are increasingly fashionable across the social sciences and humanities. Such ideas are increasingly informing ethnographic methodology in anthropology (e.g. Halstead et al., 2008; Harris, 2007) and other disciplines. Theoretical developments propose ways of understanding knowing and its relationship to knowledge that invite us to think of knowing as something that happens when we are 'doing' – that is, in practice (Wenger, 1998). Thus, the concept of knowing offers a way to think about the relationship of the individual to the social.

There are various routes through which social researchers might *attempt* to gain empathetic access to other people's knowing through various ethnographic practices. Pink (2009) discusses the idea of becoming 'emplaced' in ways similar to the research participants through participating in similar activities or imagining oneself into another person's place. Recently, anthropologists have (re)focused on the idea of ethnographer as apprentice (e.g. Downey, 2007; Grasseni, 2007; Marchand, 2007). Techniques of accessing other people's knowing, whether through the ethnographer's own actual embodied practice, or through research participants' representations of *their* own practice, involve not only the body, imaginative and memory practices of the ethnographer, but also the research participant's own attempts to articulate to the ethnographer what their experiences, memories, imaginations and inner conflicts might involve. The approach we discuss in this chapter tackles the same problem from a different (and we believe complementary) angle by seeking to facilitate a process through which research participants themselves access and articulate their inner thoughts and feelings and communicate these to researchers. This does not suggest that participants would simply reify their interior feelings and communicate them to the ethnographer through an art therapy process. Rather, it would indicate that the process of art therapy is one in which a research participant might engage in her or his own way of knowing through (art) practice, while the ethnographer/therapist is inevitably implicated in 'knowing with' the participant through the practice of art-therapy-as-visual-ethnography.

Putting this another way, we are asking how ethnographers might enable participants themselves to reflect on their own interiority through media and practices that simultaneously provide the ethnographer a route to knowing. As we have highlighted above, this approach not only assumes that certainty is not accessible, but also makes this assumption an explicit and obvious condition to the ways of knowing and understanding that emerge from feminist-art-therapy-as-ethnographic-research. It likewise poses what might be seen as a challenge to the conventional scholarly method of communicating – written narrative. Indeed, following Pink's (2007) argument for a *visual* ethnography we would suggest that they invite exciting possibilities for creating new relationships between the ways of knowing that scholarly writing involves and the uncertainty implied by the shifting meanings that are integral to the research encounter. We are suggesting that ethnographic practice, scholarship and art therapy might be co-implicated in this process. In the next section we elaborate this through a more detailed discussion of the principles and practices of art therapy and their relevance to this task.

Linking feminist art therapy and research

Social art therapy and phototherapy encompass a range of practices, but in all cases participants are concerned with self-exploration and self-expression via art or photographic materials. In her formulation of a feminist art therapy, Hogan has critiqued approaches to art therapy in which therapists interpret clients' art according to pre-existing models. Resonating with Irving's (2007) vision for an anthropology that does not reduce other people's experiences into existing theoretical structures, Hogan has proposed that a 'focus on the individual (as the site of suffering and distress) liberates art therapy from developing an over-reliance on, and rigid adherence to, set theories and a-priori categories of meaning inherent in theoretical orthodoxy, which can obscure as much as illuminate human suffering' (Hogan, 1997: 37). Feminist art therapy does not focus on interior states and the transforming self in isolation, but like social anthropology, understands individuals as *situated* in institutional, social, cultural and power-imbued contexts. Indeed, a 'social art therapy' can challenge dominant discourses – in ways that resonate with the issues of global inequalities that are made clear through Irving's (2007) work. Art therapy can act as a space in which to rehearse and explore strategies of resistance, as well as to explore and reconcile contradictory discourses (contradictions which create stress and 'dis-ease'). Thus, in art therapy, we cannot undo discriminatory practices which exist outside of the art therapy arena, but we can actively interrogate them, and explore our multiple and often contradictory selves – and the tension between these.

Indeed there is already a fertile borderline between social science research and personal therapy represented by both social art therapy and phototherapy – for example, the collaborative work of Rosy Martin and Jo Spence (1985, 1987a, 1987b) and Boffin and Frazer's *Stolen Glances: Lesbians Take Photographs* (1991), which sought to explore and represent a previously adumbrated area of social existence. Spence's work included documenting and interrogating her experience of being a cancer patient, highlighting inhumane medical practices, but using the camera as a tool to fight for a sense of self in the context of becoming a medical *object*. This was a critique of medical discourses, which also served as a tool for personal empowerment, and catharsis. Thus one of the premises of feminist art therapy (see Hogan, 1997, 2012) is that while dominance, subjugation and oppression are very real, power is not monolithic and is 'always exercised in relation to resistance' (Henriques et al., 1984: 115). Likewise, social art therapy will sometimes employ photographs (pre-existing for collage or newly taken) and might involve a simultaneous research process. An example of this is a project developed by Hogan (2003, 2008) who provided art materials in support groups for pregnant women and new mothers, to enable them to explore their changed sense of self-identity and sexuality as a result of pregnancy and motherhood (Hogan, 1997, 2003, 2008, 2011b). This resulted in a critique of discourses as well as change on a personal level for the participants. While this research produced what Edgar calls 'normative scholarly and academic outcomes' (Edgar, 2004a: 17) to elucidate the issues and concerns faced by pregnant women and new mothers, the images themselves supply another discourse on the subject (and have their own 'unpredictable' affects). Sometimes, the respondent produced an image already imagined in their head which they might subsequently talk about (the participant might be asked to imagine herself in a particular situation), but in other instances the discourse is supplied by the image and there is actually little relation between what is said and depicted, or the image is iconoclastic in the way that what is said isn't. This latter use of images to move beyond spoken discourse deserves a place in social science research methods – as it is possible to say things in images that it is hard or impossible to articulate verbally (see Figure 13.1).

Surely, for example, to translate this image as 'I felt violated by my birth experience' or 'motherhood is destroying my sexuality' is reductive? The image has power: the shock of seeing a baby bottle about to plunge into a vagina – the sense of violence about it – is hard to translate into words, and thus the image is saying something which really supplements what is written (Hogan taped and transcribed the women's spoken discourse and has quoted participants in a number of publications, as well as reproducing their art). While, for the academic art therapist researcher it is necessary to produce (some) normative written outcomes (i.e. books and articles) for academic career progression,

Figure 13.1

the exclusive translation of such research into words misses the possibility of communicating such alternative ways of knowing.

Here the art therapist as facilitator is active in the production of knowledge in a way that demands a form of reflexivity also characteristic of visual ethnography practice whereby the embodied and sensory subjectivity of the researcher becomes part of the process of knowing (Pink, 2007, 2009). In reflexive social art therapy practice the therapist is likewise constantly alert to her embodied engagements and to her role, however tangential in the creation of meaning within the art therapy encounter.

The particular benefits of imagework and 'experiential' research methods such as feminist art therapy are eloquently described by Edgar as able to achieve 'the articulation of respondents as yet dimly perceived but emotionally present aspects of self and world' (Edgar, 2004a: 21). This would seem a particular merit of these approaches. Imagework, and its amplification through the production of art works or drama, can, asserts Edgar, 'evoke both significant insights into psycho-social situations and *even change personal and group orientations*, so becoming applicable in action-research settings' (Edgar, 2004a: 21; italics added). Like imagework, feminist art therapy is interested in changing personal orientations, producing social critique and research outcomes.

There are, however, some further differences between feminist art therapy and methods and imagework. As noted above, feminist art therapy as a research tool and mode of social critique (social art therapy) retains the art work to provide a supplementary discourse which may confirm or indeed contradict the spoken word on occasions. It is important to think about the importance of working with 'contradiction' in narrative. Condor's (2000) analysis of 'resistances' in interviews, for example, has yielded interesting information about contradictory or problematic beliefs, or the recognition and resistance of certain discourses, or simply ambivalences. Cameron (2001) notes that many interview respondents give a contradictory account of an event or of their views. Furthermore, she asserts that '"normal" understandings *are* multiple and shifting rather than unitary and fixed', and should be taken into account (Cameron, 2001: 157). Responding to the ideas of Ravetz (2007), it feels important that there is an opportunity for synergy between the image and the textual accompaniment, which can also include the researcher's written and visual reflections on the process, and does not discard what the image has to contribute. More recent research work on older women's perceptions of ageing has exhibitions as a research output, which will be evaluated by relevant audiences (Hogan et al., 2011) (also mentioned in Chapter 2).

Our discussion has indicated how contemporary art (Ravetz, 2007) and art therapy can challenge both the normative (Edgar, 2004a) narrative of written ethnography and scholarship – and the 'certainties' (Ravetz, 2007) implied by it. In the next and final stage of our exploration we consider precisely how an approach informed by feminist art therapy might respond to the 'problem' of narrative in scholarly representation. In doing so we suggest that it also offers routes through which we might *represent* the 'uncertainties' and shifting/unresolved nature of the transforming self of art therapy *and* as such suggests alternatives for scholarly representations of other people's interiority.

Art therapy as a response to the problem of narrative

A narrative as described by Kerby is 'the recounting of a series of temporal events so that a meaningful sequence is portrayed' (1991: 39). Cohen and Rapport suggest that, 'It may be expressed verbally or in gesture and in behaviour. It is the individual's routine *modus vivendi* on which he or she reflects self-consciously.' They go on to assert that, 'This regular reflection may be regarded as a condition of our conscious being-in-the-world' (1995: 5). The idea of narrative then, they conclude, 'is that lasting if selective chronicle of the temporal course of experience, fixed in memory'. This is perhaps too 'neat' a definition in our view, as memory is certainly constructive, and shifting rather than fixed. Even a revisionist version, put forward by Giddens (1991: 54), which sees the storyline as actively constructed and continuously updated as events take place, is too simple. Indeed, narrative is very complex and not linear. Kirsten Hastrup suggests that 'narrative punctuates experience, awareness constantly arrests the flow of consciousness – to make room for action, as it were' (1995: 184). However, this perhaps represents a false separation between the different components in this process, since as Crang and Cook (2007) point out, that action is linked to flows of narrative and memory. Indeed, if we are (as is the case for the work of feminist art therapy) concerned with narrative in the context of the exploration of identity, this raises further issues.

Narrative as some sort of straightforward, fixed storyline is clearly over-simplistic – selfhood is complicated, our histories are embodied; as Bourdieu notes, 'internalised as second nature', yet an 'active presence of the whole part of which it is the product' (Bourdieu, 1990: 56). We should understand identity as a complex assemblage of thoughts, ways of doing things, relationship to possessions, feelings, memories, obligations, which for many of us is 'always a compromise, always pragmatic, always in flux …' (Crang and Cook, 2007: 10). Our selves are reflected in our relationships with others: 'memories may be evoked by various belongings or locales associated with different facets of people's identities' (Crang and Cook, 2007: 10; Rowles, 1983). It is also important to emphasise that people live out their lives between different locales which emphasise different aspects of their identities, produce different ways of thinking, and stimulate different memories (Crang and Cook, 2007; Valentine, 1993; Van der Ploeg, 1986). Ways in which we make sense of ourselves and our worlds result in interaction with different groups. As Crang and Cook express it, events are interpreted through:

> … discussions and debates with different groups of people as events are reported and interpreted socially through hearing about them from others, or even thinking about what someone else has said or would say about them. Reverie is part of these processes. Therefore, not only is the place where the researcher and her/his 'subjects' meet important to any study, but also the social relations of research that are (re) arranged there. (Crang and Cook, 2007: 10)

How far this complexity can be captured in interview is open to question, but it would seem fair to ask questions to draw out the importance of different milieux in creating a subject's ideas and reflections, but to be willing to acknowledge contradictions and incongruities. In feminist art therapy these complexities can be explored pictorially.

Indeed, an art therapy approach enables us to go beyond the dichotomous formulations that have framed some earlier anthropological approaches to bringing interiority to the fore. For instance, Kirsten Hastrup has suggested that:

> The process of making memory explicit, of foregrounding it from the archive of implicit recollection and habituated knowledge, has a parallel in the transformation of mere experience into *an* experience – this transformation is made by way of narrative expression; by telling we carve out units of experience and meaning from the continuity of life. (Hastrup, 1995: 183–4)

Whilst this foregrounding of certain experiences can take place in art therapy, the dichotomy is too simple. It is more fruitful to look at multiple ways of knowing and reflecting on experience *in practice* (and art being one of these, as the moment of manipulating the material is a moment of ontological uncertainty). We are all subject to contradictory discourses, and the wrenching between these is something that can be explored in art therapy. Thus we might think of art therapy as a way of 'knowing in practice' and involving a way of knowing that only comes about through and is simultaneously articulated through drawing – in other words, a knowing that cannot be expressed in words or that can only be expressed at the interface between drawing, talking and the encounter between participant/client and ethnographer/therapist. An idea may be depicted pictorially and arguably become reified – fixed, but because of the pliability of the media, whether it be clay, or paint, it can be changed; it is malleable. Understandings which *are* multiple and shifting *can* be depicted and explored. Contractions can be viewed and ambivalence can be interrogated. Therefore, art therapy invites us to participate in ways of knowing in practice, acknowledging that such knowing will only be found in practice, but that even so it has the power to impact on things that are outside of that actual moment of knowing and of practice.

If we think of humans as active agents in the production of their subjectivity through a process of *assujettissement*[2] – a simultaneous process of making and being made as a subject – then a fluidity of selfhood may be recognised, an intermediacy of being explored: reflection, imagination, reverie are part of this active process. The question of how to bring such *assujettissement* and the ways of knowing that are integral to it into the narrative of anthropological representation is indeed a challenge. However, as we have shown in the previous section, the art of art therapy has, if the uncertainty of its meaning is acknowledged, an important role to play.

Conclusion

To summarise, social researchers and art therapists are both interested in subjects' inner lives. It is complex: gender, power, class and ethnicity are all difficult and mutable notions and accessing how these are implicated in our interior worlds is not a simple task. But considering that the word cannot explain everything, and that art is a powerful medium, we propose that innovative, arts-based methods offer new routes to these interiorities. Our work is not entirely novel: we situate our ideas as part of a small, emerging group of theorists and practitioners who are interested in the inner life. In this chapter we have pushed at the boundaries of existing visual research practice. In so doing, we have initiated an exploration of the relationship between feminist art therapy and anthropological interest in inner dialogue, imaginative worlds and emotional reverie, and explored implications for visual research methodologies. This task has taken us on a short journey through arts practice, imagework, knowing in ethnography and anthropology, feminist art therapy practice, and the problem of narrative. In each of these domains, we have identified meeting points through which feminist art therapy practice offers routes to interiority that allows the shifting, contingent, and transformative nature of the self to become known to the ethnographer and/or to be represented through alternative narrative forms.

However, our conclusion is not definitive. Indeed, our ultimate objective is to invite further discussion of, and practical engagement with, this relationship and its research potential.

Acknowledgements

An earlier version of this chapter was published in *Visual Anthropology* (2010, vol. 23: 158–74). The current chapter is a revised text based on the original article.

Notes

1   Irving and Rapport posed this question as part of a call for a conference panel at the ASA 2009 conference. While we were unable to attend the conference we were nevertheless inspired to follow through to answer the question.
2   The French have a word which Henriques et al. (1984: 1) suggest encapsulates an active and complex subjectivity which acknowledges the individual as an active agent in the production of their subjectivity through a process of *assujettissement*. There is no English equivalent; however, this reflexive verb, which means 'to make subject' or to 'produce subjectivity' as well as to 'submit' or 'subjugate', is perhaps rather negative with respect to subjugation. It is conceivably a more neutral term which is needed to encapsulate our coming into being – being made and making simultaneously. The lack of a suitable word for this process illustrates an entrenched dichotomy between self and society and a conceptual 'hole' in post-structuralist theory.

Bibliography

Banks, M. (2001) *Visual Methods in Social Research*. London: Sage.
Boffin, T. and Frazer, J. (1991) *Lesbians Take Photographs*. London: Pandora.
Bourdieu, P. (1990) *The Logic of Practice*. Translated by R. Nice. Cambridge, MA: Harvard University Press (originally published in 1980 as *Le Sens Pratique*).
Breton, A. (1962) *Premier Manifestes du Surréalisme*. Paris: Jean-Jacques Pauvert.
Cameron, D. (2001) *Working With Spoken Discourse*. London: Sage.
Campbell, J. and Gaga, D.A. (1997) 'Black on black art therapy: dreaming in colour', in S. Hogan (ed.), *Feminist Approaches to Art Therapy*. London: Routledge. pp. 216–28.
Clifford, J. and Marcus, G.E. (eds) (1986) *Writing Culture. The Poetics and Politics of Ethnography*. Berkeley, CA: University of California Press.
Cohen, A.P. and Rapport, N. (eds) (1995) *Questions of Consciousness. ASA Monographs 33*. London: Routledge.
Condor, S. (2000) 'Pride and prejudice: identity management in people's talk about "this country"', *Discourse & Society*, 11 (2): 175–205.
Crang, M. and Cook, I. (2007) *Doing Ethnographies*. London: Sage.
Creswell, J.W. (1994) *Research Design: Qualitative and Quantitative Approaches*. London: Sage.

Downey, G. (2007) 'Seeing with a "sideways glance": visuomotor "knowing" and the plasticity of perception', in M. Harris (ed.), *Ways of Knowing: New Approaches in the Anthropology of Experience and Learning*. Oxford: Berghahn. pp. 222–41.

Edgar, I. (2004a) *Guide to Imagework: Imagination-Based Research Methods*. London: Routledge.

Edgar, I. (2004b) 'Imagework in ethnographic research', in S. Pink, L. Kürti and A. Afonso (eds), *Working Images*. London: Routledge. pp. 90–106.

Giddens, A. (1991) *Modernity and Self-Identity: Self and Society in the Late Modern Age*. Cambridge: Polity Press.

Grasseni, C. (2007) 'Communities of practice and forms of life: towards a rehabilitation of vision', in M. Harris (ed.), *Ways of Knowing: New Approaches in the Anthropology of Experience and Learning*. Oxford: Berghahn. pp. 203–22.

Grimshaw, A. and Ravetz, A. (2005) *Visualizing Anthropology*. Bristol: Intellect.

Gumperz, J. (ed.) (1982) *Language and Social Identity*. Cambridge: Cambridge University Press.

Halstead, N., Hirsch, E. and Okely, J. (eds) (2008) *Knowing How to Know: Fieldwork and the Ethnographic Present*. Oxford: Berghahn.

Harris, M. (2007) 'Introduction: ways of knowing', in M. Harris (ed.), *Ways of Knowing, New Approaches in the Anthropology of Experience and Learning*. Oxford: Berghahn. pp. 1–27.

Hastrup, K. (1995) 'The inarticulate mind: the place of awareness in social action', in A.P. Cohen and N. Rapport (2005) (eds), *Questions of Consciousness. ASA Monographs 33*. London: Routledge. pp. 181–98.

Henriques, J., Holloway, W., Urwin, C., Venn, C. and Walkerdine, V. (1984) *Changing the Subject: Psychology, Social Regulation and Subjectivity*. London: Routledge.

Hogan, S. (ed.) (1997) *Feminist Approaches to Art Therapy*. London: Routledge.

Hogan, S. (ed.) (2003) *Gender Issues in Art Therapy*. London: Jessica Kingsley.

Hogan, S. (2007) 'Rage and motherhood interrogated and expressed through art therapy', *Journal of the Australian and New Zealand Art Therapy Association*, 2 (1): 58–66.

Hogan, S. (2008) 'Angry mothers', in M. Liebmann (ed.), *Art Therapy & Anger*. London: Jessica Kingsley.

Hogan, S. (2009) 'The art therapy continuum: an overview of British art therapy practice', *Inscape: International Journal of Art Therapy*, 12 (1): 29–37.

Hogan, S. (2011a) 'Images of Broomhall, Sheffield: urban violence and using the arts as a research aid', *Visual Anthropology*, 24 (5): 266–80.

Hogan, S. (2011b) 'Post-modernist but not post-feminist! A feminist post-modernist approach to working with new mothers', in H. Burt (ed.),

Current Trends and New Research in Art Therapy: A Postmodernist Perspective. Waterloo, Ontario: Wilfrid Laurier University Press. pp. 70–83.

Hogan, S. (ed.) (2012) *Revisiting Feminist Approaches to Art Therapy.* London: Berg-Hahn.

Hogan, S. (forthcoming) 'Using the arts to interrogate health', in P. Fuery (ed.), *Medicine and the Arts: History & Contemporary Practice.* Rochester: Rochester University Press.

Hogan, S., Warren, L., Gott, M., McManus, C., Martin, R. and Richards, N. (2011) 'Look at me! Images of women and ageing' (retrieved from: www.representing-ageing.com).

Hubbard, P., O'Neill, M., Pink, S. and Radley, A. (2010) *Walking, Ethnography and Arts Practice*, a guest edited issue of *Visual Studies.*

Irving, A. (2007) 'Ethnography, art, and death', *Journal of the Royal Anthropological Institute*, 13 (1): 185–208.

Kerby, A.P. (1991) *Narrative and the Self.* Bloomington, IN: University of Indiana Press.

Marchand, T. (2007) 'Crafting knowledge: the role of "parsing and production" in the communication of skill-based knowledge among masons', in M. Harris (ed.), *Ways of Knowing: New Approaches in the Anthropology of Experience and Learning.* Oxford: Berghahn. pp. 181–203.

Martin, R. and Spence, J. (1985) 'New portraits for old: the use of the camera in therapy', *Feminist Review*, 19 (March).

Martin, R. and Spence, J. (1987a) 'What do lesbians look like?', *Ten8*, 25 (June: Body Politics).

Martin, R. and Spence, J. (1987b) 'Phototherapy – psychic realism as a healing art?', *Ten8*, 30 (October: Spellbound).

O'Neill, M. (2008) 'Transnational refugees: the transformative role of art?', *Forum Qualitative Sozialforschung / Forum: Qualitative Social Research*, 9 (2) (retrieved 14 November 2008 from: http://160.45.170.223:90/ojs_fqs/index.php/fqs/article/view/403/873).

O'Neill, M. (2010) *Asylum, Migration and Community.* Bristol: The Policy Press.

Pink, S. (2007) *Doing Visual Ethnography.* London: Sage.

Pink, S. (2009) *Doing Sensory Ethnography.* London: Sage.

Pink, S., Kurti, L. and Alfonso, A.I. (eds) (2004) *Working Images.* London: Routledge.

Pink, S., Hogan, S. and Bird, J. (2011) 'Intersections and inroads: art therapy's contribution to visual methods', *International Journal of Art Therapy (Inscape)*, 16 (1): 14–19.

Pink, S., Hubbard, P., O'Neill, M. and Radley, A. (2010) 'Walking across disciplines: from ethnography to arts practice', *Visual Studies*, 25 (1): 1–7.

Radley, A. and Taylor, D. (2003) 'Images of recovery: a photo-elicitation study on the hospital ward', *Qualitative Health Research*, 13 (1): 77–99.

Ravetz, A. (2007) '"A weight of meaninglessness about which there is nothing insignificant": abjection and knowing in an art school and on a housing estate', in M. Harris (ed.), *Ways of Knowing: New Approaches in the Anthropology of Experience and Learning*. Oxford: Berghahn. pp. 266–87.

Rowles, G.D. (1983) 'Place and personal identity in old age: observations for Appalachia', *Journal of Developmental Psychology*, 3: 299–313.

Schneider, A. (2008) 'Three modes of experimentation with art and ethnography', *Journal of the Royal Anthropological Institute*, 14 (1): 171–94.

Schneider, A. and Wright, C. (2006) 'The challenge of practice', in A. Schneider and C. Wright (eds), *Contemporary Art and Anthropology*. Oxford: Berg. pp. 1–29.

Schneider, A. and Wright, C. (eds) (2010) *Between Art and Anthropology*. Oxford: Berg.

Tolia-Kelly, D.P. (2007) 'Fear in paradise: the affective registers of the English Lake District landscape re-visited', *Senses and Society*, 2 (3): 329–51.

Valentine, G. (1993) 'Negotiating and managing multiple sexual identities: lesbian space-time strategies', *Transactions of the Institute of British Geographers*, 18 (2): 237–48.

Van der Ploeg, J.D. (1986) 'The agricultural labour process and commoditization', in J.D. Long, J.D. Van der Ploeg, C. Curtain and L. Box (eds), *The Commoditization Debate: Labour Process, Strategy and Social Network*, papers of the Department of Sociology Agricultural University Wageningen, 17. pp. 24–57.

Wenger, E. (1998) *Communities of Practice: Learning, Meaning, and Identity*. Cambridge: Cambridge University Press.

Young, D.E. and Guy, J. (eds) (1994) *Being Changed: The Anthropology of Extraordinary Experience*. Cardiff: Broadview Press.

14

CONTEMPLATING THE STATE OF VISUAL RESEARCH

An Assessment of Obstacles and Opportunities

Luc Pauwels

Visual research in various shapes and guises continues to gain popularity. Evidence of this can be found in the ever-increasing number of visual science journals, monographs, edited volumes, conferences and specialized organizations. Today the attraction to the study of the visual, to research using visual means to gather data, and to communicate findings more visually is definitely a good sign. But while visual practices and approaches are being invented and reinvented from a myriad of disciplinary and theoretical positions, there is also an urgent need to *integrate* knowledge and expertise in these fields of enquiry and to develop a critical constructive stance to past, present and future efforts, to truly take advantage of the rich visual dimension of society.

This chapter therefore seeks to mark out and discuss some crucial issues in the effort to advance the increasingly popular and diversified field of visual research. Some of these issues are old dilemmas (e.g. the collaboration between researchers and professional image makers); some are lingering problems (e.g. required visual competencies) that could have been better handled had they been better defined and brought to the surface; but some aspects are challenges of a more recent nature, triggered by current developments in society (e.g. globalization issues, new technologies). However, many of these can be turned into opportunities for advancement when dealt with appropriately.

My comments and observations stem from a long-standing but inevitably perspectivistic involvement with the fields of visual sociology and anthropology as well as those of visual communication, photography and scientific visualization. My position towards visual research has always been that of trying to be as methodologically explicit and rigid as possible, while at the same time stimulating and exploring efforts to use the full expressive potential of the visual, including possibly more contested arts rather than scientifically informed applications and practices. This does not imply that ultimately 'everything goes' and whatever one does is equally beneficial. However, it does call for an open-minded recognition and further development of many different types of visual research, each with specific strengths and limitations, and for a clear understanding of the potential contribution each of those approaches can bring to our knowledge of society and culture, and to our capabilities to communicate or disseminate those insights.

This chapter will take a slightly provocative, but constructive, stance to highlight essential aspects of visual research which need constant attention, even from those who are more acquainted with the field. The observations and comments made here inevitably tend to generalize and may sound somewhat normative. Both these characteristics may cause offence or put off readers who really are (or think they are) much further down the road. The effort to characterize and to some extent criticize this vast field of visual research in general terms may indeed at times seem unfair to a growing and highly diversified group of visual scholars who are at the forefront. This concise chapter will not be able to do justice to the specific and very valuable contributions that have been and are being made by these individuals. Both purposefully and because of space restrictions I have not provided many references to present day pioneers, since to indicate their specific contributions would require a detailed and fine-grained analysis that would divert from the general line of reasoning. Moreover, I think that it is sometimes better to speak in more general terms than to focus on celebrating or condemning the work of specific authors. Both examples of commendable and lamentable practices would need a very detailed and qualified treatment to be fair.

Building a more 'visual' social science, including an 'aesthetics of visual scholarly communication'

Advancing the field of visual research will first and foremost require a better understanding of the visual and of ways to deal with it in a more proficient, encompassing and explicit way. Understanding the complex nature of the visual, of visualization processes and practices, and of visual technologies are key in this respect. Clearly this knowledge base is already available, but it is first of all scattered between different fields of enquiry and, second, not always brought into practice by scholars who come from a variety of backgrounds, have at some point become attracted to this field, or who have pre-set ideas about the visual (such as: 'images should speak for themselves'). As a result, many discussions on the research value of the visual are of a repetitive and shallow nature.

A great number of issues and misunderstandings regarding visual research can ultimately be related to particular views and much confusion with regard to the iconic, indexical and symbolic properties of visual products and visual media, as they reside with commissioners, producers, users and sponsors of visual projects. Some discussion about the nature of the visual and its research potential originates in confounding 'indexicality' and 'iconicity' and in failing to consider the expressive and conceptual powers of visuals that transcend these traits. Naïve realists tend to overlook the constitutive character of the medium and the impact of its use: the fact that every act of representation obliterates many aspects of the depicted and at the same time adds new elements through the specifics of the instrumentation and the way the representational process is executed (i.e. including stylistic choices). As a result they tend to have an almost unmitigated belief in the veracity of the visual representation. The other side of the spectrum is populated by (visual) researchers, who in an unqualified manner rage against any iconic and indexical potential of images and visual representations and contend that visual representations are almost purely arbitrary constructions (oddly enough their visual work usually hardly differs from that of their opponents). But more importantly, many researchers (at both ends of the spectrum) are often overlooking the vast expressive potential of visual representations that opens up the way to scholarly argumentation and new avenues of expressing the unspeakable and unquantifiable. Visual representations not only give way to the depicted subject or object, but also tend to embody very revealing aspects about the producer and culture of production. There is no benefit in simply denying or oversimplifying the complex 'referentiality' of most images (in both iconic and indexical ways); the task ahead is to further clarify the exact nature of this referentiality and to explore its functionality for social scientific research and communication. Also, since referentiality is but one of the functions of visual communication, it is of paramount importance that the creative or constructive potential of visual representational practices is further explored and developed. Scholarly work, be it written, visual or numeric, is not (just) about describing or reflecting aspects of the outer world, but about making it more revealing, accessible, insightful, and possibly more predictable or controllable.

Thus visual scholars should no longer disregard or neglect the vital importance of style and form (the 'how') in conveying any content (the 'what'). Both are inseparable in any process of meaning making which in turn is more and more intertwined with technology (cf. the increasing impact of digital, multimedia, networking technologies, locative media (GPS; Google Earth) and eye-tracking (Olk and Kappas, 2011)). While commenting on this persistent tendency to under-utilize the expressive potential of style in scientific communication, it would be unfair not to mention that there are a number of visual scholars who in a myriad of ways are gradually building on this capacity (as exemplified and discussed in other chapters of this volume and in Margolis and Pauwels, 2011).

Aesthetic properties of media and representational practices in general should no longer be considered aspects that need to be 'controlled' in the sense of being reduced to an absolute minimum or left to 'specialists' who are trained to put things 'in proper shape'. Rather, such a functional aesthetic sensitivity should be stimulated in a thoughtful and considerate way, to result in better, richer forms of scholarly communication that will help data transfer and argumentation, and possibly even generate new types of knowledge. What constitutes an appropriate approach when producing and using imagery and media in a scholarly context depends heavily on the goals of the production: is the primary goal to educate (whom? about what precisely?), to shape, reinforce or change attitudes or behaviour, to distract or entertain, to offer 'a real life experience', to stimulate scientific or critical thought? Clearly there is no single 'right' approach, but a visually oriented scholar should very consciously select and combine all visual and non-visual elements ('signifiers') that make up the end-product.

The matter of 'functional' aesthetics and 'appropriate' expressiveness will most likely continue to trigger divergent views or feed controversies. There should definitely be room for more experimentation and, for example, for more metaphorical types of expression. This may require some more audacious and creative impetus from scholars. The main restriction that needs to be imposed on such experiments is that the audience should know what it is looking at, and/or reading or hearing. A visual product that claims the same status as a scholarly journal article should at all times be clear about its highly codified nature, even or precisely when highly iconic data (e.g. camera images) are presented, since they by their very nature tend to foster the illusion of offering an unmediated experience to the spectators.

One of the better examples of a very thoughtful and visually expressive social scientific product is the cleverly constructed (and recently revisited) film produced by Robert Aibel, Ben Levin, Chris Musello and Jay Ruby, *A Country Auction: The Paul V. Leitzel Estate Sale* (1984). Designed as social science, the authors subjected their film and its accompanying materials to similar (but not necessarily the *same*) and as rigorous standards as those that are imposed on written forms of science. At the same time they skilfully used many properties of the film medium (camera movement and position, framing, different types of editing, etc.) in an expressive way to also 'construct' visually their views on the complex social process they were depicting and uncovering. The 'study guide' that accompanied the film ensures that additional context is provided and that the theoretical framework which guided the production, as well as each of the cinematographic choices, are fully revealed and substantiated.

Visual research and visual communication of research have always entertained a strong link with technology and will continue to take stock of new opportunities they may offer to data-collection, production and dissemination. New media technologies can to a certain extent help to accommodate different audiences and purposes (e.g. users can browse menus and various options, go for further information, go back or skip information and choose their own path). However, technology does not automatically solve all problems (e.g. of an epistemological, ethical, expressive or educational nature). Therefore (new) technologies should not be the driver of a research project, as they may introduce (new) problems as much as they may help to solve existing ones. Nor should they merely be used as vehicles for old messages and approaches. While it is legitimate to turn to technology solely to make current ways of thinking and doing cheaper, the emphasis should be on what one can do with it in terms of growing research opportunities and communicating visual statements more fluently and clearly. While a modest and thoughtful approach to applying technologies is preferable, it would be inadvisable to confine scholars to a very sparse use of the many (largely unexplored) capabilities of visual media. While researchers should feel stimulated to explore new capabilities of visual media (Coover, 2011), they should not be tempted to introduce or adopt features that don't add any meaning or that conversely even introduce confusion, or to adopt practices from other fields (e.g. social media templates and practices, music video editing techniques) without rethinking them to fit their specific aims. In this regard, an at first sight more 'visual' account that does not grasp the possible side effects (confusion, distraction, unwanted connotations) may imply less adequate uses of visual capabilities in a scholarly discourse.

Given these requirements, it doesn't suffice for visual scholars to have a superficial knowledge of visual technologies and of the specific formal and meaning-related aspects of the visual media, as almost every technical or formal choice is bound to have epistemological (and various other) consequences. After all, these choices determine 'what' one is able to see, 'how' it presents itself to researchers and their audiences, and what remains hidden; they partly determine, reveal and steer the mode of thought of a given culture.

Solid social and cultural research that seeks to be more 'visual' in every respect should be characterized by precise decisions about when (and when not!) to use which kinds of visuals and for which purposes, and by an unambiguous communication of these choices and their limitations. Visual sociologists and anthropologists need to be very critical with respect to using visuals in their end products, whichever form they take (articles, slide shows, exhibitions, installations, DVDs). They should constantly ask themselves: Are the selected or created visual representations and all other visual elements (e.g. layout and design features) the most appropriate options? Do they add essential information or insights that cannot be – or would be less effectively – communicated in numbers or a verbal description and argumentation? Do they interact in the most effective way with other expressive systems and modes?

Working towards a more integrated and inclusive study of the visual in terms of themes, referents, theories, methods, disciplinary angles and experiences

Visual research in general could benefit from a better theoretical and methodological grounding and a more sophisticated analytical set of tools. Visual researchers do seem to have a broad range of theories and analytical frameworks to choose from when trying to make sense of images and visual artifacts: for example, content analysis, social semiotics, iconology, ethno-methodology, rhetoric (see Berger, 1986; Peters, 1977; Rose, 2006 [2001]; Smith et al., 2005; van Leeuwen and Jewitt, 2000). Unfortunately, they hardly offer a well-integrated and clear methodology to systematically interrogate visuals with respect to their social and cultural significance, and most methods and frameworks are ill-equipped to handle larger sets of visual data. Semiotic analysis, for instance, is arduous to apply to larger sets of visual data as it requires much time and interpretation. Content analysis may be better suited to handle larger data sets, but is hitherto not very well adapted to explore the full richness and the holistic potential of the visual, as it is often restricted to counting elements of the pro filmic or to collecting data on just a few easy-to-code (e.g. camera distance or angle) – although not necessarily the most important – parameters of an image. In short, they are often not fully adapted to deal with the complex nature of visual images, or for that matter with the increasingly hybrid, multimodal constructions (e.g. websites, see Pauwels, 2011). Whereas the analysis of existing ('found') visual products can rely on a fairly broad literature and tradition, methodologies for producing and processing (selecting and reordering, analysing, presenting) visual data are far less explicitly developed and documented. As these issues embody the core aspects and the specific contribution of a more visual social science, scholars in the field should address this matter more vigorously than they have so far.

The in-depth study of the visual typically requires a more integrated and consequently a truly interdisciplinary approach. This demand provides a good point of departure for returning to a more integrated science. Still, one cannot but observe that, hitherto, a systematic and integrated study of the increasingly important visual aspects of society is lacking, despite the growing need for a more critical approach to visual expressions – either intermediated or not – of today's high-tech cultures. Knowledge of the visual remains fragmented between various disciplines, where it is often further scattered over sub-disciplines. One could say that the visual is so much part of so many disciplines that it becomes almost invisible or taken for granted. Efforts to expand the domain in turn are too often inspired by reappropriating, extending or narrowing it to the discipline or interest of the writer/speaker.

Clearly there is no single discipline that can claim the central position in the study of visual culture (not art history, not visual communication, not cultural studies, not (even) visual sociology or anthropology, etc.). Scholars need to further clarify the distinct and at times joint or overlapping contributions each of their disciplines can make, and put more effort into trying to build on each other's insights and achievements. Visual research should not be narrowed down to researching 'image culture' nor to producing photographic records of society. The 'visual' aspect of our world does not manifest itself uniquely in the visual media, but it actually pervades our daily lives in most of its facets: in looking, being looked at, visualizing, depicting (reproducing), etc. So apart from becoming more integrated, the study of the visual and the study through and by the visual should become more 'inclusive' as well.

Looking at recent research applications, visual social and cultural science is fortunately becoming more inclusive in terms of: visual and visualized 'referents' (including now also concepts, abstract processes, visualizations of the invisible); media (not just photography and film, but also drawings, maps, artifacts, new media); and fields of interest. Consequently camera-based representations and techniques (both static and moving images), and directly observable culture, have lost the almost exclusive position they have held for years.

Moreover the insight is growing that visual (social) science is not just about analysing and producing visual data but also about visualizing and expressing insights in novel, more experimental and experiential ways (e.g. arts-based approaches). Important to note is that this mission to become more integrated and inclusive should not be confined to the humanities and the social sciences. The fragmentation that characterizes many fields and sub-fields of the social sciences and the humanities is nowhere as dramatic as the proverbial divide that still exists between these fields and the so-called 'sciences' (exact sciences, life sciences, etc.), where the visual and visualization play at least as crucial a role in knowledge building and dissemination. However, it should be clear that several fields and sub-fields of these 'science' disciplines (neurology, neurobiology, physics, scientific imaging and analysis) could enrich the social and behavioural sciences and the humanities a great deal with regard to disclosing the nature of vision and visualization. But the reverse is also true (as exemplified by the better work in the sociology of science, e.g. Knor-Cetina, 1981;

Latour and Woolgar, 1979; Lemke, 1998; Lynch, 1985), though convincing the 'other side' of this may prove even more cumbersome. While the study of images and visualization in terms of their impact on society, knowledge construction and dissemination (including discussions about visual manipulations and alterations) tends to be more recognized as an 'issue' in the social sciences and humanities than in the 'sciences' (where visualization practices are considered the site of distinct specialists and where particular visualizations are often considered uncontested state-of-the-art products), scientists could learn from social sciences about the social construction of their 'truths' and facts. For visualization – whatever its field of application – is a very complex process that not only relies on more or less transparent technologies, but also embodies numerous interventions of scientists and support personnel, not all of which are duly documented or discussed with respect to their effects. Every resulting visualization is the combined result of a long trajectory of decisions of a very varied nature. The opacity of this process may hamper the knowledge that can be derived from particular images and in more general terms foster less than adequate conceptions of the real-world aspects to which the images seek to refer. To a certain extent, every specialism tends to be locked up in its current ways of thinking and doing, often focusing on only parts of the problem and taking for granted existing practices and traditions. But what is also true is that every specialism potentially holds unique insights into what at first sight might seem unrelated aspects or fields of inquiry. A more integrated and inclusive study of the visual, therefore, should be better able to address fundamental questions with respect to the intricate relations between a visual representation and its referent (a physical phenomenon, a concept and anything in between . . .), the determining role of technology and of different scientific and representational traditions, and the hybrid set of competencies that this presupposes both for producers and users of scientific visualizations. The truly interdisciplinary nature of visual research could prove the ideal showcase in the effort to bridge the persistent and often unproductive gap between the 'Two Cultures' (the 'Sciences' versus the 'Humanities', cf. Snow, 1960) and to overcome the stereotypical conceptions about 'the other' fostered on both sides.

Ultimately the call for more integrated and inclusive types of visual research should also question the primacy of the visual and its relation to other senses and modes of expression. Notwithstanding its central and under-examined role, it is clear that the visual should not be studied in isolation and simply exclude the other senses and the many expressive modes that may address these other senses (see Pink, 2009, 2011). Yet with respect to 'mediated' experiences, even the most hybrid and advanced (multi)media technologies still only succeed in addressing two out of our five senses (sight and hearing), and usually fail to transmit tactile, olfactory or gustatory experiences. Likewise, so-called 'multimodal research' (Kress and van Leeuwen, 2001; van Leeuwen, 2011) has focused on examining the interplay of different expressive systems in the production of meaning and effect, as applied to mediated representations (and as opposed to direct encounters, e.g. a walk in the city or interactions between people), and is, in fact, limited to two (super) modes: the 'visual' and the 'auditory', ruling out all modes that address the tactile, olfactory and taste senses. But the visual mode in its wider meaning includes already a variety of expressive systems that are often not readily considered as 'visual': the textual parts (which have to be 'viewed' most of the time), typography, layout and design features. Likewise, the auditory mode (spoken or sung texts, music, noises) exhibits a growing diversity of aspects and applications and a corresponding importance in today's converging media. Important to note is that multimodal analysis not only takes different modes into account as generators of meaning, but also has a strong focus on the effects of their interplay. The older concept of 'multimedia' has a far more restricted meaning, as it refers mainly to the capabilities of a technical device or to a technology (not to a communicative act or to the perceptual processing of data by people). Multimodal research is an ambitious venture given the fact that even most forms of mono-modal or single mode analysis (for example the analysis of static photographs) are still underdeveloped, in other words, not able to tap into the full expressive potential of media and visual artefacts/performances. Moreover, to some extent multimodal research seems a mere relabelling of long-existing research traditions (e.g. non-verbal communication, sound–image studies). But the basic idea of multimodal research, with its emphasis on the effects of specific interactions between different expressive systems, is definitely a path that visual research should try to follow to some extent, without losing its focus on the specific complexities of visual perception, visual analysis, visual production and visual applications.

Whereas multimodal research today already manages to attract scholars from very varied fields, visual research in the social and cultural sciences too has benefited in recent years from interdisciplinary enrichment from fields like geography (McKinnon, 2011), design (Boradkar, 2011), arts, history, education, science and technology, etc. Thus it seems legitimate and may be more correct to say that, in fact, opposing processes of interdisciplinary enrichment and integration on the one hand, and disciplinary appropriation and fragmentation on the other, are simultaneously influencing the future of visual research.

Developing visual competencies and coping with the multiplication and integration of different types of expertise

The above elaborated recommendations for visual research to become 'more visual', integrated, inclusive, and more technologically astute will also have a profound effect on the 'level and breadth of expertise' that are needed for doing such forms of visual research, and implicate the question of how exactly the multitude of hybrid competencies can or should be 'developed' and 'combined'.

It is clear that different types of visual research may put very different demands on the researcher, depending on the method, the medium and the subject chosen. Some types of research require rather limited skills (or skills that can easily be left to technicians) and hardly tap into the expressive potential of different visual media. Others, however, are much more exigent. For example, producing cultural inventories of home settings could be left to a well-briefed (professional) photographer, who should be able to make pictures with fine detail according to a meticulous shooting script. More expressive ways of visual research, such as the visual essay or anthropological film (Rollwagen, 1988), demand more integrated skills from researchers, who need to be able to combine and amalgamate their scientific and visual abilities in a kind of 'visual scientific literacy' (Pauwels, 2006).

Whether or not 'assisted' by visual professionals or technicians, sociologists and anthropologists should actively seek to develop their visual research and communication skills in order to gradually appreciate the difficulties and problems of the different media and their sheer limitless expressive capabilities. Producing photographic materials with the right levels of mimesis and expression is quite different from creating conceptual representations as an aid to knowledge building and communication. When studying or applying any representational medium or technique, researchers should be aware of their specific transformational qualities, and of the fact that no representational technique can produce 'complete' and 'objective' records, let alone undeniable statements. This should not imply, however, that such records cannot be used as 'reliable' data of some sort. Constant researcher attention is required, to avoid stepping into a naïve realist trap of implicitly equating 'representations' with full and objective records of reality. A broad and thorough knowledge of the visual media and of the many interconnected transformational – technical, social and cultural – processes in which they are rooted is needed to employ the visual in the varied processes of scientific data-gathering, processing and communication. Currently this requirement is not always met, nor recognized to its fullest extent (see Grady, 2011; Pauwels, 2006).

The issue of how to develop and combine or integrate different types of expertise in fact goes back to the heated discussions in the field of ethnographic and anthropological filmmaking: whether the anthropologist should be the filmmaker, or better, work together with a professional filmmaker to produce 'visual ethnography or anthropology' (Mead, 1963; Rollwagen, 1988; Rouch, 1975; Ruby, 1986). But this old question becomes ever more pertinent as media opportunities continue to grow and a commensurate development of visual competencies remains to be desired. In fact, currently so many types of expertise are involved in performing and presenting visual research that these can hardly be mastered by the same person at the best possible level of proficiency, so that forms of collaboration seem unavoidable to some extent.

The question of the 'ideal' division (and combination/integration) of labour and expertise is not confined to visual data production or to the more innovative forms of presentation, but also comes into view when results are presented in a more traditional scholarly format. Today even the more basic multimedia features (typographic, graphic and design elements, the interplay of visuals and captions or text) are not capitalized in science communications to their fullest potential, despite the fact that they are an intricate part of communicating scientific ideas and results and can help to embody or express the unspeakable or unquantifiable. But a further complication is that even if researchers have the many skills and types of expertise required, they often have little control over the final 'look of things', especially when publishing in scholarly journals. Publishers usually have fixed design templates, which as a rule are not very well adapted to accommodate creative (and meaning generating) treatments of word, image and layout. As mentioned above, simply delegating the different types of expertise to separate specialists may also fail to produce an optimal result. It is not just a matter of adding up distinct skills, but of normative systems and traditions that may work together or against each other. Growing pressure falls on the users of visual technology who really want to use it in the most meaningful manner to assimilate and integrate a multitude of skills. These skills will not be acquired automatically and go far beyond reading the operations manual of a device or knowing how a software package 'works'. Video editing or website authoring, for example, is not just about learning software packages but about acquiring a multitude of insights and skills in highly specialized fields, such as typography, graphic design, narratology, camera work, etc. These 'technologies' also presuppose a thorough understanding of the human learning process and of social and cultural characteristics of the target audience. Thus, in conclusion, the further development of visual scientific competencies should be put high on the agenda of visual researchers and in fact on that of virtually all scholars of most disciplines.

Fostering more self-critical, constructive and reflexive visual approaches

Looking further at how visual research could make significant progress in the years to come, it might benefit from becoming somewhat more (self)critical, modest and reflexive.

When discussing or advocating different options in visual research, visual scholars should try to avoid taking too rigid a position, for example, by believing that there is only 'one right way'. It is not very productive to over-emphasize or celebrate one kind of visual research at the expense of other kinds. For instance, one should not dismiss more mimetic-oriented research as naïvely realist, or conversely reject the more aesthetically inspired, experimental or expressive approaches as unscientific. So, for instance, meticulous re-photography projects aimed at reading social change (Rieger, 2011) through the reproductive capacities of the camera, or micro-analytical studies of interaction using video recordings (Heath et al., 2010; Knoblauch and Tuma, 2011) in very standardized ways, should be able to blossom next to more implicit and ambiguous artistic approaches (O'Donoghue, 2011) which perhaps lack the rigour and control of the more basic and accepted approaches, but in return excel in expressing what cannot be put in words or numbers or in transmitting holistic capacities of the visual as intricate amalgamations of content and form.

The field needs to remain open to approaches that try to go further than using visual media as mere transmitters of characteristics of the depicted, but which instead creatively use their features as vehicles of expression of scientifically informed insight, and at the same time continue to recognize the research potential that resides in the reproductive capacities of visual media.

A genuinely (self)critical stance implies that one constantly questions both one's own and borrowed mental frameworks. Insight into the structure (the building blocks, expressive means, codes) as well as the culture of the image and the visual material world in the broadest sense (production, reception and practices) remains a precondition both for being able to formulate well-founded criticism and sound scientific statements. Such an attitude requires consciously taking the transformational properties (the 'mediation process') and the stylistic choices (the 'aesthetics') of the visual representations and the wider – visual and other – context of their use into account.

Some visual scholars would benefit from abandoning an 'author celebratory mode' (often leading to very predictable and repetitive findings) to a truly more critical mode that seeks to confront established ideas with one's own viewpoints and visual experiences. First and foremost, visual scholars should try to 'look more closely' at what is offered visually, and not simply adopt interpretations of authors with a guru-like stature. While theories ideally serve as 'eye-openers', they should not stimulate prejudice or inhibit a fresh and original look. Also, scholars should drop the urge to invent a new term for a field, a method or technique each time they are dissatisfied with the current version, and in particular when they have only a very limited view of the current offer (and history) of the discipline, method or technique. Paradigms or ideological positions should not be promoted to whole disciplines, and a critique on a particular paradigm of a discipline should not lead to the dismissal of the whole disciplinary tradition. Often too much effort is put in delineating and appropriating the visual field, at best out of ignorance and at worst for self-gratifying purposes. A rather innocent example of this urge to reinvent and relabel practices and techniques can be found in the variety of idiosyncratic and overlapping descriptions of very similar (or the same) forms of respondent generated image-making: participatory video, photo voice, shooting back, etc. One could also refer here to unproductive discussions or struggles around terms like 'visual culture', 'visual studies', 'visual cultural studies', 'image based research', 'visual communication', 'media studies' and 'visual rhetoric', which are often too focused on the presumed unique character of one's approach (or discipline), but often result in vain efforts to reinvent the wheel and while doing so just add confusion rather than insight.

Constructive self-criticism should go hand in hand with more appropriate types of 'reflexivity'. Reflexivity encompasses a clear recognition that all scientific knowledge is 'provisional', 'positioned' and incomplete, but it should go beyond that recognition.

Reflection upon the generative process of knowledge production and the role of the researcher as a culturally positioned individual is not new, and indeed in some instances it again is simply attaching a new label to existing practices. But the concept may also point at broadened insights, principles and focal points that should be incorporated in a more contemporary version of knowledge building and dissemination. Yet, it often remains unclear what this notion means precisely and how it should be brought into practice. A better understanding of what reflexivity entails, not as a mere buzz word but as a complex and never-ending task, is key in this regard. MacDougall (2011: 111) sees reflexivity essentially as contextualizing the content of a visual production, anthropological film in his case, by revealing aspects of its production in both explicit (interactions between filmmakers and the field, voice-over commentary, etc.) and implicit ways (e.g. editing choices as signs of the presence of the filmmaker).

How the various aspects of a reflexive approach should be dealt with more concretely is not always very clear and this often leads to new misunderstandings. Closer attention to one's own influence and positioning need not gain the upper hand over the actual topic of a visual production. While reflexivity should result more in self-relativization and a more modest qualification of the results, some visual researchers do sometimes use it as a means to put themselves to the fore in an almost self-glorifying manner. Such strongly autobiographically oriented explorations can, paradoxically enough, be at the expense of insight into the broader 'meeting of cultures' that they believe themselves to be making a contribution to. The same holds for exaggerated reflexive approaches that in turn may quickly degenerate into a repetitive meta-discourse on visual research, against a changing background of given cultural contexts. There are no quick or simple procedures for a reflexive approach: occasionally putting oneself or members of the crew into the picture, or a merely verbal acknowledgement of reflexivity, provides little insight into the driving forces behind a researcher and the research value of the product. Ruby (2000: 155), a fierce advocate of a thoughtful and well-balanced reflexivity, does admit that it is extremely difficult to determine exactly how much knowledge and precisely which aspects of the producer and the production process are needed, and conversely, what should be considered excessive or superfluous and thus detrimental to the end result.

Evidently reflexivity or reflexive action does not imply a liberation from a rigid and explicit methodology, but rather a necessary and demanding expansion of it. After all, non-recognized subjectivity or the denial of subjective influences and the unmistakable epistemological consequences of all choices made, inevitably leads to far less scientifically useful insights, although this might not always appear to be the case at first sight. Reflexive contextualization is key to assessing and qualifying the strength and limitations of any technique in its specific application, and therefore should become a recognized and stimulated aspect of any methodology.

Conclusion

This chapter has addressed different but often interrelated challenges and opportunities for visual social science. It started with a call for a more explicit methodology and a more truly 'visual' practice, for which the development of a more explicit 'aesthetics of scholarly communication' in close conjunction with rapidly evolving technological opportunities is deemed necessary. Next, reflecting on how visual research could make progress in years to come, this contribution also emphasized that visual scholarly activities should become more 'integrated' and 'inclusive' in terms of subject areas, disciplinary angles, media, modes and sensory experiences. Closely related to the first two proposals it was argued that there is an urgent need to further define and specify the diverse visual competencies that are needed to perform innovative visual research from start to finish, including the complex duty to actively develop these competencies as well as to stimulate productive forms of co-operation between the highly divergent types of expertise and their sometimes somewhat conflicting professional norms and expectations. Contemplating some unproductive paradigmatic quarrels of the past and present, this contribution then argued that at least a portion of the growing hordes of enthusiastic visual researchers could benefit from a more self-critical and reflexive attitude towards their visual work and a more open and constructive attitude towards that of others.

Both novice and seasoned scholars should constantly be challenged to go back to their work and ask 'self-critically' (as I and my students sometimes do, with a humbling effect): What is the status of the visuals I am employing? To what extent do these images really matter? What types of unique data do they contain or which kinds of insights are expressed in my visuals that are largely inexpressible in words and of value for the particular points I want to make? And what about the interplay of different expressive systems; do the images work together with the words? Does the layout add any meaning? And so on. These are questions one should pose and should keep on posing, no matter how experienced one is, or thinks one is.

While visual research, as discussed above, faces many challenges that need to be addressed by researchers themselves, there are also some obstacles from outside that continue to encumber its progress. Most of these hurdles have to do with persistent misconceptions or ignorance with respect to dealing with the implications of the visual in different segments of society. One could think about: the need to prepare the diverse audiences of visual research in a society that is not as visually literate as one would rightfully expect; the impact of the legal void and the ethical confusion with regard to the production and use of imagery; and the various institutional practices (reviewers, publishers) that are still ill prepared for the visual.

How the future of visual research is finally going to play out, whether progressing as a more highly integrated trans-disciplinary venture, or simply continuing its course as specialized pockets of interest and expertise dispersed over different disciplinary areas of inquiry, is hard to predict. Though again, the idea should be nurtured that visual research and visual studies offer a domain 'par excellence' for revisiting the way the sciences, social sciences and humanities are currently organized and that failing to make this happen will hold back chances for more captivating ways of knowledge building and dissemination.

References

Berger, A.A. (1986) *Media Analysis Techniques*. Beverly Hills/London: Sage.

Boradkar, P. (2011) 'Visual research methods in the design process', in E. Margolis and L. Pauwels (eds), *Sage Handbook of Visual Research Methods*. London/Thousand Oaks/New Delhi: Sage. pp. 150–68.

Coover, Roderick (2011) 'Interactive media representation', in E. Margolis and L. Pauwels (eds), *Sage Handbook of Visual Research Methods*. London/Thousand Oaks/New Delhi: Sage. pp. 619–38.

Grady, J. (2011) 'Numbers into pictures: visualization in social analysis', in E. Margolis and L. Pauwels (eds), *Sage Handbook of Visual Research Methods*. London/Thousand Oaks/New Delhi: Sage. pp. 688–709.

Heath, C., Hindmarsh, J. and Luff, P. (2010) *Video in Qualitative Research: Analysing Social Interaction in Everyday Life*. London: Sage.

Knoblauch, H. and Tuma, R. (2011) 'Videography: an interpretative approach to video-recorded micro-social interaction', in E. Margolis and L. Pauwels (eds), *Sage Handbook of Visual Research Methods*. London/Thousand Oaks/New Delhi: Sage. pp. 414–30.

Knor-Cetina, K.D. (1981) *The Manufacture of Knowledge: An Essay on the Constructivist and Contextual Nature of Science*. New York: Pergamon.

Kress, G. and van Leeuwen, T. (2001) *Multimodal Discourse: The Modes and Media of Contemporary Communication*. London: Hodder Arnold.

Latour, B. and Woolgar, S. (1979) *Laboratory Life: The Construction of Scientific Facts*. Princeton, NJ: Princeton University Press.

Lemke, J.L. (1998) 'Multiplying meaning: visual and verbal semiotics in scientific text', in J.R. Martin and R. Veel (eds), *Reading Science*. London: Routledge. pp. 87–113.

Lynch, M. (1985) *Art and Artefact in Laboratory Science: A Study of Shop Work and Shop Talk in a Research Laboratory*. London: Routledge & Kegan Paul.

MacDougall, D. (2011) 'Anthropological filmmaking: an empirical art', in E. Margolis and L. Pauwels (eds), *Sage Handbook of Visual Research Methods*. London/Thousand Oaks/New Delhi: Sage. pp. 99–113.

Margolis, E. and Pauwels, L. (eds) (2011) *Sage Handbook of Visual Research Methods*. London/Thousand Oaks/New Delhi: Sage.

McKinnon, I. (2011) 'Expanding cartographic practices in the social sciences', in E. Margolis and L. Pauwels (eds), *Sage Handbook of Visual Research Methods*. London/Thousand Oaks/New Delhi: Sage. pp. 452–73.

Mead, M. (1963) 'Anthropology and the camera', in W. Morgan (ed.), *The Encyclopedia of Photography*. New York: Greystone Press. pp. 166–84.

O'Donoghue, D. (2011) 'Doing and disseminating visual research: visual arts-based approaches', in E. Margolis and L. Pauwels (eds), *Sage Handbook of Visual Research Methods*. London/Thousand Oaks/New Delhi: Sage. pp. 639–52.

Olk, B. and Kappas, A. (2011) 'Eye-tracking as a tool for visual research', in E. Margolis and L. Pauwels (eds), *Sage Handbook of Visual Research Methods*. London/Thousand Oaks/New Delhi: Sage. pp. 433–51.

Pauwels, L. (2006) 'A theoretical framework for assessing visual representational practices in knowledge building and science communications', in L. Pauwels (ed.), *Visual Cultures of Science: Rethinking Representational Practices in Knowledge Building and Science Communication*. Hanover, NH, and London: Dartmouth College Press/University Press of New England. pp. 1–25.

Pauwels, L. (2008a) 'Taking and using: ethical issues of photographs for research purposes', *Visual Communication Quarterly*, 15: 243–57.

Pauwels, L. (2008b) 'A private visual practice going public? Social functions and sociological research opportunities of web-based family photography', *Visual Studies*, 23 (1): 34–49.

Pauwels, L. (2010) 'Visual sociology reframed: an analytical synthesis and discussion of visual methods in social and cultural research', *Sociological Methods & Research*, 38 (4): 545–81.

Pauwels, L. (2011) 'Researching websites as social and cultural expressions: methodological predicaments and a multimodal model for analysis', in E. Margolis and L. Pauwels (eds), *Sage Handbook of Visual Research Methods*. London/Thousand Oaks/New Delhi: Sage. pp. 571–90.

Peters, J.-M. (1977) *Pictorial Communication*. Claremont, CA: David Philip.

Pink, S. (2009) *Doing Sensory Ethnography*. London: Sage.

Pink, S. (2011) 'A multi-sensory approach to visual methods', in E. Margolis and L. Pauwels (eds), *Sage Handbook of Visual Research Methods*. London/Thousand Oaks/New Delhi: Sage. pp. 602–15.

Rieger, J. (2011) 'Rephotography for documenting social change', in E. Margolis and L. Pauwels (eds), *Sage Handbook of Visual Research Methods*. London/Thousand Oaks/New Delhi: Sage. pp. 132–49.

Rollwagen, J. (ed.) (1988) *Anthropological Filmmaking: Anthropological Perspectives on the Production of Film and Video for General Public Audiences*. Chur/London: Harwood Academic Publishers.

Rose, G. (2006 [2001]) *Visual Methodologies: An Introduction to the Interpretation of Visual Methods* (second edition). London: Sage.

Rouch, J. (1975) 'The camera and man', in P. Hockings (ed.), *Principles in Visual Anthropology*. Chicago, IL: Aldine. pp. 83–102.

Ruby, J. (1986) 'The future of anthropological cinema – a modest polemic', *Visual Sociology Review*, 1: 9–13.

Ruby, J. (2000) *Picturing Culture: Explorations of Film and Anthropology*. Chicago, IL: The University of Chicago Press.

Smith, K.L., Moriarty, S., Barbatsis, G. and Kenney, K. (eds) (2005) *Handbook of Visual Communication: Theory, Methods, and Media*. Mahwah, NJ: Lawrence Erlbaum Associates.

Snow, C.P. (1960) *The Two Cultures*. Cambridge: Cambridge University Press.

van Leeuwen, T. (2011) 'Multimodality and multimodal research', in E. Margolis and L. Pauwels (eds), *Sage Handbook of Visual Research Methods*. London/Thousand Oaks/New Delhi: Sage. pp. 549–70.

van Leeuwen, T. and Jewitt, C. (eds) (2000) *The Handbook of Visual Analysis*. London: Sage.

INDEX